# Alone in the Fortress of the Bears

## 70 Days Surviving Wilderness Alaska: Foraging, Fishing, Hunting

Bruce L. "Buck" Nelson

ISBN-10: 1517399092
ISBN-13: 978-1517399092

# Acknowledgments

My thanks to Gayla Marty, author of *Memory of Trees: A Daughter's Story of a Family Farm*, for her expert advice with my manuscript. Thanks also to my good friends Jim Griffin, Allen Biller and Tom Boatner for their suggestions. Finally, thanks to Rod Dow, author of *Just a Few Jumper Stories: A Collection of Smokejumper Adventures* for his generous assistance.

*Please visit my website at www.bucktrack.com for ordering information, to see a list of gear I used on this trip, to purchase my other adventure books and videos and much more.*

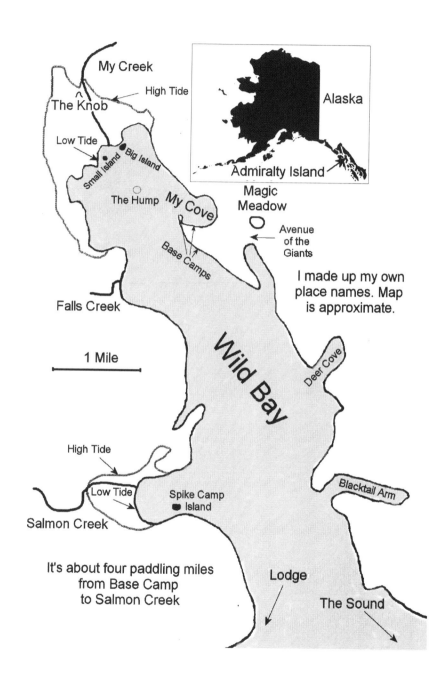

# Contents

# Introduction

I grew up on a dairy farm in East Central Minnesota, the second of four kids, the oldest of two boys. We had a big barn to goof off in and a large woods to roam. Sometimes in the fall, starting when we were about five and nine, my brother and I would head off into the woods for two or three days at a time to "live off the land." We'd pack a tent and our sleeping bags and a .22 rifle but no food. We'd eat what we could find, mostly squirrels and wild grapes as I recall. Since those days, now long ago, I've always dreamt of making a much longer expedition into much wilder country.

When I was nineteen I began a career in wildland firefighting. Firefighting took me to Wyoming and Oregon and finally to Alaska, and Alaska firefighting led me to smokejumping. Parachuting to wilderness fires was the job I was meant to do, an adventurous job where strong friendships are forged. I was mighty proud to be an Alaska Smokejumper for well over twenty years.

In the winter of 2013/2014 I decided this was it, this was the year I'd go on my epic "Living Off the Land" trip. The first question was "where?" Well, Alaska of course, and the coast seemed like the best bet, specifically the Southeast. It's the most food-rich area of Alaska.

Although I couldn't hunt seals and whales nowadays, there would still be salmon, halibut, crabbing, shellfish, berries, blacktail deer, grouse, waterfowl, and more. The biggest drawback was my lack of experience in that ecosystem. I didn't know how to crab or fish for halibut or to identify most of the local plants. And of course, just because the food is there doesn't mean that a person can find it, or catch it, or put up with the associated hardships and challenges. Therein would lie the challenge and the adventure.

One concern was rain. The Southeast is notoriously rainy. Ketchikan gets over 150 inches of rain a year. Using rainfall maps, I found an area on Admiralty Island that reportedly gets less than 60 inches. Huge difference! I also liked Admiralty because it is in the Inside Passage and relatively protected from the open ocean. I looked up Admiralty Island on Wikipedia:

*Admiralty Island is an island in the Alexander Archipelago in Southeast Alaska...the seventh largest island in the United States and the 132nd largest island in the world...*

*The Kootznoowoo Wilderness encompasses vast stands of old growth temperate rainforest. These forests provide some of the best habitat available to species such as brown bears, bald eagles, and Sitka black-tailed deer...*

*Known to the Tlingit as Xootsnoowú, which is sometimes interpreted as "Fortress of the Bear(s)", Admiralty Island is home to the highest density of brown bears in North America. An estimated 1,600 brown bears inhabit the island...*

The National Park Service had this to say:

*While bears outnumber people, bald eagles outnumber bears and provide one of the more outstanding features of Admiralty Island--an estimated 2,500 reside on Admiralty Island--more than all bald eagles known to exist in the remainder of the United States.*

Many of the same foods that support the high bear and eagle populations would support me. I would be very aware of bears, but I wouldn't worry about them.

I didn't want to mess with a satellite phone, so I studied cell phone coverage maps and found a bay with pockets of coverage, presumably signals coming over the ocean through gaps in the mountains. Perfect. I could be "off the grid" most of the time, with the option to occasionally let people know I was OK. I called a government office. One of their employees remembered getting a signal near the mouth of the bay. Berries were reportedly widespread in that area, so finding them shouldn't be a serious problem. I also found reports of halibut fishing and crabbing there. Fish and Game salmon run charts indicated the first salmon would be showing up around the very end of June in several local streams. I took a good look at the bay on Google Earth and topo maps. There were mountains and islands and numerous streams. It sure looked good to me. It had its own name but I would call it Wild Bay.

So how long did I want to be out there? Maybe a couple of weeks just to get a good taste of the experience? Or how about a couple months or more? Would that be too brutal? Charts showed the rain starts picking up in September and peaking in October. This year's hunting regulations weren't out yet, but deer season traditionally starts in August, waterfowl season in September. Flying out around July 1 and returning in early September might work well for weather and salmon runs and hunting.

I needed to firm up my gear list. It's tempting to bring a mountain of gear, "just in case." That's a good way to have all your bases covered, but it's a sure way to over-pack as well. I'd done several long hikes like the Continental Divide Trail, and on those hikes my pack usually weighed from fifteen to thirty pounds total, including food and water. This would be a dramatically different situation however, living out there with no chance to resupply or replace gear. I would be bringing no food, not even emergency food. Salt and pepper would be it.

I asked around for some ideas on boats, and experts mentioned skiffs and sea kayaks and even boats with sleeping quarters! I considered the boats I owned. My old Scanoe would be too difficult to transport. My fourteen foot inflatable raft would be really difficult to row for long distances but would be roomy for camp moves. My inflatable kayak would be light, but too small to haul all of my gear at once during camp moves. I could do several shuttles though. My inflatable would be slower than a sea kayak but easier to transport. That was my choice.

Firearms would be a big consideration. I wanted to hunt deer, ducks, and geese, and grouse. And I wanted a gun for bears, just in case. Saltwater and rain mean rust. My stainless Ruger 30-06 would be great for blacktails and acceptable for bear protection. I considered a shotgun/.22 combo for birds and small game, but my research showed there wouldn't be much for edible small game, other than game birds. The only shotgun I own is an old side by side. It was tempting to buy a new stainless shotgun but I elected to just use my old shotgun and keep it oiled.

I ordered a foldable crab trap, rope and buoy, and researched halibut fishing gear. I pictured many cold, rainy days and elected to spend the money for a large, tipi-style tent with a tiny collapsible wood stove so I could dry wet clothes. My gear list slowly came together.

Food preservation has always been a big issue for people living a subsistence lifestyle. What would I do when I shot a deer or caught a big halibut? How would I preserve a good catch of salmon? Smoking and drying was a standard practice in Alaska and sometimes still is. But all that rain and humidity! And how about when I left camp? How would I keep bears and birds out of my drying racks? Pressure canning in glass jars would allow me to preserve food for long term storage in just a few hours. This was an issue I'd been thinking about already, and I'd canned up some deer meat for practice. I'd go that route.

It's a long, long way from Fairbanks to Petersburg, the nearest airport. About 750 air miles. I had a lot of bulky gear, too. I worked on a plan to drive to Whittier, Alaska, about 400 miles, and then take the Alaska ferry system to Kake or Petersburg. The ferry schedule would require me to leave on certain days and spend at least one night in Juneau. When I called to ask about my taking my gear on the ferry they said they'd have to see how much room was available.

"So I won't know if there's room until just before the sailing?"

"I'm afraid not."

That put the kibosh on that plan. Flying down wouldn't be as scenic or adventurous and it would be several hundred dollars more expensive, but it would work and it would save me days of travel time. I made a plan to air freight most of my gear and then fly down and back.

I called a couple of air taxis in Petersburg. They quoted a thousand dollars round-trip to fly out to Wild Bay and back. One air taxi was a bit cheaper and seemed cheerful and helpful.

"Could you fly me out the afternoon of June 30?"

"Let me check our schedule... Yes, that would work. Do you want me to pencil you in?"

"Sure. And how about you put me down for a tentative September 10 pickup?"

"OK. We've got you scheduled."

It was exciting to have a plan. It was no longer just a dream. I picked up a copy of the fishing regulations. As my trip approached I kept checking to see if the hunting regs were available yet. Just before I left I stopped by the Fish and Game office and found a copy hot off the press. Waterfowl regulations are a separate booklet, and this year's regs wouldn't be available on time. I'd have to try to get the basic regs with my smartphone from Wild Bay somehow. Bummer. I had my hunting and fishing license but still needed a duck stamp. A sporting good store had them. Good news!

"My boss said we can't sell them yet."

"But today is their official issue date!"

"Sorry. We were told not to sell them until he says so." I was running out of time, fast. I called the U.S. Fish and Wildlife Service.

"Do you have duck stamps yet?"

"Yes we do."

"Can I buy one?"

"Sure."

When I got there the friendly lady selling them was curious why I needed a stamp now. I told her my general plan. A law enforcement officer overheard part of our conversation.

"Where are you headed?"

"Admiralty Island."

"Where do you live?"

"Fairbanks."

"You can't hunt on Admiralty Island."

"Of course I can!"

"You're not a resident of that area. You don't qualify for subsistence hunting." (Some people, primarily Native peoples, qualify for spring "subsistence hunting" of waterfowl. Although I would be living a pure subsistence lifestyle on this trip, legally it wouldn't qualify.)

"I'm not going to hunt waterfowl until regular duck season opens."

"So why do you need a stamp today?"

"Because I'm leaving to start my trip on Monday."

"Season doesn't start until September."

"I'm going to be out there until September."

He finally understood. I thought it would have been wiser to find out exactly what I was doing before making his legal pronouncements.

A week before my trip, I gathered all my gear and packed most of it up to be shipped via the slowest and cheapest form of air cargo. When I dropped it off at the air cargo office I knew the lady working at the counter making a simple process even easier and more pleasant.

For a long trip with sporadic communications like this, there are many important tasks to take care of before leaving. Freezer emptied. Coffee pot off. Arrangements made for mail pickup. Bills prepaid or on auto-pay, etc. One by one, I checked them off my list.

Finally the big day came. At 4:14 AM, full daylight in June in Fairbanks, my old smokejumper buddy Ken pulled into the yard. We loaded up his Subaru with my gun case, a big gear bag and my carry-on. I locked the door. This was it.

# Chapter 1

## Into the Wilderness

June 30, 2014 3:30 PM

Rain streaks the plane's window. Far below, the rugged, forested coastline and rocky islands of Southeast Alaska scroll past. The plane banks gently. Ahead, I get my first glimpse of Petersburg, a small town facing a harbor crowded with fishing boats.

In the small terminal, I put on my rain coat and wait for my bags. My fellow passengers look like typical Alaskans, lots of Carhartt jackets and rubber boots. Many wear sweatshirts or caps featuring some reference to Alaska. No one is prouder of their home state than Alaskans.

The baggage door opens. Cool, damp air rushes in. I grab my large, blue pack. The door shuts but my gun case hasn't appeared. I spot it behind the ticket counter.

With my big pack on my back, my gun case in one hand and my daypack in the other, I walk out the front door into the rain and turn left. In a few steps I spot the PACIFIC WINGS sign. That was easy! A middle-aged fellow spots my load and opens the door for me.

"I'm Bruce Nelson" I say to the smiling lady at the counter.

"Hi Bruce, I'm Sarah. If you like you can take your gear through that door."

"Sounds good. Are my air cargo and jars back there?"

"Yes. The hardware store brought your jars over yesterday. Cole can show you where your stuff is." Cole, one of the pilots, steps forward to shake my hand.

"Are you flying me out today?" I ask.

"Mike will be flying you out, but I'll give you a hand getting ready."

"Thanks. Do we have enough ceiling to fly?"

"Yes. It should be fine."

In the back bay, I take the cover off the steel drum that holds my most fragile gear. It arrived ahead of me. Cole helps me transfer the glass jars from their cardboard boxes into their strong plastic crates. I change out of my flying clothes and put them in the drum which will stay here in Petersburg. As I sort through gear I notice Mike is loading the plane.

"How about we wait a few minutes before we load? I want to make sure I've got everything." We aren't scheduled to fly out for another half hour. I know from experience with other air taxi flights that I can't assume all my gear has been accounted for and loaded, and unloaded, if I haven't verified it myself.

"Sure. No problem."

When everything is ready we load a big cart with gear. The Cessna 185 sits high off the tarmac, on wheels that extend beneath the pontoons for runway landings. Mike climbs the stairs and loads while Cole and I hand him stuff.

When we are loaded I head back inside.

"All set?" Sarah asks.

"Yup. So you've got me down for a tentative September 10th pickup?"

"Yes. Do you have a satellite phone?"

"No. But there's supposed to be cell phone coverage out there in places."

Cole says "There's a lodge within paddling distance if your cell phone doesn't work."

I take a photo of the page of the schedule book showing my pickup time and date. [A friend and I had once had a different air taxi fly out on the wrong date to pick us up, despite our having verified at least twice that they had recorded it right. These people seem very squared away though.]

"If I need to change my pickup time I'll let you know."

"OK, if we don't hear from you before then, on September 10 we will pick you up where we dropped you off."

Only in Alaska, I muse, would a business, without batting an eye, drop a stranger off for months alone in the wilderness!

After putting on my waders and wading boots I walk out to the plane. Mike has me sit in the right front seat, briefing me on the location of the ELT (emergency locator transmitter) and survival gear. I put on my seat belt and shoulder harness as well as a headset and mic.

We taxi for takeoff. Reaching the runway, Mike looks both ways for incoming aircraft, then pulls out onto the runway facing into the wind. He guns the engines to full power, releases the brakes and roars down the airstrip, quickly gathering speed and suddenly we are airborne. It's always a thrill to leave the ground on a big trip like this. We are soon several hundred feet in the air and speeding along over the cold ocean.

"Do you fly out to this bay very often?" I ask.

"Sometimes. To drop people off to meet their bear guides."

"Hunters, or bear watchers?"

"Bear watchers. There's a couple of whales." He banks the plane slightly and points.

"That's awesome!" I say. The whales spout as they break the surface.

"They say this area has the greatest concentration of humpbacks in this part of the world. There's a couple more."

"Cool! The whales must be a big draw to this area."

"They are."

"There's some seals. On that island." I say, pointing.

"Sea lions I think."

"Oh. OK." I suppose by the end of this trip I'll be able to tell them apart at a glance.

Here and there, small blue and white icebergs drift with the tide.

"Where is the ice coming from?" I ask.

"The LeConte Glacier."

LeConte is the northern hemisphere's southernmost tidewater glacier. It's also known for its ice calving under water and then shooting to the surface. That would be fun to see!

We spot two or three more humpback whales, and more sea lions (or maybe seals) hauled out on some rocks.

We turn into Wild Bay, a fjord running several miles up into the mountains. I begin to recognize the islands. Ahead is the peninsula I have selected for landing [after studying topo maps and Google Earth.] Mike banks the plane around to bring it into the wind, lowers the flaps and descends until we are barely skimming over the water. When the plane is just above stall speed he sets it down. The pontoons hit the water with a metallic sound, like an aluminum boat bouncing off the waves. Spray arcs up on both sides. Mike taxis towards shore, then cuts the engine and we drift the last few feet.

He opens the door and jumps out. He is so skillful we are soon grounded tail-first to the shore without him even getting his feet wet.

"Do you know if the tide is going in or coming out?" he says.

"Going out," I reply, proud to know the answer. I'm surprised he thinks the tide moves fast enough to make a difference, though.

Unloading goes fast and the footing is gravelly and firm. I check inside the fuselage to make sure I've got everything while Mike pulls the last few items out of the floats.

"I had a pilot fly away with our stove fuel one time on a week-long trip." I tell him. "And then our water filter broke the very first time we used it. We were boiling water on alder and willow fires to purify it. We got kinda tired of smoky flavored water." I carry the last items to shore.

"Well, that's everything. Good luck!" Mike says.

"Thanks for the ride," I say and step back out of the way.

The engine sputters, then roars to life. The plane quickly picks up speed, gets "on step" then lifts off the water. After gaining some altitude it begins a slow, gentle bank back towards Petersburg. The thundering engine fades and the blue and white plane shrinks to a speck before disappearing behind the mountains. I won't see him again until September.

I am alone in the Fortress of the Bears, home to the highest density of brown bears in North America. This is not a drill. This is the real deal.

I like the looks of this place. Firm seashore. Nice big trees. There should be a good camp spot somewhere. I was concerned the shore might be too steep to camp. It's not raining. It's got a good feel. I'm really lucky.

I walk into the trees to look for a campsite, but there's no flat, open ground near the beach. I climb a twenty-foot slope and find myself on a fairly flat ridge among giant hemlock and Sitka spruce interspersed with smaller trees and scattered brush. My tent will need an opening about fifteen feet across. After walking a couple hundred yards to the left without finding an appropriate spot I turn back the other way and search towards the end of the peninsula. Should I have brought my rifle? But I'm not too worried about bears. The peninsula narrows to a

grassy strip seventy-five feet wide. This is the spot I'd seen from satellite photos that had looked like it would be serviceable for the first night if necessary. And it might be necessary from the looks of things.

But then in the very next patch of trees I find two mossy openings, each barely wide enough for my tent. Neither are perfectly level, but close. There is a good screen of trees all around for wind protection and it's nice and close to the water. The level spots are about five vertical feet above the highest tide mark. Finding a campsite was a concern of mine. It wasn't hard to imagine landing in the rain and finding a forest too thick and too steep for my tent. That would have been a bummer.

I duck through low-hanging branches and head back towards my stash of gear. I shoulder my big blue pack and grab my gun case in one hand and my daypack in the other. The next trip I fetch the dry bag with my camping gear along with as much additional gear as I can carry.

With the tent laid out in the center of the opening I look for dead branches above. Luckily the big branches above my head are still living and should deflect any smaller dead branches falling from above them. Plus the trees here are relatively short compared to the 100-200 footers not far away.

I peg down the front tent stake, and then find the rear stake loop of the tent, pulling it out taut. Using the measuring mark I've made on the tent pole, I move the loop 40 inches back towards the center and then temporarily stake out each side of the tent. Inside the tent I lift the peak of the tent with the extended tent pole then go back out and place all the rest of the tent stakes. A few adjustments results in a nice taut setup of my silnylon tipi, about seven and a half feet high at the peak and maybe thirteen feet across.

Soon my lightweight cot is set up with a closed-cell pad for insulation. I pull my down sleeping bag out of its stuff sack and give it a good shake to fluff it up. It's always nice to have a secure camp set up, especially in this rainy country.

Walking back for my last load something above me catches my eye. It's an eagle with a huge load that must be 4 feet long! What is that anyway, some kind of sea creature? The eagle passes so close I can hear its wing beats and only then do I recognize the long trailing stringer of moss it is carrying for nesting material. Cool!

I glance at my wrist to check the time. Where's my watch? I definitely looked at it while I was packing in Petersburg. Knowing the correct time is going to be important for keeping track of the tides. I check my pockets, and my daypack. Is it possible it fell off when I was cramming clothes into the dry bag? When I dump my clothes out I'm relieved to see my watch. One wrist band pin had pulled loose. Pretty lucky it fell off in a bag and not on the ground somewhere.

It's nearly 10 PM by the time camp is all squared away and sorted out. I'm tired, mentally and physically. It's been a long day traveling all the way from Fairbanks to Anchorage. After a layover there I flew to Juneau. After another long layover it was on to Petersburg. Then there was the repacking, the flight out, and setting up camp. I take my 30-06 from the gun case and put four rounds into the magazine, leaving the chamber empty. I set the rifle within easy reach, then take off my shoes and lie back on my cot. It's a good feeling to be settled in at the beginning of this big adventure. I'm really out here. The dreaming and planning are over. It's time to live it.

# Chapter 2

# Night Bear

July 1, Day 2

I wake up at about 4:30 AM. I often do. My main priority is obvious, find something to eat! I pack some basic survival gear including rain gear, lighter, GPS, and drinking water and start walking east down the peninsula towards the mainland. Salmon berries are supposed to be ripe and it would be great to have some for breakfast. At first it's fairly open forest and I weave my way through without much trouble other than climbing over a huge log or two. But near the mainland it gets much brushier with more of the wicked, spiny Devil's club mixed in. Some of the brush, though, is head-tall blueberry bushes, a few with sparse, green berries. In an hour I manage to find a small handful of half ripe blueberries. I follow a brook back down to the salt water and walk the beach back to camp. Looks like it might be harder to find berries than I'd hoped.

Back at camp I study my topo map. "I'll check the stream at the head of the bay" I say out loud. "There should be some salmon there. I want to set my crab trap, too." I unroll my inflatable kayak on the shore, open one of the valves and start pumping it up with the tiny hand pump.

I chuckle thinking about one of the silliest mistakes I ever made. I'd bought a remote cabin in the foothills of the Alaska Range and bought this kayak to try to paddle down the tiny creek to a larger creek and finally to a major river on my way to the road, a hundred miles away. At first the kayak started inflating nicely but then it seemed like I was doing a lot of pumping without much progress. I tested the pump. It was pumping air just fine. I went back to work. Did it take this long when I tested everything out? I kept switching hands. It was tiring work. It's pumping air, so it must be going into the boat, right? There is air in it, but it just won't fill up.

Finally, after what must have been a half an hour or more, I take another look at the boat valve. On my raft I always leave the one-way valves open to lessen pumping resistance. The pump valve keeps the air from leaking back out. When the raft tube is full, you turn the valve. When it's time to deflate the raft, you turn it again, without the pump attached, and the air rushes out. Just to experiment I close the one-way kayak valve. In about ten minutes I have the whole boat pumped up. Unlike my other pumps with their own valve, the hand pump allowed air to flow right back out on the up stroke! What a knucklehead! Having learned my lesson last time, the kayak is inflated in minutes. I ponder placement of the removable seat, finally clipping it in just to the rear of center.

Back at camp I assemble my collapsible crab trap. I tie a 100-foot weighted rope to the top of the trap. It would be a serious bummer to lose the trap, so although I've tied a good bowline knot, I wire AND duct tape the tag end of the knot. The buoy at the other end of the rope is tied and secured already. The law requires that crab trap buoys be marked with the angler's name, address and the boat name or number. I find a pen, and on the white part of the buoy I write:

B. Nelson
867 Esro Rd.
Fairbanks, AK
Kayak

I take off my rubber boots and change into my Gore-Tex waders and wading boots. There are some strong opinions on whether it's safe to wear waders in a kayak. The main argument against it is that your waders might fill with water making it difficult or impossible to climb back in the boat. I watched a few videos, however, with people purposely falling into the water with waders and climbing back out without a serious problem. I have fallen in with hip boots and waders without serious problems myself although I haven't tried it in the cold ocean. Ultimately, I figure I've already been wearing waders while on boats for years. On this trip I'll always wear a tight belt around the waders to keep them from flooding if I should fall in. The belly band of my life jacket will act as a second "gasket." I think that used this way the waders will actually help prevent the overwhelming shock of cold water.

A small dry bag contains my daypack with survival gear and fishing tackle. I carry the bag, crab trap, my fishing rods, and an empty bucket down to the water's edge. With the kayak in shallow water I arrange the load, crab trap across the front, then step in and push off. Soon I'm paddling out into the open bay. It's about a mile to the stream at the head of the bay. Far from shore the ten foot kayak seems very tiny and the bay very big. Near the mouth of the stream I'm surprised to see several buoys. Commercial crabber traps, no doubt.

In thirty minutes I reach the tidal flats at the stream's mouth, which I paddle up as far as I can before beaching my kayak. After unloading I carry everything fifty feet from the water. The bucket I leave near the water's edge to see how fast the tide rises. I shoulder the forty pound kayak and paddle and carry them to the edge of the trees two hundred yards away. Turning back I notice my bucket starting to float away! I trot over there and grab it in shallow water. Yikes, the tide really comes in fast!

It's just about low tide and it's pleasantly easy walking across the tidal flats. I'd expected the flats to be muddy and soft, but the ground is a mixture of gravel, mud, shells, and sand, making it nice and firm.

The stream cuts a channel across the flats. It's about twenty feet wide and six inches deep on average. I walk upstream, hoping to find a nice pool past the flats and in the trees. There's a good pool in the shadows of the first timber. No salmon are visible in the clear water. With just my spinning rod and pack I walk upstream, weaving through Devil's club bushes with their wicked thorns. There's another nice pool at the confluence of two branches of the stream and... no salmon. This doesn't look good at all. I haven't had anything to eat except for a few berries for nearly a full day. According to the fish map, pink and chum salmon run in this stream. The run timing chart indicated that both pinks and chums should be running in freshwater already. I try walking farther upstream. Thick alders and Devil's club and the lack of fish turns me around. Back at the first pool I sit down and ponder. Something dimples the water against the far bank. Then again. The fish map shows no Dolly Varden or trout in this stream, but it sure looks like trout rising to me!

Excited and hungry, I put a small reel on my spinning rod and tie a small silver spinner on the light line. On the first cast a fish darts of out the deep water after the lure but turns away in shallower water. I cast again, a little farther this time, and let the lure sink before starting an erratic retrieve. A fish strikes but escapes almost immediately. If only I can catch a couple of fish, even small ones!

Then I feel a solid strike and the thrumming of a fish on the end of the line. I reel and when I have him in the shallows I drag him up onto the gravel bar and pounce on the flopping fish, pinning him down. I break off a nearby dead stick and rap him solidly on the head. YES! A six inch Dolly Varden. The first fish of the trip! [Dolly Varden are technically a kind of char, but they are often called trout or "Dollies."]

The next few casts yield no strikes so I switch to a black spinner. The next cast several fish come after it, and bang! Black spinners is what they want. I hook another fish and soon have him beached, bonked and laid next to the first fish in the cool shade. By the time the hungriest fish have been caught and the cautious fish spooked there are five small Dolly Varden lying in a row. I've got my first meal! I'm going to call this beautiful creek "My Stream."

From branches at the base of nearby hemlocks I break off a handful of tiny dead twigs, then some pencil size, bark-less branches. Most break with a dry snap, largely protected from rain by the thick, overhanging canopy. Lastly I gather a few one inch thick dead branches. Any wood laying on the ground, or not protected by overhead from the rain, is soaked.

On the gravel bar near the water I crumple up a couple pieces of scrap paper, break up the smallest twigs and criss-cross them on top, followed by the rest of the twigs. I break up the pencil size branches and the rest of the bigger firewood and set them within easy reach.

Using the lighter stashed in the front pocket of my pack I light a bottom corner of the crumpled paper. It catches and the tiny flame spreads and grows, the twigs catching one by one then several at a time until there is a four inch flame. I slowly add the pencil size sticks. When they are burning well, I add criss-crossed pieces of the larger wood. When the fire is burning nicely I clean the Dollies and arrange them on one side of the broiler grill, then flip the "clam-shell" top part down and slide the locking ring in place.

While I wait for the fire to burn down to coals I look at the beautiful, mossy camping spot among the trees only a few steps away. A much better spot than where I'm camped. The disadvantage? When the salmon finally show up there will be brown bears parading through here left and right. That's what I call a downside!

When there is a good bed of coals I lay the grill right on top of them and put some of larger coals on top of the fish. In only a few minutes the eyes of the fish have turned white. When I poke them with the tip of my knife blade the flesh flakes nicely and I pull the grill off the fire.

From the plastic bag in the side pocket of my pack I retrieve the salt and pepper shakers. My mouth is already watering when I flip up the top half of the grill and peel a chunk of meat off the back of the largest fish, juggling it briefly in one hand as it cools. I pop it in my mouth. Wow, that's good! That's *really* good!

After sprinkling salt and pepper on all the fish I eat the rest of the meat off the top of the big fish. Seasoned, it's even better. The skeleton peels cleanly from the bottom half. I eat the rest of the meat including the cheek meat, the best part of all. One by one I polish off the last four fish, peeling off and eating the bits of skin still sticking to the grill. That was an awesome meal, but I'm going to be needing a lot more food to last 70 days out here.

The heads, tails, guts and skeletons go into a plastic bag. After hiking the half mile back to the boat I carry everything down to the water, then put all the fish scraps into the wire crab bait cage, six inches long and four inches square, which I bungee on the center of the trap's bottom. Looking around I find a rock to put in the trap for a little extra weight. It will help prevent the tidal current from moving the trap. Is it necessary here? I don't know. I've never set a crab trap anywhere before.

I've read that in this area the best crabbing is off to the side of stream mouths at about sixty feet deep. I figure the commercial crabbers must know what they're doing, so I paddle out and find spot a reasonable distance away from, but between, two buoys.

The trap line is coiled at the bottom of the kayak. Making sure my feet and legs are free of any tangles I lower the trap into the water. The trap disappears from view at about 20 feet but a sheen of fish oil remains on the surface. That should draw some crabs.

There's a nice island of perhaps two acres nearby that I want to explore. I paddle over and pack everything above high tide. I watch for berries and campsites but I'm not finding much of either. At the high point, maybe twenty feet above the water, I find and eat a few more half-ripe blueberries. Not exactly a berry bonanza so far! There's a nice little opening near the opposite side of the island. It's not perfectly level but it will work as a campsite. It's an easy walk to the water, too, and a pretty good spot for avoiding bears as well. For most of the day this is an island, only at low tide could a bear reach this place without swimming.

The crab trap has only been out an hour but I paddle back out to check it. I pull the buoy and slack rope into the boat. At first it's easy because the water is only about 75 feet deep and there's 100 feet of rope. I don't make any special effort to coil the rope as I pull it in.

When the rope tightens I pull with both arms, to about nose level, holding what I have with my right hand and reaching down to grab the rope at boat tube level with my left. It's tiring. When I glance down after hauling for a while there's still no sign of the trap. Why are my hands stinging? I notice white stringers of something on the rope. Jellyfish tentacles! No wonder. The trap comes into view far below the surface and it now holds a reddish object. Is that a crab!? Yes!

The trap comes over the side and balances easily across the boat in front of me, dripping. I ponder my game plan. Getting a Dungeness, or crab of any kind, out of a trap is a new challenge for me. I retrieve the yellow crab caliper from my pack and put on my neoprene gloves. When I reach through one of the trap doors the crab makes a grab for my fingers. I distract him by reaching towards the side of the cage with my left hand, then grab him from behind with my right. He reaches back with his claws and manages to pinch one finger. Ouch! Those are some strong claws! Luckily my finger slides out from the tip of the glove and I escape. Taking a grip farther back I pull him towards the door. He hangs on briefly, then gives up.

Using an inside edge of the caliper I measure just behind the spines, which are the widest part of the shell. My caliper has a series of stepped notches on one side. The crab just fits inside the one marked 6 1/2", meaning he is *barely* too small. I'm disappointed but encouraged. If I caught one that soon I will certainly catch more!

I paddle the mile or so back to camp and get geared up to try my luck for rockfish. Young crows are calling hoarsely from the tree crowns, begging their parents to bring them some chow. There are big rocks at the end of my peninsula and also along the shore towards the main Sound. It seems like it would be good rockfish habitat. I put the large spinning reel on my salmon rod. I skewer a large white double-tailed plastic jig onto a heavy jig head and tie it on. I feel good about catching a fish or two. I jig around the end of the rocky point. This seems like a great spot. I feel the jig bounce off the rocks occasionally, but no strikes. Paddling upwind a quarter mile or so along the shore I stow my paddle and drift, jigging steadily.

Is that a strike?! Nope, snagged on a rock. Paddling back upwind a bit the snag comes loose. About halfway back to camp I feel something on the end of my line. It's no rock. But it's also not fighting. When it reaches the surface I see I've snagged a sea cucumber.

Now, I *know* part of sea cucumbers is edible, but when I lift it out of water it's like jelly in a plastic bag, or a huge slug. It could hardly be less appetizing. I consider eating it anyway to get some food and also for the adventure, but I'm not hungry enough yet. Instead, I put it in my bucket to try it for crab bait.

After an hour or two I haven't gotten a strike. Seems to me they either aren't biting or this is a bad spot or both. Or possibly I don't know what I'm doing.

I paddle the mile back to my crab trap. A seal bobs to the surface and follows me off to the left. With his dark eyes and the top of his head barely above the surface he looks cute, but sneaky.

My red and white buoy is easy to pick out from the commercial crabber buoys. When there's a pile of wet rope in the boat I start glancing into the water hoping to see the trap red with crabs. I see red, but not a whole lot. It's a single crab. I grab him from behind again, but this time with my thumb underneath, rather than my fingers, and as far back as I can maintain my grip. This keeps all five fingers clear of his claws. The caliper shows what I was already afraid of: he's slightly smaller than the last one. Oh well.

Half of the char scraps are already gone. The grid of the bait cage is a little too big and some of the smaller scraps have simply slid through No doubt the crab ate some of it, too. I add the sea cucumber to the bait. I decide to use one of the huge halibut jigs as additional bait. They are made of scented plastic, and to add to the appeal I add a few drops of halibut bait oil. If it smells like fish to a halibut, it should smell like a meal to crabs, too.

I paddle for home, thinking about tomorrow. The kayak bow crunches against the gravelly bottom. I relax for a moment, leaning back against the boat seat. I'm tired. I unload the boat and swing it up onto my head to carry it to high ground. I suddenly recognize a plant. Sea asparagus! I'd been expecting a plant about the size of standard asparagus, but these plants are a few inches tall and a little thicker than a spaghetti noodle. I pick one and take a bite... it's crisp and salty, with a taste like string beans. I grab a bunch to munch on.

It's great to get out of my waders. I take off my sweat-dampened socks and put on nice, dry, clean socks then crawl into my sleeping bag. Extra clothes in a fleece jacket serve as a pillow. An eagle is calling from his treetop perch. I read for a little while until I get sleepy, then check that my rifle is within easy reach and that I know where my headlamp is. In no time, I'm sound asleep.

July 2, Day 3

It's already getting light when I wake up.

What are my best odds of a meal? I'll check the crab trap first.

I'm concerned about losing my paddle or crab caliper overboard. Sitting in the kayak seat I tie a length of parachute cord to a floor loop then, checking for plenty of slack, tie the other end to the center of the paddle with a good, tight, bowline knot. With another length of cord I make a lanyard for the caliper.

On the way to the trap, there is a little chop on the water. Once again, the trap holds a single Dungeness crab. This one looks a bit bigger.

"Is he legal?" I ask myself. With the caliper handy I pull the crab out and measure him; he won't fit inside the six and a half inch notch.

"He's legal!" I say aloud, triumphantly. But then I remember it has to be a male crab as well. I turn him over, and, sure enough, he's got a narrow, triangular-shaped belly plate. Yes! This is going to be a real meal. I put the crab in a bucket, add bait oil to the jig and drop the trap overboard.

Back at camp, I fetch my wood-burning rocket stove, frying pan, lighter, and tarp. It's time to establish a cook camp. 150 yards down the beach I find an open area. There's a tree with a big branch about eighteen feet high with no other branches below it. That should work well for hanging a food cache. Nearby there is a brush-free spot with some smaller trees spaced nicely for hanging a tarp.

I carry the crab bucket down to the shore. I've never cleaned a crab before, but I know the theory. With the crab facing away, I grab his left legs near the shell with my left hand and his right legs with my right. Now he can't pinch me. I step over to an angular rock and, squaring the crab's shell to a rock edge, bring it down hard once, twice, and the whole top of the shell breaks off cleanly. I break the crab in half on the same rock edge, then fling the innards out and pluck the remaining pieces of gill off. All that's left is crab legs and the meat of the body. That was remarkably easy, and a fast, humane way to dispatch him.

After rinsing, both halves are thrown in the bucket with a gallon of saltwater. I notice limpets below high tide. Limpets are a conical shaped aquatic snail. These aren't very big, less than an inch in diameter, but they're edible and safe from paralytic shellfish poisoning. I can use the food and want to give them a try. I add a half dozen to the bucket.

I gather up the driest wood I can find, twigs and small sticks, then set up my rocket stove for its first-ever use. I put the crab and limpets in my frying pan and add seawater until it's nearly full. I crumple up two pages from the airline magazine and put them in the combustion chamber. With a loose pile of dry twigs on top of the paper, I light it. The tiny fire grows quickly as the chimney begins to draw. I quickly add larger sticks and, when the fire is going good, put the frying pan on top. In no time, the water is steaming. When it begins to boil I set the timer on my watch and cover the pan with foil.

The stove concentrates the heat perfectly. The boil is easy to maintain with foot-long sticks of finger thickness which I push into the stove as they burn. Steam curls up from beneath the foil. After twelve minutes I stop adding wood and at fifteen minutes I pull the still boiling pan off the fire and set it aside to cool.

This is the first crab I've ever cooked. I'm so hungry it's hard to wait for the meat to cool. I break off a small leg and juggle it around a bit, then crack the shell of the largest end with my teeth, peeling off the broken shell and plucking out the steaming white meat. I pop it in my mouth.

It's too hot. I hold the meat briefly between my front teeth, blowing on it, then chew.

Oh man, that is sooooo good, sweet and slightly salty. It could not possibly be better. I crack the next section and the next, tossing the empty shells in the bucket. I break the next leg off along with the attached body section. There is more meat on this larger leg and big pieces of meat on the body section. I make sure to salvage every bit of it. The claw shell is the strongest, but it also yields large pieces of delicious meat. This is awesome!

I pick out the limpets one at a time. The meat is good, like escargot maybe, but they are just so tiny it doesn't amount to much. When they are gone I tackle the second crab half. It's time consuming cracking shells and getting at all the meat, but it's like eating peanuts in the shell, there's satisfaction in the process itself. When I finish the last claw and the meat is all gone I feel as if I've eaten my first full meal of the trip. That was great!

I've brought a blue, nylon tarp to establish a proper "cook camp." I tie the center grommets at each end of the rectangular tarp to two small trees spaced nearly perfectly. It takes a little more imagination to tie off each corner. One cord goes to a blueberry bush, one to a stake, and the others to branches, resulting in a nice, taut pitch. I set the stove beneath the tarp and scout around for firewood. Other than some sprinkles it hasn't rained much since I arrived and I want to get some dry wood under cover. Most of the dead wood is mossy, soaked and heavy, so I'm selective. In an hour there is a small stack of dry wood under the tarp.

Bringing the bucket of crab shells I paddle back to the crab trap, which is empty. I add the crab shells figuring they will leave a nice scent plume. I stash the kayak and excess gear above high tide and hike back up to the Dolly pool to catch some supper. In a few minutes I hook, land and keep a small fish. While casting I notice movement. A blacktail deer is walking out of the sunny meadow into the shadows of the trees where I'm fishing. He hasn't seen me yet and I freeze. His summer coat is very brown. Insects are harassing him. He flicks his tail, bats his ears and bobs his head, kicking with one hind leg at an especially bothersome bug on his nose. Obviously he can't smell me. He's startled to notice me so close. He can't quite figure out what I am but finally loses his nerve and bounds off.

I'm not hooking any more fish, nor am I getting "follows." I change spinners, but no dice. I check the next pool upstream. Nothing. What happened to all the fish? They either moved or aren't biting. I'm not seeing them in the clear water so maybe they headed farther upstream?

I lean my fishing rod against a tree and head out with my daypack looking for berries. I walk across boggy ground, noticing deer tracks in many places but not much recent sign of brown bears. I follow a low ridge to higher ground. I recognize blueberry bushes but few have any berries, not even green ones. When I do spot a reasonably ripe berry, I eat it immediately. Good thing I caught that crab because there sure aren't many berries. Where are the salmon berries, anyway? What kind of places do they like? Sun, shade, high ground, low ground? Walking in my waders is tiring. It must be in the low 60's and there's even some sun from time to time. I'm starting to sweat. I sit down, leaning back against the trunk of a giant hemlock. It's quiet back here in the ancient forest, away from the seagulls along Wild Bay. I watch for blacktails, or brown bears, approaching along the paths that wind down the low ridge, but see nothing but a few insects and an eagle soaring high overhead.

After a while I stand up and work my way back towards the creek but only find a few more partially ripe blueberries. The deer tracks are encouraging though. I should be able to get a buck when the season opens.

On my way back to camp I check the crab trap once more, but it's empty. A brisk east wind has sprung up. It really slows my progress. Even the thought of having to fight the wind is tiring.

I fry up the small Dolly at cook camp. It's good but there's not much to it.

Back at the tent I pull off my waders, put on dry socks and lie back on my cot and close my eyes. It's only 5 pm but I find myself drifting off.

I wake up in the pitch black of night with my heart pounding. A brown bear is sniffing loudly just outside my tent! In five seconds my headlamp is on and my rifle in hand with a round chambered. I listen again but hear nothing. I unzip the tent and step outside and sweep my light in a circle... All I see are the dark trees and brush. He must have run. For a minute I stand quietly, listening. My heartbeat is back to normal. Hopefully he hasn't trashed my cook camp. Bears often destroy gear out of curiosity or just for fun.

I walk along the beach, rifle in hand, my headlamp casting a pool of bobbing light ahead of me. Almost certainly the bear is long gone. Cook camp is undisturbed. Down at the water I turn the headlamp off and stand in the dark. It's amazing how quiet it is here compared to the day with its wind, waves, gulls, eagles, crows, ravens.

Back in the tent I open the bolt of my rifle and get back into my sleeping bag. I'm not worried. More than once I've had brown bears in camp on past trips, even when I was unarmed. It's a good sign when they run off right away.

I think back to a bear that DID worry me. I was hiking the Continental Divide Trail a few years ago. I was "cowboy camping," sleeping on the open ground, somewhere along the Montana/Idaho border. I was just drifting off to sleep when I heard something breathing nearby. Something big. It was nearly dark but when I sat up I could see the outline of a black bear maybe twenty feet away. He stood, staring at me. I jumped up and yelled and he stepped back. I picked up a stick and rushed at him and he walked slowly into the trees. What I didn't like is that he wasn't very scared. Typically, wilderness bears are terrified of people. When they bolt, that's usually the last you see of them. When they aren't scared, they tend to come back to snoop around, looking for food. I lay back down and watched and listened for a while. It was now full dark. I was sleeping again when the strong smell of bear wakened me. He was right there! I jumped up and grabbed a big stick and my light. This time I wasn't screwing around. I rushed him, trying to get close enough to hit him. He hustled off and I picked up a series of rocks and threw them at him. This time he got the message. He didn't come back. Bears should be scared of people, for their own good.

I glance at my wrist, but of course the band broke and it isn't there. Where the heck did I stash it? I look around for a bit with no luck. I check the time on the LED of my weather radio. 10:17. I should find my watch in the morning when the alarm goes off. I am soon falling asleep again.

# Chapter 3

# Hunger and Exhaustion

July 3, Day 4

The next thing I hear is my watch going off. It sounds like it's outside. In the pocket of my life vest. That's where I put it! Since the alarm is still set for my 3:45 airport wake-up I fall back asleep.

I wake up again in the gray light of dawn and turn on the weather radio. They are predicting three foot seas, or higher, out on the Sound in coming days. I don't know what that will mean for here on Wild Bay, but I'm concerned about having to stay off rough water and worrying people back home by being out of touch for weeks. Hopefully there will be cell coverage out towards the Sound somewhere so I can let people know I'm OK. If there is sufficient coverage to use my iPhone, I'll update my online journal. I've told people I'd try to update my journal periodically and I feel I owe it to them if it's possible. Worrying people unnecessarily is my greatest stress right now. That's a problem with the ability to contact people. If people think you can let them know you're OK, they will worry if you don't. Imaginations run wild. I want to get this issue resolved, and I want to resolve it today.

It will likely be a long paddle round trip. I'll plan for an overnight expedition. I'm glad to have the electric bear fence to protect my camp while I'm gone, especially after hearing that bear last night.

The fence will have to be pretty close to my tent due to brush and trees around my campsite. I set up a fiberglass stake in each of four corners, then string out a strand of polywire and run it around the perimeter, then do it again for two more strands. I install the tensioning device on each wire then hang the wire on the clips of each stake and take the slack out of each wire.

The fence energizer, the component that actually does the "zapping," is powered by two D batteries. I install them as indicated, then latch the battery cover shut. For a moment I'm stumped. How does the electricity get from the energizer to the wire?? Then I realize the energizer hangs directly on the wire by a metal clip which conducts the power to the wire. After grounding the fence I turn on the energizer and the light begins blinking. Is it working? There's an easy way to find out. I touch it as briefly as possible. Nothing. Again. Nothing. A third time. Nope. Damn. What's the problem? I try again and let my finger linger this time. *Zap!* I felt that! I'd simply been touching it so fast I'd missed the brief pulses. Electric shocks are strange. Harmless, I guess, but boy do I hate'em. So do animals. Specifically bears, I'm hoping.

OK, so what do I need for this trip? My little tarptent for one. Usually one end of this shelter is held up with a hiking pole. I don't have a hiking pole so I bring a nail to put in the end of a stick. The head of the nail will go through the grommet at the peak of the shelter and keep the stick in place. I put the nail in a small pocket of my daypack so I don't lose it. The tent, my sleeping bag and sleeping pad go in a dry bag, along with a change of dry clothing. So I'm set to sleep warm and dry.

I bring my iPhone along with it's charging cord and solar charger. No need to pack any food because I don't have any! Instead, I'll bring fishing gear, a spinning rod, fly fishing rod and a landing net, along with tackle. I'll bring a bucket and lid in case I have fish to haul back to base camp. The broiling grill. Lighters. A quart jar for berries. Headlamp. Water filter. Fork. Salt and pepper. Fillet knife. I plan to camp on islands so I'll leave my rifle. Kayak and paddle, of course. Repair kit. Life jacket. Wader belt. Tide tables. Watch... Yes! It's in my PFD

pocket. I run down my gear list print-out and add a few more odds and ends.

I carry my gear and kayak down to the water's edge and load the boat, trying to keep everything low for stability and to lessen wind drag. I bungee down my fishing rods and some smaller gear. A couple items I leave loose, the large dry bag and the sealed plastic bucket which holds my daypack and other smaller items. If, heaven forbid, I flip, it will be easier to right the kayak that way. But flipping is highly unlikely. I've sat on one side of this kayak as a test, and it didn't flip. I plan to avoid going into the water at all costs, that's for sure.

The kayak glides into the bay. My watch and the tide tables show I will have about two and a half hours of falling tide to give me a gentle push towards the Sound. The water is calm and I paddle steadily, making good progress. The sun breaks through the clouds and sparkles on snow-capped mountains that have magically appeared above Wild Bay. It's a higher, more colorful world. A seal head pops out of the water nearby and follows along, creating a V of tiny ripples. After a few minutes, he sinks soundlessly into the water. Ahead I see what must be seals, or sea lions, resting on a bare rocky island a few feet above the water. As I approach they panic, jumping into the water in all directions with great splashes. The excitement is immediately replaced with the calm of many seal heads cruising along, watching me curiously.

From time to time I glance at my iPhone, in its waterproof case that hangs by a lanyard around my neck. Not a hint of coverage. I stop paddling to put on my neoprene gloves, not for warmth but to prevent blisters. There are many miles of paddling ahead of me.

Before the trip I'd seen a cabin plotted on the USGS topo map of the area. As I near that island I watch for it. I'd considered landing at this island to establish a base camp. The AT&T map showed good coverage there, so I'm hopeful. But as I pass the island there is no sign of any cell phone signal nor the cabin. I've already paddled nearly five miles as the crow flies. This isn't good. As I paddle onward I hear a boat motor and turn to see a small boat racing towards me. As it nears the engine slows then stops completely. Two 60-something fisherman glide towards me in their skiff.

"How's fishing?" asks the one.

"I haven't wet a line yet today. How about you guys?"

"We caught a rockfish. We got a halibut yesterday. Do you have a boat?"

"Nope. Just this kayak. I'm camped near the head of the bay. Any idea how far I'd have to paddle to get a cell signal."

"About ten miles or so. That's the last place we had coverage." My heart sinks.

"Ouch."

"Do you need to use a phone? Our boat is over by the lodge until tomorrow. If you want you could leave a message with our wives and we can make a call for you when we get back to coverage."

"I appreciate that. I'm going to be out here a while though. From time to time I want to be able to let people know I'm OK."

"That makes sense. You should talk to the lodge owners, they have a cell booster. They seem like nice people.

"I think I will, thanks. Good luck!"

"You too."

It's about two more miles to the lodge, protected in a cove off the bay. There are several buildings. As I get closer I try to pick out the office. I never like asking for favors, especially from strangers. Man, if I had only brought a satellite phone. It's going to be a long haul to paddle here to use their cell service. Assuming they let me.

I see what looks like the main lodge. A friendly, 30-something, bearded fellow greets me. I briefly explain my situation. He tells me they have satellite internet as well as the cell booster. He directs me to the business office.

A female voice answers when I knock on the office door.

"Come in."

"Hi, I'm Bruce Nelson."

"Hi Bruce, I'm Jody."

"I'm camped at the head of the bay for a few weeks. According to AT&T there was supposed to be good coverage here in areas. Apparently there isn't. I promised people I'd update my website to let them know I'm OK. I don't want them to worry. I'd be happy to pay you for use of your internet service every week or two."

"To be honest we've had some trouble with people arriving by boat and hanging around the lodge just to use our internet."

"I understand that. I'd be as brief as possible and try to stay out of the way."

"How much time would you need?"

"Maybe 30 minutes each time."

"What kind of device do you have?"

"An iPhone."

"OK, we'll give you an hour."

I thank them profusely then head over to the main lodge building. Wanting to make sure I don't overstay my welcome, I keep my update brief, check for critical emails, then head back to the office.

"I'm off. Thanks again. You really helped me out. It's a huge relief knowing people won't be worrying about me.

"You're welcome. We'll see you next time. Be safe!" They've already warmed towards me. Very nice of them.

I didn't even take my waders off so it doesn't take long to get back on the water. It's great to have a plan. It's not Plan A, but it is a Plan B that will work.

"I'll probably shoot for updating my site every two weeks or so," I think. "I don't want to bother the lodge too much. And it's a long paddle, especially round-trip. Plus I want to make this a wilderness trip as much as possible. Actually, I guess that's one advantage of not having cell coverage. I'll really be cut off from the outside world."

I'm going to explore another cove on my way home. Hopefully there will be salmon in the stream at its head. There's an island I should be able to camp on. Looking at the map I see that a short portage across a peninsula will save me close to mile of paddling. That's what I'll do.

I haven't eaten since last evening, but having resolved the commo issue I'm in a fine mood. I stop to take several self-timer photos of myself and kayak in the sun, with a backdrop of spectacular green and snow-capped mountains. The portage is short, a spit of land that is awash at high tide, so it's completely free of vegetation now and easy walking.

It's about a mile to the cove. I pass the island where I plan to make camp. It's small, but has nice, high ground, big timber and what appears to be some open, flat spots. It will be completely bear free. The tide is coming in again, so I carry my kayak and gear to high ground on the mainland, then grab my fishing gear and head for the creek, still about a mile away. After arriving I walk along the bank, looking down into the clear water. One, two, three large fish are cruising in the lowest pool. Salmon! It's always fun to spot salmon when out fishing, but now, after almost a full day with no food, I am especially excited. I really want to catch them. I really NEED to catch something. I tie on a spinner and cast it past the salmon and begin reeling. It flutters past them but they ignore it. Several more casts draw no reaction at all. I change to a spoon but they ignore it completely.

I walk upstream to a bend in the stream. There, a beautiful riffle empties into a deep pool in the shade of big trees and overhanging Devil's club. In the crystal water I see a single salmon holding, and many, many Dolly Varden! Now I know I will catch fish today. I will get something to eat.

I tie on a black spinner and on the first cast get a solid hit. I battle the struggling fish to shore and drag it onto the gravel. I whack it on the head with a handy stick and lay it in the cool shade on a green, mossy log. I pause to admire this beautiful fish that will become my meal. It is about thirteen inches long, covered with faded pink and orange spots. The fins are orange-ish, some with the white edges typical of char.

My second cast draws a strike as well, but I lose the fish. On the third cast I catch another fine Dolly of about fourteen inches. One by one I add fish to the growing line on the log. After I have a half dozen I keep only injured fish or the biggest ones. I cast into the riffles of the bend and allow the spinner to sink deep into the pool. There is a solid strike and I feel the heaviest fish so far fighting its way towards the brush on the far bank. I tighten the drag and stop him in time then work him towards shallow water and up onto the gravel bar where I pounce on him and give him the coup de grace. He has some real heft as I pick him up. He must be an eighteen incher! What a magnificent fish, an absolute giant compared to the Dollies I've caught so far on this trip. At about 5 PM I have my limit of ten fish and the good weather holds. Luck is on my side.

At the edge of the trees I gather dry twigs and dead branches and build a fire on the gravel bar where high water will later wash away all traces of it. As the larger wood burns to hot coals I clean all my fish and line them up on the grill until it is full, setting the rest of the fish in the cool shade. I lay the grill on the coals and put some large coals on top of the fish to speed the cooking. It will be especially helpful with these larger fish. I find a stick about twelve inches long with a three inch fork on one end and run the long end through the gills and mouth of the remaining fish, and slide them down until they are stopped by the short arm of the Y.

The fish are ready. I find a comfortable place to sit, open the grill and sprinkle salt on a fish. I peel away a steaming chunk of beautiful meat. It's good, but I don't feel very hungry. With each bite my appetite

rapidly wanes. My appetite evaporates before the first fish is gone. I should be starving. What's going on? I drink some cold water and wait for a bit but I don't want to eat any more. I flip the top half of the grill back down and slide the ring to lock it in place. I pack my daypack again and pick up the grill in one hand and my fishing rod and the stick with the uncooked fish in the other and head back towards the kayak.

After walking only a few hundred yards I'm tired and stop to rest. After recuperating for a few minutes I resume hiking but once again run out of steam and sit down, leaning against my daypack. I don't like this feeling. Why am I not hungry? How come I'm so tired? It's unsettling. I remember a time, many, many years ago, during another, much shorter "living off the land" trip. I was maybe ten years old, sitting by a smoky campfire in the dark woods of Minnesota with my little brother, about six years old. I was struggling to get a kettle of squirrel meat to boil. I liked squirrel meat. I was hungry. But I had the same feeling of no appetite.

On adventures like this I have great confidence in my ability to put up with challenges, to persevere even when it's uncomfortable, to not be lonely when I'm alone, to be unintimidated when things aren't going well. One of my biggest concerns for this trip, however, is that I will get so tired of fish that I'll find them difficult to eat. But certainly I'm not tired of fish yet. I must just be tired, so exhausted I'm just not hungry. Right? It staggers my confidence, but doesn't shatter it. After resting a couple more times, and switching my loads from hand to hand many times, I finally make it back to my kayak.

What a relief to get camp set up, to have my sleeping pad rolled out and my sleeping bag waiting for me. I'll feel better tomorrow. Tomorrow I'll tie into those Dollies like I mean business. I take a big drink of water, read for a while, then nestle into my bag and drift off to a sound sleep.

# CHAPTER 4

---

# Independence Day

July 4, Day 5

When I wake up there is no hurry to find food, no pressure to do anything but eat. I'm going to make this an easy day. A recovery day.

I fetch the grill of cooked fish from the cool shade where it was covered with a huge Devil's club leaf with green moss on top. The fish are in perfect shape. With a quart of cold drinking water at hand I peel meat from a fish, season it with salt and pepper, and chew contentedly. After two and a half fish I'm full. Although I'm not nearly as hungry as I expected, those big dollies made a fine breakfast.

It's another nice day and it's not difficult to find reasonably dry firewood. I build a small campfire to cook the last of the fresh fish so they will keep better. When they are done I eat some more fish, then wash my hands and return the remaining fish to their moss "cooler."

I lie back on my pad and sleeping bag, reading the last of the Alaska Airlines magazine and working on the crossword puzzle. Already a bunch of pages have been used for fire tinder but now the rest will be available. Dual use!

After a nice nap I get up and eat some more fish. There were two fish in the eighteen inch range, and all the rest in the eight to sixteen inch range, so it's a lot of good meat. What's for dessert? Berries maybe? With an empty quart jar and my daypack with rain gear, space blanket, lighter, etc, I head over to search for berries on the nearby mainland. At a beautiful little brook I filter two quarts of cold water.

There are many berry bushes but the berries are sparse. It's fun exploring though, and the jar slowly fills with mostly ripe blueberries. It would fill faster if I didn't eat so many of them! Varying my diet is important, for enjoyment, digestion, the challenge of harvesting different types of foods, and for wide array of necessary nutrients. Blueberries are good for vitamin C, for example, as well as their fiber. Where are the salmon berries? I thought they would be a main food source at the start of this trip and I still haven't found a single berry.

Suddenly it strikes me, it's the 4th of July! Not much to set this day apart from any other here in the Kootznoowoo Wilderness.

With a quart of berries in my pack, I return to camp, triumphant. I eat some more char for a late lunch then relax in my sleeping bag, reading an old issue of Backpacker magazine. Today is the first day of the trip where I have as much as I can eat and now, with my jar of blueberries, and fish in the cooler, I have variety as well. With eating, napping, reading and berry picking I've managed to putter away an enjoyable day of wilderness living.

As evening approaches I look for my headlamp. Where the heck did I put it? With so few belongings it doesn't seem like it would be that difficult to find. I look through every bag and pack, shake out my sleeping bag (a favorite hiding place of missing small gear) and check under my sleeping pad. After nearly going through every pocket in all my clothing I find the missing headlamp in the pocket of my fleece jacket.

I end a fine day with a full belly, and with one last cooked char in the "cooler," most of a jar of blueberries in reserve, and my morale and confidence fully intact once more. What a difference a single day can make!

# Chapter 5

# Home in the Wild

July 5, Day 6

I sleep in until 6 AM or so, fairly late for me! It looks like another nice day. I've saved the biggest Dolly for last, the eighteen incher. There must be over a pound of meat on it. It provides a big, delicious breakfast. As I wander around camp I notice the best patch of blueberries yet. I had completely missed it, even though it is in an obvious spot, along the path down to the kayak. That's funny. Now the blueberries serve as the freshest of breakfast fruit, straight from the bush to my mouth.

While packing leisurely, I make another discovery: a salmonberry, a first for this trip! Now I know what the bushes look like. This patch is growing in a sunny opening. I'll keep an eye out for these head-high bushes with leaflets in groups of three. Especially in sunny spots. I only find two half-ripe berries but I eat them anyway.

After breaking down camp and loading up, I paddle back to base camp, aided by a gentle tailwind. The sun has come out, occasionally hidden by passing clouds. I beach my kayak on the near side of the spit, opposite from where I usually land. I weave through thimbleberry bushes then duck under low-hanging hemlock branches to leave my excess gear inside the electric fence. Everything just as I left it. If my tent had been ripped to pieces it would really have ruined my day!

Back at the kayak I paddle towards the head of the bay to check the crab trap. Hand over hand I pull the heavy trap out of the depths until finally I see the trap and... red, quite a bit of red. Crabs! When I pull the trap over the side of the boat and set it, dripping, across the tubes in front of me there are three crabs scooting to the sides. YES!

I pull on my neoprene gloves, and reach for the crab caliper. Carefully grabbing the first crab I measure him: 6 ¼." Damn! Over the side he goes. The second: also 6 ¼." Rats! The last one looks a bit bigger. I hope. 6 ½." Barely. *YES!* I lay him upside down on the floor of the kayak behind me where he can't get a grip to right himself. Grabbing the bucket behind me I unscrew the top and set the bucket between my legs. I release the little bungee holding the bait cage to the bottom and pull it out. In the bucket are fish heads, guts and tails. I fill the bait cage and bungee it back to the bottom of the crab trap. I put the crab in the bucket and set it behind me. The wind has pushed me nearly to shore so I paddle the two hundred yards or so back out to deeper water and lower the trap into the ocean, throwing the red and white buoy over last. I mark the spot with my GPS.

Heading back to camp my tailwind is now a headwind, but no matter, it still only takes 30 minutes or so before my kayak crunches ashore.

After carrying everything above high tide I get my camp chair and head to cook camp. I clean the crab, fill the frying pan with seawater, and add the crab halves, letting the excess water slop over the sides. I start a fire in the rocket stove and when it's going well set the frying pan on top and cover it with foil. In no time it's boiling. Soon I'm eating my second full meal of the day. Now I'm living!

I'd brought a Kindle for this trip for it's multi-use. Primarily it was going to be a backup for my smartphone so I could update my website even if my iPhone failed. Back when I was going to depend on cell service, that is. Expecting to spend many rainy hours in my tent, I'd downloaded numerous books on it, and also photos of pages of some books I had at home, pages about rockfishing, halibut fishing, salmon run timing maps, topo maps. While waiting for my connecting flight in Juneau, however, I'd plugged it in to top off its charge and to check my email before I headed afield. I noticed the battery was draining even as it was plugged in. Customer service tried walking me through possible fixes but then finally said:

"OK. Looks like your Kindle has charging issues. Just return it and we'll send you a replacement."

"That's not really an option right now. I'm, ahhh, heading out on a trip for a couple of months. There's no other options?"

"I'm afraid not. It will have to be replaced."

Just like that I was down to one commo device. That's exactly why I brought a backup. Electronics can be undependable, especially in such a wet climate.

The sun is out again and in this country it pays to make hay while the sun shines. Knowing it might be a week between good sun I want to keep all electronics fully charged when possible. I lay out a solar panel and plug in my Kindle, figuring "what the heck, it can't hurt to try." I lay out my iPhone's small, folding charger and when I plug it in the phone gives a satisfying "ding" signifying it's charging. When I check the Kindle I'm delighted to see it's gained 1 per cent charge already. Sweet! Maybe I'll be able to read all those books after all!

My gear is a bit of a disorganized mess. I'm the type of person that likes to BE organized, but I'm not super disciplined to stay organized. In the tent I study all my gear and ponder a system. My gaze falls on the plastic jar boxes, the two separate halves lying side-by-side looking like an opened egg carton. I set one out and put pens in one section, headlamp in another, medicines in a third, spare glasses in a fourth, and so on. The smallest items I organize in empty quart jars, handy because they are clear. I put all the empty bags and stuff sacks together. All the hunting stuff is gathered together, my 30-06 and 12 gauge, ammunition and cleaning kit in the opened gun case. I put all the repair stuff together, duct tape, super glue, needle and thread, wire. Socks, gloves and underwear go in one stuff sack. Other spare clothing goes in another. I sort out fishing gear as well, stashing most of it in a bucket while keeping smaller kits of saltwater and freshwater fishing tackle separate. It feels great to be organized. I'll know exactly where my headlamp is if I need it at night, where my toothbrush is in the morning. It's good to have a system.

While I work, young crows holler insistently from the treetops. They become background noise after a while and I don't notice them, but if a person focused on it and let it become bothersome it would get pretty annoying! Regardless, they leave, and/or are quiet at night.

I gather and eat some raw sea asparagus which is plentiful on the beach nearby, and munch on blueberries. Checking the solar charging operation, still leaning against the boulders, I find my iPhone at 100 per cent and the Kindle at 96 per cent. Very good news.

It's been a great day. Things are organized and dry. I've eaten well. Everything is recharged, the electronics, and mind and body. I've made a home out here.

# CHAPTER 6

---

# Wildfire: Looking Back

July 6, Day 7

It was twenty years ago today. Twenty years! How can that be? On July 6, 1994, I was working in the Alaska Smokejumper parachute loft when a voice came over the loudspeaker.

"All jumpers please come to the Box." The Box is Operations. Usually an announcement like that means big news. Maybe good, maybe bad.

"There was a blow-up on a fire in Colorado. A bunch of firefighters are missing, including some smokejumpers."

There wasn't much information. Apparently the fire had been jumped by smokejumpers out of the BLM spike base in Grand Junction, and there was a hotshot crew on the fire too, as well as some helitack. At least a dozen firefighters were unaccounted for.

"They'll show up." I said to another jumper. People are worriers. There was a blow-up. It was confusing. People scattered. When it calms down and things get sorted out it would be OK.

But it wasn't OK.

"We've got an update. It's bad news. It looks like about fourteen firefighters are dead. At least three smokejumpers. And we think a couple of BLMers." The Alaska smokejumpers are BLM, Bureau of Land Management. So is our sister base, Boise, Idaho.

That was punch in the stomach. People we knew were dead. I headed over to a phone to call my family to let them know I was OK.

We later learned three fellow smokejumpers had died. One was my friend Jim Thrash, a smokejumper from McCall, Idaho. It was really hard to believe. He was a careful firefighter. A real sensible guy. I remembered an interview he had once done in a national magazine. When asked about minimizing fire danger he'd said "You never want to get down to your last option." In other words, have several ways to escape a fire when things go wrong: the ability to move to a large unburnable area nearby, or to an area that has already burned well enough that it cannot "reburn," or allow enough time to move out of the fire's path completely.

That day the fire was fairly calm and didn't seem particularly dangerous. But at some point a cold front hit and the wind started blowing, hard. They noticed a spot fire had started below them. The smokejumper-in-charge, Don Mackey, was aware of the danger and moved down to a group of hotshots and smokejumpers that were in a bad spot. Thrash was there. It was time to get out and Mackey wanted to make sure they made it. The fire below them grew rapidly. There was now a 40-mile-an-hour upslope wind on that steep mountainside. With the fire below them in the dry scrub oak it was a worst case scenario.

They were suddenly faced with the deafening roar of 200 foot flames below and only moments before the fire would engulf them. Thrash said "Shelters?" and he began to pull out his fire shelter, a last-ditch option, a foil pup-tent that has saved numerous lives. Another friend of mine, Eric Hipke, was third in line. He looked up the ridge and saw his only chance to escape. He began to hike up the slope as fast as he could. If he could beat the fire to the ridge-line he might survive. One hotshot followed him. The other firefighters attempted to deploy their shelters. Some, like Thrash, a cool head, somehow managed it in the crazy wind. Others didn't. It made no difference. Conditions were far too severe to survive, even with a fire shelter. In moments they were all dead.

Eric was just short of the ridge when the radiant heat reached him. He dropped his fire tool and covered his burning ears with his hands and kept running up the steep mountainside. In the unbearable heat he reached back and pulled out his fire shelter, thinking to use it as a shield as he ran, but it slipped from his hands. He scrambled frantically up the mountain. Ten steps from the ridgetop a wind-blast from the fire hit him and knocked his hardhat off. He fell forward, screaming in pain, face first onto the hillside. He scrambled to his feet and stumbled ahead. His upper pack-straps had burned off and his pack hung by the waist belt, bouncing off the back of his legs. Stumbling forward he reached down to unclip his waist belt to release the pack and noticed the skin from his arms hanging in tatters.

In a few steps he was over the ridge and running down the other side, protected from the intense radiant heat by the ridge itself. He bounded down-slope until he encountered two other firefighters. Together they looked back. No one else made it over the top. Unbeknownst to them, the only other firefighter who'd attempted to outrun the fire, a hotshot and former Marine, died only 40 yards from the safety of the ridge-line. Missoula Smokejumper Don Mackey had died with Jim Thrash and the firefighters he'd tried to save. As jumper-in-charge he'd made mistakes that day, everybody makes mistakes regardless of profession, but rushing down into the danger to help everyone escape is the very definition of heroism in my mind. Also perishing with him were McCall smokejumper Roger Roth and nine members of the Prineville Hotshot crew

Two helitack firefighters died during that same blow-up, on a different part of the same fire, showing just how dangerous and unusual conditions were. It was the worst wildfire tragedy in nearly thirty years.

Jim Thrash left behind a wife and two young children. These twenty good years since that day he never got to enjoy. But he died with his boots on. He lived the life he loved. A risk-free life isn't worth living. Eric Hipke recovered incredibly quickly. In September, just a few months after the deadly fire, he parachuted to a fire near Crater Lake.

Just this year Eric completed a film about the deadly fire he survived, a fire now known as "South Canyon."

This morning in coastal Alaska I paddle to the crab trap and am surprised to find it empty. All that good bait, and in a good spot, too. But that's subsistence living. You just never know.

It's near high tide. I'm headed to My Stream but the tidal flats are flooded and things look very different. *Where exactly is the creek anyway?* It was obvious before. I paddle up the bay until I see a stream coming out of the trees. When it gets too shallow I get out of the boat.

A brown bear stands up on its hind legs near the edge of the timber, staring, green grass hanging from its mouth! After long moments, it slowly drops down on all fours and runs into the forest. There was nothing threatening about his body language, and he was far enough away so it wasn't at all frightening. Standing up is just what a bear does to get a good look.

This area doesn't look familiar though. Something isn't right. This isn't My Stream.

I'm too far left. My Stream must be on the other side of that peninsula . I carry the kayak to the edge of the timber, then grab my fishing gear. I follow the high tide around the head of the cove and hike into the treeline to take a shortcut across the timbered peninsula. Soon I'm running into thorny Devil's club, death to thin Gore-Tex waders. I backtrack out of the trees and follow the grassy edge, building a light sweat. It's worth it though, the easier walking. In a few minutes I recognize My Stream. A spotted fawn jumps up in the tall grass, hops a few times, then watches me. He's cute, maybe a month old. He watches me curiously as I walk by, then bounds away into the rainforest.

There is no sign of salmon, but a few Dollies are visible, finning in the shadows. I've got my fly rod. Remembering that black spinners worked the best, I tie on a black wet fly. After a few false casts the fly line rolls ahead and extends out, gently dropping to the water, the fly sinking in the dark pool. There's a swirl and the rod pulses as a Dolly struggles for freedom. I land him, an eight incher. There are plenty of fish in the pool today because on the next cast another fish strikes and on the third cast I hook him. He's a dandy for this stream, a solid ten-inch fish. It's fun to be fly fishing, and effective. It's not long before I have five fish lined up on the shady gravel bar.

Something catches my eye and I look up. Three deer are walking towards me through the sunny tall grass on the far bank, only forty yards away. They haven't noticed me in the shade of the trees. Insects swirl around them; the deer swat at them with their big ears and bob their heads. All three deer pause, looking around for danger. Suddenly one spots me. Noticing their companion stiffen, the other two look my way, ears forward, all senses alert. One turns to run and the others instantly follow, all thudding hooves and clattering gravel. Just as quickly I am alone again.

Although I didn't bring the grill I decide to cook the fish here anyway. I build a fire and clean them while the fire burns to coals. When the coals are ready, I lay the fish directly on them, putting some large coals on top. They cook quickly. When they are ready I flick away the largest coals with a stick, then quickly pick up each fish with my bare hands and set it on a clean rock to cool. The skin is slightly burned and tattered on the outside, but the meat is nearly perfect. I enjoy every bite.

When I get back to the flats the tide has fallen dramatically. I beeline across flats that were flooded before. Only one channel requires wading. Back at the boat the warm sun streams across the green grass and dark green trees. There are blue lupine and red Indian paintbrush flowers, and white and yellow flowers I can't identify. My overturned kayak offers a perfect air bed. I lie back upon it, my head propped up on my life jacket, and fall asleep in the warm sun.

I awake, looking up at drifting white clouds in a blue sky. I grab my daypack and an empty quart jar and head inland to look for berries. There are patches of Devil's club but I weave around them, only occasionally do I have to crawl over a big log. Blueberries are sparse but I find a few here and there, maybe a cup total, eating them as I go.

I follow a good trail back towards the kayak. In a nice flat spot overlooking the bay there is charcoal from an old campfire, a hunter's camp from decades ago. I wouldn't care to camp here on this bear trail.

It's amazing how far the tide has gone out. I swing the kayak up on my shoulders and start walking to the edge of the receding water. I finally drop the kayak with a bounce. It must have been a half mile! After making the long round-trip hike to get the rest of my gear I carry the boat to the water then drag it out until the water is a foot deep before hopping in.

The crab trap is empty again. Bummer. And at some point another crab boat has been here because there are new, orange buoys.. With the trap resting across the front of the kayak I paddle several hundred yards closer to camp, hoping a new spot will change my luck.

Back at camp I read from a paperback book called *The Way West*, about Oregon Trail pioneers. I unscrew the lid of a jar and treat myself to blueberries for supper.

# CHAPTER 7

## Making Meat

July 7, Day 8

When I wake up this morning, I reach over and turn on the weather radio. Light winds are predicted. I'm going to go back to the stream with the big Dollies. Maybe there'll be more salmon this time, or at least ones that will bite. It's about three miles, maybe four, so camping gear is part of my load, just in case.

I bee-line diagonally across Wild Bay. It's cloudy, and raining lightly. As I pass a forested point of land I hear an unusual sound. Looking up I see a mature bald eagle plunging towards the ocean's surface, wind sizzling past his wings, flaring dramatically at the last second, his prey having disappeared. Cool!

After securing the kayak, I head towards the creek. When I pass the trees, I see the grassy area along the lower part of the creek. Two brown bears lope towards the trees 200 yards away! They glance back at me from time to time as they run. Yearlings. They'd been looking for salmon. They ran immediately, a good sign. Their mother likely beat them into the trees. I'm not worried. They are almost certainly long gone. I'll just walk out in the open where I won't surprise any of them.

At the lower pool, three salmon cruise in the clear, rain-dappled water, perhaps the same ones I saw last time. I walk a gravel bar upstream to the pool below the bend, the one below the riffles, in the shade of the trees. My heart jumps. There must be thirty salmon in the pool!

Tying on a small spoon, I cast to the opposite bank and reel the fluttering spoon past the nose of the upstream salmon. Nothing. When the spoon passes through the middle of the school on the next cast one salmon moves out of the way but other than that there is no response. The next casts are no more successful. I switch to spinners... still nothing. All those salmon. All that meat swimming out there. It would be so easy to tie on a big treble hook to snag them, but I cannot and will not do that.

I switch to flies. I tie on a big, green bugger, weighted with just enough split shot to cast with my spinning rod. A Dolly strikes immediately and I land him. At least I'll have something to eat if the salmon won't bite. I catch another Dolly, then another. Looks like the Dollies are liking green flies almost as good as black flies.

On the next cast a huge salmon swings its head and grabs the big green bugger. He's on! He charges downstream while the drag screams. I stop him before he gets out of the pool and he heads back upstream. He's beginning to tire. I look around for the best place to land him: the shallow tail of the pool on a gently sloped gravel bar. He makes one last run towards a submerged log where several stout branches break the water's surface. I've got to stop him before he gets tangled up. When I slowly tighten the drag the line snaps with a pop. Sonofabitch! He's gone! My heart sinks. But that was still incredibly fun. I'll get another one. I'm not really geared up for a fish that big. Eight pound test line I think. I thought pinks were only about five pounds or so. At least the few I've caught were about that size. This one was *way* bigger.

I am getting lots of Dolly strikes. Confident I can catch my limit I start keeping only injured fish or the very biggest ones.

A salmon strikes but isn't hooked. The next cast another salmon follows briefly, grabs the fly but shakes it's head and escapes. A couple more casts trigger no reaction but on the next I see a salmon grab for the fly in the clear water. I set the hook and have a solid hookup! This fish is a good fighter, but isn't as strong as the monster that broke off. I stop it short of the sunken log and the Devil's club sweeping the water along the opposite bank. When the time is right I fight it towards the shallows and quickly slide the flopping fish six feet onto the gravel bar where I pounce, pinning it to the wet stones. I reach for a rock to rap the struggling fish on the head, and miss. The second attempt does the trick, the fish stiffens, stunned. I take a few steps to my daypack and find my Swiss army knife in the front pocket. After opening the big blade I slash one side of the salmon's gills to bleed it. Blood spurts out with each heartbeat then ebbs away. My prize lies dead, a day's worth of fine food! Yes!

He must weigh, what, eight pounds? Dramatic stripes mottle his sides in an irregular pattern, reddish, dark green, light green. This isn't a pink salmon. It's a chum salmon! That explains the big fish I lost earlier. It was a big chum. If this one weighs eight, that one would have been a fifteen pounder. This is a surprise, to catch chums before pink salmon. If anything, though, it's good news. Bigger fish mean more meat.

My day is already a huge success with this nice salmon and four Dollies on the cool, shady gravel bar, but the fish are biting and my enthusiasm, already high, has soared even higher.

As I try for another salmon I hear the whoosh of wings. A mature bald eagle flies past, staring at the salmon in the clear water. He lands in a tree, ten feet above the creek, only thirty feet away. It's a dramatic sight, the branch still bouncing, his white head and tail contrasting beautifully against his black body. He suddenly looks up from the fish and notices me. Startled, he abruptly launches himself with loud, powerful wing-beats and quickly vanishes around the bend.

It's been raining off and on. Not pouring, but it's wet out. With my good rain jacket and my waders, it makes little difference.

From the uppermost pool, just below the riffles at the bend of the creek, the current has scoured a dark pool of water below green, dripping hemlocks draped with moss. The fly sinks into the depths and as it swings a big char strikes. He fights valiantly, but I successfully land him and add him to my catch, a fine eighteen incher.

Most of the salmon are holding in the middle pool, so I head down there again. In a few casts I have a solid hookup with another chum, slowly tiring him with steady pressure. In five minutes, I have my second salmon lying next to the first. What an awesome day!

I've actually been pulling the fly away from many small Dollies as I concentrate on salmon, but now a large Dolly darts towards my fly and I hook him. I have my limit of ten.

I clean the fish and ponder my plan. I'm tempted to cook up some Dollies right here, but I want to keep the fish as fresh as possible. Plus, I don't want to have to build a fire here and then a second fire when I get back to base camp. It's about 4 PM. I've been so focused on fishing I haven't eaten a thing all day except for a half dozen blueberries.

I'm surprised by a couple of things today. One, why are these chums (also known as dog salmon or calico salmon) in spawning colors? I mean, they are already clearly striped. I've seen bright, silvery chums thirty miles or more up rivers. These were less than 200 yards from saltwater. They've been in freshwater for less than 3 days, probably only for hours. Even more surprising is that when I dress one of them it is a female, even though it has male spawning colors. I throw the orange eggs into the stream. "I'd eat them if I really needed the food." I think. It's funny how big of a role culture plays. I've never eaten salmon eggs. Why? They must be loaded with high-quality nutrients.

A couple of Dollies dart out and began grabbing the drifting eggs, attracting more and more fish. I throw the remains of the rest of the fish in the water as well and it creates a feeding frenzy of at least two dozen fish, a good illustration of the circle of life.

With the bucket heavy with fish I hike back to the kayak and paddle for base camp. There, I gather up stuff for the canning operation, including the pressure canner, a box of jars, and the fillet board. It takes a couple of trips to cook camp to carry everything.

My canning experience has been primarily the canning of maple syrup. But my pressure canning experience, a very different procedure, is limited to canning up last fall's whitetail deer. I've never canned fish at all. I review the canner instructions:

*Split fish lengthwise. Cut into jar-size lengths. Pack tightly in jars, skin side out. Drain off excess moisture. Leave 3/4" to 1" of headspace in order to achieve a good seal and help avoid boil-out of oily liquid during processing.*

I take a salmon out of the bucket and clamp it to the fillet board. The first fillet is doing it's best to fall off the side of the board onto the sandy gravel of the shore. Knowing that it's much easier to "keep meat clean than to clean it," I fetch a square piece of plastic, three feet across, that I've brought for just such a purpose. I concentrate on filleting close to the bones. I slice each fillet to jar length, then in half, lengthwise. When I start packing the jars, the slices are still too big to fit into the jars easily and they are leaving large gaps of air, so I cut them into narrower strips. *That's the ticket!* I save out the biggest char to eat now, but cut off the tails of the other fish. They are already gutted. After giving them a good wash I decide to can the char heads and all, cutting them to length. With the fish, salmon and char in their own jars, I redistribute some of the meat to achieve proper headspace. After cleaning the rim of the jars I put the lids and screw caps on. Each jar is hefty. That's a lot of fish. Usually people can fish in pint jars, even half pints. Maybe I should have brought some pints. Regardless, I have eight nice jars of fish.

I rinse the bucket with salt water, then scoop up some clean water a few feet away and pour it in the canner until it's about three inches deep. Next I put in one of the racks to keep the jars off the bottom of the canner. After arranging seven jars inside on the bottom layer, I add the second rack with the last jar on top. I put the canner lid on, lining up the arrow on the lid with the groove on the canner, then make a slight twist to lock it in place. Lastly, I flip up the clamp bolts all the way around, slightly tightening one of the knobs, then the opposite one, then on around on alternating sides before doing the final tightening. I pick it up to carry it to cook camp. This sucker is heavy! The canner itself weighs over twenty-five pounds. Each full jar must weigh about three pounds. There are eight jars, so twenty four pounds there. I'll bet there is about twelve pounds of water at the bottom of the canner. The whole shebang must weigh over sixty pounds. No wonder you're not supposed to put them on glass top ranges!

With a nice little fire going in the rocket stove I split the big Dolly down along the backbone so it will lie flat and cook faster. It's way too long for the frying pan though. I cut it to so it will fit, then cut the shorter piece in half so it will fit on each side of the main piece. I cover the pan with foil and put it on the fire. In a minute it's sizzling. It really smells good.

When the fish is done I set the pressure canner on the stove and add more wood. Then I take the foil off the frying pan, salt and pepper the fish, and chow down. It's 6:45 and other than a few berries this is the first meal of the day. It's very, very good.

As the canner heats I put together the windscreen I made for the stove. It's a piece of aluminum flashing. I have a small ziploc of small bolts, nuts and wingnuts. I assemble the aluminum into a cylinder so it will fit around the canner with a half inch gap all the way around. I cut two pieces of wire and suspend the assembled windscreen from the canner's handles. It looks good and should work well.

The canner sure seems to be taking a long time to heat, but at about sixty pounds it has a lot of thermal mass and it's a long way from 55 degrees or so up to 212 degrees! The stove has a little wire rack at the same level as the door which allows longer pieces of wood, about twelve inches or even longer, to be fed into the stove as they burn. As each piece burns I push it in a little way, adding new wood as necessary. Finally steam begins coming out of the vent on top and I hit the stopwatch button on my wristwatch. After ten more minutes I put the pressure regulator weight on top of the vent. It's a clever, simple design. When the pressure is less than 10 pounds the weight prevents steam from escaping and pressure builds. When pressure exceeds ten pounds the weight lifts up enough to release the excess pressure, keeping it at ten pounds. There is also a safety plug on top. If the pressure regulator would fail for any reason the safety plug would blow off before the whole canner exploded. It's actually no joke, steam under pressure is far, far hotter than normal steam. At ten pounds pressure the pressure gauge dial says the temperature is 240 degrees!

The pressure dial slowly climbs towards the ten pound mark. A moment after reaching it the regulator begins bouncing and hissing. Yes! I restart my stopwatch. It needs to cook at this pressure for 110 minutes. I have to think a moment. It will be done at... 9:20.

With everything set I gather supplies for hanging my food and walk over to the best tree. I tie parachute cord around the neck of my half-full canteen and look up for a good branch for hanging the cache. I'd spotted it earlier, nice and stout, about eighteen feet up, with no other branches beneath it. I gather twenty feet of slack line, tie the loose end to a small tree behind me and, keeping my eye on a spot about two feet over the branch, send the canteen flying with an underhand toss. The canteen sails over the branch and falls until the cord tightens, leaving the canteen swinging. Although I can hear the canner regulator chattering, I quickly check the operation, adding a little wood, then head back to the tree.

I remove the canteen and tie on the lightweight block and tackle. Extending the block and tackle full length it stretches about ten feet. I will be using TWO lines for this operation. One will be the line that pulls the top of the block and tackle up to the tree branch. The second line will be the line that runs through the pulleys. That's the one I'll pull on to raise and lower the cache. There's not going to be enough line on that cord, so I add fifteen feet of parachute cord. At the little tree I untie the other cord and pull the top end of the block and tackle up to the branch and tie off the cord to the tree again, leaving the bottom end of the extended block and tackle about head high. Done for now, I head back to the canner.

I've been pretty busy today, but now it's relaxing and fun: sitting back on my chair, keeping an eye on the pressure, adding a little wood now and then, and reading. But why isn't the regulator "chattering" more and hissing less? Maybe the fire is too hot? When I tap the hissing regulator it chatters a bit then goes back to mostly hissing. I back off on the wood and it chatters more. Either way, the pressure gauge stays at 10 pounds.

The light is failing at 9:20 on this cloudy evening when 110 minutes has finally passed. I lift the canner off the stove but when I try to set it down, the windscreen, which extends beyond the bottom of the canner, gets in the way. I set the canner back on the stove, then unhook the wire on each handle allowing the screen to fall free around the stove. I set the canner off to the side to cool.

When I canned the deer last fall I learned why the instructions say to let the canner cool before opening it, naturally allowing the pressure fall to zero. I figured it was a safety thing, to prevent people from getting scalded by steam. Thinking I could do it safely I took the regulator off with a glove, my face off to the side, allowing steam to shoot out of the vent. When I opened the canner I found that the jars had still been under pressure, forcing venison broth out of the jars. Bad move.

The canner slowly cools and the pressure falls on it's own. When it reaches zero I take the regulator off, then loosen the knobs all the way around and take the cover off. With a leather glove I remove each jar and set it on the moss to cool more. The liquid continues to boil in the jars for several minutes. I saw this before but it still surprises me. Look at all that meat! About sixteen pounds. I've gotten ahead of the curve. Having this reserve food is a big deal and a great feeling.

One by one the jar lids "ping" as the contents contract, pulling the lid down and verifying a good seal. Finally all eight have sealed. When they've cooled a bit more I put the jars in a jar box and wire each end shut, then carry it to the cache tree. I slide the jar box into the gear bag, tie the bag to the bottom of the block and tackle, then grab the end of the block and tackle line and pull. With all the pulleys it takes a lot of pulling, six feet of pulling only raises the bag about one foot, but it's easy. When the bag has reached the branch I tie it off. Food in the bank!

I walk back to camp as darkness falls. It was a big day. A good day.

## July 8, Day 9

Rain is pattering on the tent walls. It's still so dark I can barely see. It must be about 4:30 AM or so. The days are long here, but not as long as they are back home in Fairbanks. In Fairbanks, over seven hundred miles northwest of here, it doesn't get dark at all this time of year. There, the sun sets briefly, after midnight, but it barely goes below the horizon. Here, sunrise is about 4:15 and sunset about 9:45. The usual overcast nature of this area makes it seem darker, though, and so does camping in the trees. Even the mountains hide direct sun when it first rises.

My pee bottle saves me a trip outside into the rain. I've kept the rest of the jar of berries in the tent, so I eat some blueberries for breakfast.

In no hurry, I crawl back into my sleeping bag and read *The Way West*. Reading is great. I'm happy to be here but it's nice to live in another world for a while. The decision to head west on the Oregon Trail was huge, almost irrational. I think I would have gone as a single person. I probably wouldn't have taken a family if I knew what the dangers were.

About mid-morning I put on my rain gear and waders and step out into the rain. My wader belt is clipped to my PFD so I can't forget it. I put the belt on, then the PFD and paddle over to the crab trap. Where's my buoy? I should be seeing it. Did my rope break? Did somebody take it? There it is. No doubt exactly where I dropped it.

When I pull it up, it's empty. How can that be, with all that good bait? Well I've got more bait now, fresher bait. I paddle over to shore where I can work. I wire the salmon heads inside the trap, on top, and empty out the bait cage and fill it with fresh fish scraps. That should do it! In case the crabs have abandoned this spot I paddle over to near the commercial crabber buoy closest to base camp, maybe a quarter mile out. I lower the trap down until I'm nearly out of rope. The rope is too short. It's over 100 feet deep here! It's a long pull getting it back up. That would have been a major bummer if I had let go. The trap with its stone weight is likely heavy enough to sink the buoy. I paddle closer to shore. This time it's about forty feet deep. We'll see how this works.

Back at camp I walk over to the food cache and lower it down. One issue I've been pondering is how to lower the bag all the way to the ground. The way it is now I have to lift the bag about nose high. Makes it hard to tie and untie. Once most of the jars are full it will be even more difficult. The big issue is that knots won't go through the small pulleys, so I can't just add cordage. I reroute the rope to only use two pulleys. It cuts my mechanical advantage to 2:1, but that will be enough. If the bag of jars weighs 60 pounds I'll still only need to pull 30 lbs. This is a much better option than constructing a high platform and a homemade ladder, something I'd considered. This is simple. Simple is good. And anytime I can avoid climbing a ladder with a heavy box of glass jars I will! I retrieve two jars of salmon and pull the cache back up, then head back to camp.

It's nice to get out of the rain. I find a fork and sit down on my camp chair. I open a jar, salt and pepper the topmost fillet and raise a chunk to my watering mouth. Man, that is good! Really good. I have all-I-can-eat for the rest of the day. Ready to go. It's a good feeling. I eat most of a jar, take another drink of cold water, then crawl into my sleeping bag. What items do I wish I had brought on this adventure? A satellite phone, first of all. It would save me the long paddle to the lodge every couple of weeks. It would also be nice just in case, and so friends and family would worry less. Shoe Goo. I should have brought some. My rubber knee boots are cracking. I have to laugh at myself. During the river portion of my Alaska traverse, from Canada to the Chukchi Sea, my hip boots started leaking and I was wishing I had some then as well. I forgot to add it to my list. Better rain pants would be nice. That was simple carelessness. I had several pairs of rain pants hanging up and grabbed a pair that looked to be in good shape. But I hadn't looked closely enough. They were a pair I'd already worn on the Pacific Crest Trail. They'd worn considerably after hundreds of miles of wear. They are still useful, but it's not too smart to head into this country with anything less than the best when it comes to rain gear.

One thing I'm good at is staying entertained just puttering around. I easily while away the afternoon making minor repairs, napping, eating, organizing and reading. Hopefully I'll have more days like this in the weeks to come.

July 9, Day 10

In the morning it's fairly calm as I paddle to the crab trap, a much shorter paddle since I moved it closer to camp. A doe and fawn are feeding in the grass along the shore. A lone deer feeds farther along.

I grab the buoy. As soon as the slack is out I can feel the trap is heavy. Lots of crabs, hopefully! When the trap reaches the surface it contains three or four huge starfish, each with a dozen arms or so, countless tiny tube feet on each arm wriggling through the trap grid. Bummer. I paddle over to shore and open one side of the trap to dump them out. They've eaten a bunch of the bait but there's plenty left. Why did I catch starfish? Because it was too shallow, or just because of the spot? I didn't even know starfish were an issue with crab trapping. Obviously this location isn't going to work. I paddle back to the head of the bay and drop the trap near where I first put it, in about sixty feet of water, off to the side of the creek.

Now that I have a good cache of canned fish, berries are a priority. Back at camp I pack a couple of empty jars along with survival gear (rain gear, lighter, space blanket, etc.) and eat a good brunch of canned salmon and finish up the last of the blueberries. There's still some salmon left in one jar I have in camp, as well as an empty fish jar. What's my strategy for these food jars? Ideally I suppose I would carry it back to the cache, lower it down and haul the jars back up in the tree. Realistically, I know I'm not going to do that for every meal during the whole trip. Instead, I'll compromise. I put the jars outside the tent just inside the electric fence wire. If a bear walks up to sniff the jars it should zap him on the nose.

If there are any good berry patches around here I've yet to find them. I'm going to check out a completely new spot. I bee-line for a mile, straight across Wild Bay, picking the steepest shoreline so I can land near the trees, saving me a long carry back and forth across tidal flats to the water. It's a short twenty foot carry. I stash the kayak near a big boulder and hike into the trees. There is the usual bear trail just inside the tree line. After climbing the mountainside for a few minutes scattered blueberries appear here and there. I eat them as I go. Rather than pushing my way along a predetermined route I let the easiest walking guide me. There are a few more berries up higher, enough so that I get a jar out and start adding berries to it. Ahead the trees thin and the hill flattens into a mostly open meadow. Along the edges is the best berry-picking I've found. They certainly aren't thick, I'm picking them one at a time, but I can walk from bush to bush, making steady progress filling the jar. For a while I pick from clumps of bushes growing on high spots in the meadow. It's a different ecosystem here. There are Labrador tea bushes, and different subspecies of blueberries growing on lower bushes. There are also some cedar trees here, some of them dead and bark-less. One of the young smokejumpers who grew up in Southeast Alaska had told me to look for them as the best firewood in this wet country. Most surprisingly, there are a few lodgepole pines. I just didn't picture lodgepoles growing in this area.

At last I fill a jar and screw the lid on, exchanging it for an empty jar. As I pick along the meadow's edge I notice very old stumps of small dead cedars. There must have been an old cabin nearby. Maybe there still is. I'm going to watch for it.

I've followed this open "bench" for several hundred yards and have managed to fill the second jar about three quarters full. The berries are getting harder to find. I'm going to call it good for today. I stash the jar in my pack. I can hear a creek nearby. Many times I've located cabins in remote country by finding old stumps and looking around for a nearby cabin. I search along the bench first, then walk upstream along the creek looking for a cabin roof. Wouldn't it be cool to find an old abandoned cabin, especially one that was intact with a good roof? Would I stay there if I did? At the very least it would be fun to explore. Following the creek bank downstream I hear a growing sound of falling water. The creek drops out of sight ahead of me. I cautiously approach the edge and look down over an honest-to-goodness waterfall. Awesome! Now that's exploring, discovering a waterfall like this, all on my own.

I follow a bear trail that skirts the cliffs and falls, making extra noise to avoid encountering a bear at close range, a bear that might not hear me in the roar of the falls. I can catch glimpses of the falls as the trail skirts around on high ground overlooking the creek. Finally I can get a good look at the falls from an opening in the trees. The main falls plunges in a white plume, crashing into a deep pool of clear water suspended over dark green rocks. A second, smaller cascade arcs from the right, meeting the larger falls where it hits the water. Everything is surrounded in greenery; hemlock and spruce, Devil's club and berry bushes. Bears have climbed up and down the steep ravine but it looks like tough going. Instead, I follow the descending ridge until it meets the stream, then walk back up to the falls. The thundering water makes me want to laugh. It's thrilling. I love this spot, the roar of water, the rich green colors, the fertile wet scent of the rainforest.

I walk the creek back to the saltwater. When I wade the shallows I feel water leaking into my knee boots. The cracks are getting bigger. Bummer.

It's nice to get back to camp and into dry socks. I head over to my food cache and get a couple more jars of salmon. I eat the rest of the jar I had at camp and start on another. I've eaten two and a half quarts the past two days! I was going to take tomorrow to dry everything out but it looks like it will be cloudy. Instead I'm going to head back to my salmon stream, so I get gear ready for a fishing trip. I'm going to call that creek "Salmon Creek."

I finish the book *The Way West*. One unrealistic aspect is the never-fail judgment and skills of the old mountain man guiding the party, including his brilliant memory for a route he hasn't seen in twenty years, including how many days it takes to get from place to place. People forget. But people need larger-than-life heroes. Real people are all too fallible.

Still, it's a good book. What a struggle it was on the wagon trains migrating West. Heading out into the unknown, things are never quite the way you expect them to be. But it was also the greatest adventure of their lives. I can imagine how the aging pioneers told their stories to children and grandchildren, tales of a world and a time that was gone forever, an experience they could relive only in their memories and in the stories themselves.

July 10, Day 11

I slept great. I look at my watch while gathering the last of my gear. It's still only 4:30. This should qualify as an early start! I carry my gear down to the water on the opposite side of the spit from where I usually land. Clams squirt water out of the mud, the first time I've seen that here. There are starfish near shore too, also a first near camp.

It's a smooth paddle across Wild Bay, mountains towering into a mostly clear day. I reach the mouth of the salmon stream cove at about 6 AM. It seems like it should be obvious where the stream runs into the cove, but I end up too far left and follow the shallows to the right, looking down into the clear water to see what I see: countless shells, starfish and... a crab, nearly a legal one by the looks of him! A few yards farther is another, and then another! Ahead I see the current of my stream and I beeline towards it. Just before I land I see a nice crab in three feet of water. I beach the boat, untie my paddle and wade out to the crab in my waders, trying to scoop him up somehow with the paddle. The crab faces me, claws up, defensively, grabbing at the paddle blade but letting go and sliding off when I try to lift him. I try again with the same result. But each time I push him a few feet towards shore. Finally I stick to just pushing and herding him along until I have him in six inches of water, where I manage to scoop him onto shore. Yes! I take a few steps back to the boat and measure him with the caliper: 6 ¾"! He's legal!

I got here at almost exactly low tide which means the water will be rising soon. I pull the kayak up a little higher and wade back into thigh deep water. Strange how I've barely seen a crab in the water and now there are many of them, enough so I only target the larger ones. I soon have another crab, also legal. I untie the caliper from the boat and retie it to my wader belt.

Too bad I don't have a landing net. It would be a lot easier. But I soon have a third legal crab. It seems like the large males have more whitish looking claws, and their claws are definitely more massive. I get a fourth crab, also a nice legal male. Wow!

My kayak is right on the edge of the rising water. This would be exactly the kind of scenario where a guy could get himself in trouble: distracted by the excitement of crab hunting, while the tide comes up unnoticed and the kayak drifts away and/or I get trapped by rising water. I stop and carry the kayak a couple feet above the water and vow to keep a close eye on the rising tide.

Two crabs have gotten away, maybe three. They've skittered off to the side in swirling mud and sand and disappeared or escaped to deep water. Still, I can't believe how successful this crude method has been. I've caught seven now, the biggest over seven inches! Finally my bucket is stacked full with eight big male crabs! It's only 7 AM. Man, did this day go differently than I'd expected!

Common sense tells me to fill the bucket with water so the crabs can breathe, but experts say they will suffocate that way if new water isn't kept circulating or if air isn't added. Instead, they say to make sure the crabs are kept cool and damp so their gills can get oxygen directly out of the air. So I splash water over them and shade the bucket, then paddle back to camp.

After carrying everything up to the trees I flood the bucket with fresh water, then after a minute or so dump the water out and set the bucket in the shade. Hey, the sun's out! I hang my inverted waders, boots, raincoat and socks to dry, then lay out the solar chargers.

I splash water on the crabs one last time, then carry the bucket to the shore near cook camp and clean them. Cleaning crabs is easy, even with a bunch of them. I concentrate on killing them quickly while trying to knock the top of the shell off cleanly. Just for fun I hang the biggest shell on a broken branch sticking up from a log near cook camp.

After rinsing the crab halves I put some salt water in the canner, then add the crabs and a bit more water to cover them, then start a fire in the stove. This will be a two-part operation. I don't put the regulator weight on the canner yet. I'm just using it as a big kettle right now.

After they've cooked I take a crab half out, set it in the frying pan and break a leg off. Man, that is good. When I start getting full I continue to crack the crab shells, pulling out the meat and putting it into a clean jar. I'm getting all the meat, way down each leg, so it's very time consuming, but yikes, what a lot of great crab meat I'm getting. I end up with an all-I-can eat meal and two quart jars full of shelled crab meat. I add saltwater to within an inch of the top of each jar.

Canning goes great. While the jars cool I wander around gathering firewood. I drop each armload back at the tarp, break it to stove length and stack it under the middle of the tarp. I lower the food cache, add the jars of crab and pull it back up. This cache system works great. I'll have to keep an eye on the rope for fraying though. That would be a major bummer if the whole thing fell and all the jars broke!

It's been another good day. The sun is going down. I ate well today: salmon, crab, blueberries and sea asparagus. I have two jars of delicious crab meat added to the larder, and my gear is dried out, charged up, and organized. I'm in the groove!

July 11, Day 12

It's raining this morning. The tide tables predict a 6:58 low tide so I launch my kayak at about 6 AM and arrive at the head of the bay in plenty of time to look for more crabs. I've got a landing net this time, but now that I'm here, where are all the crabs? Yesterday was something of a fluke, no doubt, but I was hoping I could catch several legal crabs. Instead, I see only two. Luckily one is legal. That's the good news, the bad news is I don't want to go back to camp yet, I want to check out My Stream to see if the salmon are in. I put the crab in the bucket and paddle out to the trap. There are three crabs inside, including two keepers! Now we're talking. I ponder my options and come up with a fairly simply one: I'll put all the crabs back in the trap and submerge it in shallow water, with plenty of slack line to keep the buoy afloat. I bet that isn't done very often; netting a crab, putting it in a trap, and then throwing the trap back in the ocean!

I stash my boat and extra gear in the trees and switch to knee boots, then walk across the tidal flats until I hit the stream, watching for salmon all the way to the first pools in the timber. There isn't a single one. Not only that, but nearly all the Dollies seem to be gone as well. Maybe they followed a run of salmon upstream? It's doubtful. If the salmon are in, there should be some in these lower pools. I pull out my topo maps and ponder. I haven't explored the other stream at the head of Wild Bay. Maybe the salmon have arrived there. At the very least it will be fun to explore new country and maybe find some new berry patches.

Walking with just light rubber boots is fun, easier and cooler than wearing waders. If they don't start leaking like sieves, anyway. It does mean I can't just splash across the stream, though. Upstream there is a place where a log has fallen part way across and debris have built up a

precarious bridge at the other end. I work my way across and take a last giant step to reach the other bank, grabbing onto bushes to avoid falling backwards into the creek. I walk around the point of trees, across a grassy meadow, and then across another big tidal flat. There is a channel in the middle, clearly deeper than my boots, so I walk upstream for a hundred yards or so to where it's shallower, then quickly wade across. I feel some dampness from water leaking through the boot cracks.

There isn't much water in the next stream. I follow it up into cottonwoods. There is no sign of salmon or Dollies or any other kind of fish. The brush is thick and it's tough going. Cursing the brush helps repel bears! I see some salmonberry bushes though, and a few green berries. At last I push my way through the jungle and out into the more open spruce/hemlock forest. There is Devil's club and fallen logs, but once I get past the lowest ground they are easy to weave around.

Ahead is giant old stump, six feet tall. Half way up there is a rectangular notch, maybe eight inches wide, two inches high, and four inches deep. It's an old springboard notch. Loggers would chop out a notch like this, then put a springboard (plank) in it, standing on it to chop a "face-cut" notch in the direction they wanted the tree to fall, finally falling the tree with a crosscut saw. The nearest cannery opened in 1918, so this notch was likely cut in 1917 or so. The mossy stump has a small tree growing out of the top, tendrils of its roots following the outside of the stump to the ground. Someday the stump itself will have decomposed to the the forest floor, leaving the young tree on stilts. When I'm long gone, the stump and its springboard notch will still be here.

Thinking that more blueberries will be higher on the mountainside, I climb a gentle ridge. Soon I'm picking a few. A pine squirrel sits, unmoving, on a branch a few feet away. This is only about the second one I've seen. Good thing I'm not subsisting on squirrels.

The blueberries are sparse and the situation doesn't seem to be improving as I climb. I turn around and head down the mountain to look for salmonberries in the sunny areas along the bay. Sure enough, there are some nice patches of bushes. I find a clump with a few that are just starting to ripen. I manage to pick about twenty, not very sweet, but it's a victory just finding them.

I walk through tall grass and then start angling out across the tidal flats, still only about half flooded. An eagle wheels overhead. Eagles are as common as robins here. After passing a small island out in the flats I look back and see a deer walking along the water, eating a bit of something now and then. Suddenly he looks up and spots me, then bounds off in stiff-legged jumps, all four legs together like a mule deer.

Ahead is a forested hill about twenty feet high, a hill that becomes an island at the very highest tides. I've seen a bunch of deer around here. Maybe there's a good vantage point to watch for deer. When I reach the base of the hill I look around. This is a good spot. I think I'll sit here on opening day of deer season. Less than a month away!

By the time I make it back to the kayak, I've put in a lot of miles. The crab trap, barely flooded when I left it, is now under several feet of water. I pull it up, transfer the crabs to the bucket, then paddle out and drop the trap in deep water.

Back at camp I clean the crabs. The frying pan isn't big enough so I put the crab halves in the canner and add just enough water to cover them. For supper I eat all the delicious crab I want, and end up with 2/3 of a jar of shelled crab meat to have for breakfast.

Before I know it it's dusk. Where did the day go?

# CHAPTER 8

---

# Salmon!

July 12, Day 13

It rained pretty much through the night. I guess it's... Saturday? The day of the week has little meaning out here beyond listening to the weather forecast. The date, however, is very important to keep track of tides.

About 6:15 I launch, on my way to Salmon Creek. It's the same cove where I caught the salmon of course, and the place where I caught the crabs with the paddle. The creek near the good berry picking, the one with the falls, I'm calling Falls Creek. Then of course there's My Creek at the head of Wild Bay.

I paddle into a stiff headwind on the paddle over. With a headwind it pays to keep paddling steady and hard. If I stop I'll blow backwards. If I don't paddle hard it will take forever.

I stop near my old spike camp to look for my water filter cap, which I find. I also look for berries and get a half dozen salmonberries and a handful of blueberries. Better than nothing!

The tide is already coming in so I don't try to net any crabs. Salmon are jumping in the salt water though, and I can see dorsal fins and tail fins sticking out of the water here and there as salmon cruise preparing to enter freshwater. That's a good sign! The run should be improving.

I stash my kayak above high tide and walk upstream. There's a bear! He walks along heavily, patrolling along the grassy bank 200 yards away, oblivious to my approach. I rap on the side of my plastic bucket. He turns my way and stands on his hind feet, sniffing the air, then lopes off into the trees. In less than a minute another bear appears around the corner! This one immediately spots me, likely alerted by the sound of the bucket or seeing the other bear run. He doesn't hesitate, instantly bolting for the trees.

There are almost no salmon in the lower pool, or the next. Strange. The bears probably chased them away. I hike upstream, exploring past the area I've visited before. It is very brushy in places with plenty of Devil's club, and there are numerous downed logs among the giant hemlock and spruce. I sing aloud and rap on the bucket occasionally. There will be more and more bears showing up along the streams now that salmon are running. It's important not to surprise one at close range. Bears rarely attack, contrary to what people seem to think. Their default reaction is running. People and animals are more dangerous when they are frightened. A sudden, close-range encounter is best avoided.

It's a relief to get out to an open gravel bar and easy walking. Two chum salmon are holding in a pool along the far bank. I keep heading upstream hoping to find more fish. It's a beautiful stream without a single human track other than my own. I'll bet years pass without a single person fishing these pools. Where the creeks fork there is a log jam. Beneath it is a deep, dark pool of clear water with numerous big chum salmon cruising around or holding quietly. Nice! I set my fly rod up, making a special effort to thread the line through *every single line guide*. If I had a dollar for every time I finished stringing up a rod and tying on a big fly only to find I'd missed one of the guides... well, I bet I'd have a pile of dollar bills.

I make a few casts with a big, green bugger fly. I get snagged on one of the many waterlogged branches lurking below the surface. There's no way to wade in there without spooking all the fish so I break the fly off. I try for a few more minutes without hooking a fish. After losing a second fly I have to admit that there are so many snags a hooked fish would be sure to get tangled up and break off anyway.

I hike back, taking a shortcut over high ground, following ancient bear trails through park-like stretches of open walking. At a pool I stand looking into the clear water. Below, a group of five salmon swims upstream, under a log jam and through the riffles into the pool. I cast above them but they don't react to the fly. For a while they hold in two feet of water at the head of the pool. I can see them easily. It's fun to sight fish for them where I can see both the fly and the fish. Finally I see one swing his head. The fly disappears and the line tightens. I set the hook. A big chum makes a run upstream, scattering the other fish. He turns to make a run downstream, through the deep water of the pool where I want him, then continues downstream towards the log jam. I put more and more pressure on him, tightening the drag of my fly reel as much as I dare. If he makes it to the log jam he'll break off for sure. Just as it seems the line is sure to break he begins to tire and slowly heads back to the main pool, my fly rod still in a hard arc.

When his runs begin to slacken I lead him towards shallow water, then quickly drag him out onto the gravel bar. I grab the stout club I'd prepared, rap him on the head and slash his gills. *One down!* He's a dandy, a big striped male.

Small groups of chums continue to cruise upstream, some passing through with barely a pause, others holding in the pool for a while. I like having new fish moving through, a chance at fish that have never seen a fly before. I hook and lose a fish, then hook another solidly. The key is keeping them out of the log jam, if I can do that there are no other nearby snags and I will most likely land them. Soon I have another big male on the bank next to the first.

The green bugger seems to have lost its appeal so I switch to one of the Thor flies I tied years ago. It has an orange body, a white hair wing and a red tail. They are good colors for Alaska salmon streams. It takes a half an hour or so but with it I land a third fine fish.

I gut the fish and put them in the pail and head downstream. Pushing through the thick brush and climbing under and over logs, with

a heavy bucket of fish trying to fall out, adds to the challenge.

The lowest pool is now flooded with saltwater from the rising tide. In the next higher pool a large school of salmon keeps cruising through, then disappearing back downstream. They are totally uninterested in biting. Of course, salmon seldom if ever feed once they are in freshwater, but they do sometimes strike out of instinct or aggression. Like any fishing, they will only strike when they choose. Sometimes it's easy to catch salmon, sometimes it's nearly impossible. Finally some new fish appear in the pool and hang around, resting. I hook one and think I'm going to add him to my goal of five fish, but he gets tangled in a branch in three feet of water. I wade out from above, trying not to spook the other salmon. My fish is pretty tired. Just when it looks like I might succeed at getting him untangled, he breaks off.

I look up. A brown bear is following the creek towards me, maybe 150 yards away! When I yell at him he spots me and starts loping my way! His body language isn't aggression, though, it's curiosity. Although my heart has sped up I'm not too worried. Not yet anyway.

"Hey bear!" I yell. "Hey!" He stops and stands on his hind legs, maybe 75 yards away, staring at me. His front legs look extraordinarily long as they dangle, his front paws with their long claws hanging loosely. His expression changes to "Oh-oh." He drops down and acts like he's trying to just disappear. "No bear here. Just go about your business." He slowly turns around and then sprints for the forest. Cool! I kinda wish I'd reached for my camera though!

More new salmon move into the pool and I switch to another old Alaska standby fly, a purple egg-sucking leech. It's basically a purple woolly bugger with a marabou tail and a yarn "egg" tied in near the eye of the hook. This one has a reddish-orange head. I like the theory that it looks like a small fish grabbing a salmon egg. Whatever it looks like, it's a great producer for many species of fish and often triggers salmon strikes. And it does today. I land another big fish, and on the very next cast I hook and land another big male. By my estimate these five big fish will fill up about fourteen jars, the most the canner will hold.

I clean the last fish and put all five in the bucket, tails sticking out, and head for the boat. The bucket must weigh close to 50 pounds. I have to stop repeatedly to switch hands. It's nice to set the heavy bucket in the floating kayak. Water is the way to move weight!

I try to keep an eye on things around me and I always like to spot animals. I notice a brown bear sow and small cub feeding in the grass along the timber several hundred yards away. They don't even notice me. In the shallows of the bay several schools of salmon are cruising around, a couple are close enough that I can clearly see the "tiger stripe" spawning colors of the males. I'd never known before this trip that some salmon "turn" in saltwater.

At the shore next to cook camp I fillet my catch, putting the fillets into the jars as I go. When I get down to the last fish it barely fits into the fourteenth jar. Perfect!

It takes a long time to heat all those jars of fish up, but once the canner pressurizes it goes smoothly. Still, here I am canning in the dark. Except for when I flip on my headlamp to check the canner pressure I am sitting in the blackness with only the glow of the fire through the rocket stove door for light. Fire is good. Friendly and warm. Think of how valued it was before the days of stoves and headlamps and powerful rifles!

It's after midnight when I finally pull the canner off the stove, and nearly 1 AM before the jars are hung up and I head back towards camp. The tide is the highest I've seen on the whole trip. The water has crept up beneath the branches of the shoreline trees. It's eerie walking back in the dark along the shore with the cold ocean pushing me into the trees and brush. It makes a guy think. How dependent I am on nature doing what it usually does rather than what it MIGHT do. It wouldn't take much for an earthquake somewhere, maybe hundreds or even thousands of miles off, to set off a tsunami big enough to wash my camp away. It almost certainly won't happen. But it could. My camp is maybe five feet above the water. In the Alaska earthquake of 1964 waves as high as 220 feet were reported!

Years ago we jumped a fire on a remote area of Kodiak Island. The area had a different look than most of the fires we fight. It was mostly grass on small hills near the sea. There were patches of alder brush and a few cottonwood trees growing along creeks. We made good progress, swatting out some flames and backfiring from creek bottoms and snow patches to stop the flames advance. Finally we were down to patrolling for "hot spots," smoldering cottonwood stumps and driftwood and the like. It was the middle of nowhere.

Another jumper and I were walking along a little creek when something caught my eye, something out of place. I stopped and looked down through three feet of clear water.

"Look at this," I said to the other jumper. He came back and looked into the creek, glancing up at me and then back into the water.

"That's pretty spooky." It was a doll's head, its blue eyes staring upward past us, through the cold water and into the sky. It was undoubtedly swept here in the 1964 earthquake, thirty-eight years before, when the resultant tsunami struck many places along the Alaska coast. Here on Kodiak, the wave destroyed a nearby village, now abandoned.

Tonight there is no earthquake or tsunami, at least that I know of. It is so nice to get back to my tent and out of my sweaty waders and damp socks, and crawl into my warm, dry sleeping bag, a successful day of hard work and wild food harvesting behind me.

# CHAPTER 9

---

# Killer Whales

July 13, Day 14

In the morning I wake up and ponder the day's plan. I turn on the weather radio. It sounds like it won't rain. On most federal lands you're supposed to move camp every two weeks, and this area is no exception. It's a reasonable rule, really. It prevents people from claiming the very best camping spots. In this case it's probably a rather pointless regulation, there's no campsite competition, but I will try to honor the rule just the same.

When planning this trip I expected to shuttle my camp by boat, but I walk along the shore to see what there is for campsites. There are some places that look good at first, but many have tall trees with huge dead branches over them, some with dead branches already on the ground. It's a significant risk to the tent and my own health. It's a bit of a hike but I finally find a good spot, well above the high tide but near the shore, reasonably flat with stout living branches overhead.

I have purposely started early in the day to take advantage of the low tide. I begin packing gear down the beach. There are thimbleberry bushes here. The leaves look something like maple leaves, and their berries, when ripe, similar to raspberries. I've been watching their beautiful white blossoms develop into green berries. Soon I'll be able to pick some thimbleberries near either camp. I look forward to it.

I lay out the tent in the best spot. This is a new tent I bought for this trip. Every time I set it up it's a little easier. It's always satisfying to get a nice taught pitch. It sheds rain and condensation better and it's just good for morale.

I flew in with ten gallons of fresh water, there was plenty of payload on the plane, and amazingly I still have about six gallons left. How is it I've only used four gallons, a quart a day? A big part of my low water usage is that the water is only used for drinking. Crabs I cook in salt water. Fish, crabs, plants and berries have their own moisture. I filtered two quarts to drink at spike camp one day. I am hardly sweating at all and the humidity runs high.

I'm carrying over the two collapsible water jugs by their handles, one in each hand, when a handle pulls off one and a jug falls onto the rocks. The handle ring has straightened right out. I'm not surprised to find a small leak in the thin plastic. How can the handle be so &$@# weak that it can't hold the weight of a full jug? And to be so wimpy that it punctured with that short fall? Pretty poor. I carry the leaky jug over, and set it, punctured side up, so it won't lose any more water.

This move has been time consuming. If I were thru-hiking I could have completely packed up, unpacked and set up again in less than an hour, probably a half hour, with a pack of maybe twenty pounds. Now, with all the bulky equipment requiring many trips I don't get done with moving chores until about 4 PM. Just moving the electric bear fence is something of a project. It's very satisfying, though, when I place the four corners stakes in strategic positions and find the wire is exactly the right length even without adjustments.

At last everything is set up and organized. I take a break, lying back on my comfortable cot, reading *Bear Man of Admiralty Island*. It's fascinating to read about this man who lived among the bears on this island for so many years. It definitely gives me a unique perspective reading about him while I'm actually here in this remote rainforest. It is interesting to see how his views changed through the years. Like most stubborn old hermits he thought he knew it all. He surely knew a whole lot more about Admiralty Island than I'll ever know. He and others were slaughtering large numbers of bears, way back when, to the point where bears rarely showed up along the coast. In later years he became, to some degree, against bear hunting, and chased most hunters, even deer hunters, away from "his bay." It was interesting how much his winters varied, from brutally cold and snowy to fairly mild. Deer populations often rose and fell with the severity of the winters.

Suddenly a whale blows nearby! And again! I slip on my boots, grab my camera and binos and run outside. In a few steps I'm through the screen of trees. A plume of steam shoots up three hundred yards away and a long, black dorsal fin pierces the surface of the bay. A second later I hear the loud *Whoosh!* Orca! It plunges beneath the surface, immediately replaced by a second orca and another plume of steam, tall dorsal fin, and whoosh. It is thrilling. I run along the beach and out to the end of the point, watching the whales traveling to the head of the bay. I think of my seal friends that have followed me the last two weeks and hope they stay out of reach of the whales. How cool is it to be reading in your tent, hear whales, and be able to step outside and watch them? It's a big deal to an inlander like me.

I take advantage of some blue sky and sun and deploy the solar chargers. It was mighty nice of the rain to give me a break today.

Exploring the high ground above my camp I find some blueberries. Not many, but it's nice to know there are *some* blueberries within walking distance. This morning I finished off a jar of salmon and now I'm working on a jar of trout. Or Dollies. Or char. Whatever you want to call them, they are delicious.

This camp has a slightly different feel. It's bigger timber. It's darker here. It also faces the main bay rather than "My Cove" though, so maybe I'll see more whales. It also might be a bit quieter. Crows liked to sit around my other camp, out on the end of the point. Crows enjoy yelling.

It's nice to have the move done and to be resettled. With food on hand, tomorrow I'm free to do anything I want: explore, read, nap, eat, write, work on repairs. Options are nice. Freedom is good. It's gratifying to have reached this point on the adventure. I'm glad to be out here. I write in my journal until I get tired, then fall asleep.

July 14, Day 15

Man, I slept great last night. What's the date, the 14th? I've been out here for two weeks! I have some salmon for breakfast, salted and peppered. I've decided to head straight across the bay to the area near Falls Creek where I found the most berries before. A crab boat is in that area though, working their traps. I don't want to talk to them. Why? I guess because I don't want to explain what I'm up to. And I want to keep my summer as "wild" as possible. As I start paddling the boat is straight out from where I want to land so I steer more towards the creek. The shore is much less steep here, so rather than a carry of a few yards it's nearly 400 yards. Ouch! I switch from my waders to rubber boots.

I walk the shore looking for berries, not finding much except for a few of what I would have called gooseberries as a kid in Minnesota, but the proper name is black currants. They are tart, but good. I follow a bear path just inside tree line.

There's movement just ahead. Two brown animals. Medium sized. Low to the ground, shiny and dark. Otters! The nearest one, the largest, calls for the younger one, who hesitates. The adult runs over, grabs the half grown otter by the scruff of the neck, and runs clumsily to a nearby log behind which they disappear down an unseen hole. That was really cool! They were river otters. The young one was pretty big, several pounds. He didn't react fast enough in response to potential danger, so the parent took over. Very impressive! I walk over to inspect their burrow. There are red crab shells scattered all about. It must be a favorite food.

I climb the mountain but I must be taking a different path than last time because I'm hardly finding a berry. For some reason my legs feel weak. Low blood sugar maybe. Near the flat spot on the mountainside, the "bench," berries start showing up. There are the shiny black ones I call huckleberries and the similar, bluish ones I call blueberries. There is also a shorter species of blueberries like the ones in the Alaska Interior. Once I've found them, I can pretty much walk from bush to bush. Still not thick by any means, but fairly steady picking.

It's misting. I haven't bothered to put on rain pants. The wet bushes soon soak my pants. They sag, heavy and wet. The cracks in my boots have leaked enough to get my wool socks wet as well. With my rain jacket on and hood up, my torso is warm and dry.

Despite eating my fill of berries I finally fill the second jar to the top and replace the lid. When I hold it up there are alternating stripes of blue and black. There is a buzzing sound behind my head. When I turn a humming bird is looking me in the eye. It's the second time it's happened today. My hood is now down and he's spotted my red anti-mosquito bandana hanging below my hat and figures he hit the jackpot on giant flowers.

When I start seeing the small firewood stumps from years ago I keep an eye out for a cabin but I still don't find it. Maybe it rotted away long ago. The descent to the ocean goes smoothly, my energy lapse was brief.

I change back into waders, put on my waist belt and PFD and paddle for the crab trap a mile away. The trap feels heavy and I can see several crabs when it comes into view. Two of four crabs are keepers, one over well over 7", the biggest crab of the trip!

An hour after pulling them from the sea floor I'm eating steaming hot crab meat. If it's possible to cook them some way where they don't turn out great, I haven't found it! I eat my fill and bring two unshelled halves of cooked crab back to camp. I hang them in a tree outside my tent and just inside the electric fence.

The sun pierces the clouds. It's good timing. I take my damp waders off and hang them, inside-out, on a branch in the sun to dry, along with my wet pants and socks. Comfortable in my dry clothes I sit back to write in my journal and read. Sun streams through the trees and onto the screened door and casts dark silhouettes of hemlock branches on the nylon fly. Variety is the spice of life. This evening sun is especially beautiful at the end of a soggy, cloudy day.

July 15, Day 16

It's morning. I pull on my rubber boots and walk down to the water's edge. The low sun is hidden by the big timber behind me, but sunlight sparkles brilliantly on the white snow of mountaintops across Wild Bay, a striking contrast to the green-carpeted hillsides. What a pretty morning.

I'm going to take advantage of this perfect weather and get all cleaned up. A few days ago I found an empty blue bucket hidden in tall grass, washed up in a storm. It's weather-beaten but perfectly usable. I bring that bucket and my fish bucket, along with dirty clothes and shampoo, then head down the beach to a spring about a quarter mile away. There is plenty of water in the spring but it's hard to find a deep enough pool to dip clean water. I pick the deepest spot, scoop up as much water as I can in one bucket, then top it off to the very top with the other bucket. I scoop the empty bucket about 2/3 full then even out the two buckets.

It seems like a long walk back to camp. I'm accustomed to carrying heavy loads but I have to stop to rest several times. At cook camp I fill the canner with water and start heating it with the rocket stove. When it's nice and warm I pour it back into the bucket and carry it down to the gravely shore. The sun has finally reached this spot. I strip down in the warm sunlight and dunk my head in the hot water. Nice! The first hot water in two weeks! I shampoo up my head, then use my soapy hands to scrub my face and ears and neck and arms and on down to my waist. I step into the bucket and take a moment to enjoy the nice hot water on my feet and legs. What a luxury! I use the last of the shampoo suds from my head to thoroughly wash each foot, carefully scrubbing between my toes. I gingerly step out onto the dry gravel and rinse my head and all the way down to my waist. With a little more shampoo I scrub my unmentionable areas and rinse off.

A dirty cotton t-shirt serves as a towel to dry my feet. I put my boots on, and that's it. The sun will dry the rest of me. Now I know it's highly unusual to wash your clothes in your bath water, but that's exactly what I'm going to do. I turn my socks inside out and put a little shampoo on each sole. With one sock on each hand I scrub them together briskly. Each article of clothing, my pants, nylon shirt, underwear, etc. get a similar scrub, then go in the bucket. With everything soaked full of hot, soapy water, I push it to the bottom, squeezing water through everything. I pull it back up, letting everything soak up water once more, then squeeze it to the bottom once more. The water gets dirtier and dirtier, so it's working. After ten minutes I call it good. I twist as much dirty water out of everything as I can.

All the wet clothes go into the bucket of clean water. I take off a boot and stomp the clothes down to the bottom, over and over until suds stop coming out. Once more I twist out as much water as I can, then carry the buckets up and dump them in the trees.

The sun has dried me nicely. I put on clean socks and a pair of boxers and carry everything to the beach near camp. I hang most of the wet clothes on dead branches in direct sunlight. It's a good day to dry. Soon my sleeping bag, sleeping pad, waders, boots and just about everything else that can soak up moisture, are baking in the warm sun. That includes my tent fly. I bought it figuring it would be handy for condensation and to help retain heat when I use my stove. I haven't even fired up the stove yet, and condensation hasn't been an issue. Finally I lay out my solar panels to charge everything up. Free solar energy is a big delight for me. I try to aim the panels square to the sun to maximize their energy collection.

Back at the tent, I put on my camp shoes and place my rubber boots in the sun to dry. I inspect my rifle and shotgun. My shotgun is speckled with rust. It's an old shotgun, the bluing worn by years of use, but at the very least I want to keep it in good operating condition. I even find some speckles of rust on non-stainless parts of my stainless rifle. I get out my gun cleaning kit and give everything a good cleaning, finishing up by wiping both guns down with an oily rag.

I reorganize things in the tent. I carefully go through the two quarts of berries, cleaning out all the leaves and twigs and bugs, then lay the berries out on a space blanket in the sun to dry off excess moisture. They were wet from yesterday's rain. As I putter in the tent I hear wind in the trees followed by the sound of needles raining down on the tent fly. I walk outside and find the berries I'd so carefully cleaned are sprinkled with needles. Bummer. I let them dry then re-clean the whole batch.

With rubber boots in hand I inspect the cracks. There's one bad one in back of one boot, one bad crack near the toe, too. I wish I had Shoe Goo. Looking at my repair gear I ponder my options. Boat glue should work, right? I smear boat glue on each crack, extending the repair well beyond the cracked area. I also coat an area where cracks are just starting. I set the boots in the sun. It looks very similar to a Shoe Goo repair. Hopefully that will work.

I climb the ridge above camp. After a few more steps I look down and am surprised to see my current cook camp! I hadn't realized how much farther the easy, low route circled back. Going over the top is one third the distance! Perspective is interesting. Distances and angles can be very deceiving.

I'm writing in my journal as the sun sinks, relaxing in my chair. There's a whoosh nearby! I run outside. A huge orca fin appears above the placid water with a sudden plume of steam and another sharp report. As the fin sinks two smaller dorsal fins surface with small whooshes, then the calves dive too. Once more the adult appears with a sharp breath, followed moments later by the calves. I wait but they are gone. What a great way to end the day.

# CHAPTER 10

## Spike Camp

July 16, Day 17

When I wake up I turn on the weather radio. It sounds good. No rain, light winds. I'll go to the lodge to update my website and let people know I'm OK. I want to stay out of their way during their busy mornings when guests are being fed and getting ready for a day of fishing, so I get a late-morning start. There is a quartering tailwind, one of the few down-bay winds I've seen on this trip. It is an unusually nice day, a few clouds in a blue, sunny sky. Eagles soar overhead or perch in prominent trees, watching me paddle by. Seal heads pop out of the water and watch me curiously. Several times I hear whales blow and see their spout, but not the animal.

Scoters (a kind of sea duck) cruise past, low over the water, white wings contrasting with their black bodies. And as usual I see many of my favorite sea birds. I'm not sure what they are called, maybe auklets?

I should have brought a bird book. I was thinking I could look up birds and stuff with my smartphone if I needed to, but that's when I was counting on occasional cell phone coverage. Whatever they are, they have a number of endearing qualities: the way their heads tip back as they look at me from the water, the way they dive so suddenly, plunging their heads into the water with splash and disappearing instantly; the way they take off, barely able to maintain altitude at first, frequently skipping their bodies off the water; their plump, lemon-shaped bodies in flight, their rapid wing beats on too-tiny wings, holding a small, silvery fish in their beak as they head back to their nest.

[I find out later they are marbled murrelets. One of the most remarkable things about them is that the first nest known to science wasn't found until 1974! One reason the discovery was so late is that they don't make a true nest. Instead, they lay a single egg on a broad, moss covered tree limb near the trunk of an old growth tree. Murrelets use their stubby wings to "fly" underwater. Their low reproductive rate and dependence on old growth timber make them an endangered species.]

I stop at an island to pee and notice a strange creature exposed by the receding tide. It looks like an oblong, fist-sized dollop of chocolate pudding. It's a chiton, another critter than I haven't seen before. After a long paddle I arrive at the lodge and land at the dock. I climb out and stretch my legs, then pull my kayak out of the water and set it out of the way on the dock. I take off my waders and change into running shoes. Before leaving I invert my waders to dry and make sure nothing can blow away in a sudden wind.

The lodge owners greet me warmly at their office. I haven't talked to anyone in two weeks! I head over to the main lodge where the WIFI signal is the strongest.

"Hi Bruce!"

"Hi Anna." Anna is one of the lodge employees. She's young, pretty and cheerful. I'm sure she charms everyone with her genuine, warm personality. While I update my website I chat off and on with Anna and the cook. The cook once worked as a boat captain here in Southeast Alaska, but left for chef school to pursue his true calling. From what he says it appears he's found his niche in life.

I've promised to keep my WIFI time brief, so I've written up my website update before my arrival. It begins like this...

*It has been a great adventure so far.*

*Don't know if I've described the area in the last post. I'm at the head of a bay with my own little cove. There is huge, mostly virgin timber along the coast, primarily Sitka spruce and hemlocks, I believe, with some cedars in places. It's green country, and branches are often draped with moss. Mountains several thousand feet high rise above the bay. On the sunny days when they're visible, brilliant white snow sparkles against the green.*

*In places the forest is nearly impenetrable, a tangle of thorny Devil's Club or alder and huge, slippery fallen logs. But in many others it's fairly easy going through 4-5 foot tall blueberry bushes.*

*The ocean is clear with drifting seaweed. Sea lions and seals are common and often follow me. Out in my kayak there are usually eagles in sight. Sea ducks and seagulls fly to and fro. Mink scamper the beach. Blacktail deer sometimes appear along the edge of the forest...There are countless billions of shells. There are many starfish of several species to be seen at low tide...*

After updating my online journal I email my family to let them know I'm OK, and ask my brother to check on the duck hunting regulations for me. This year's regs weren't out yet when I left. It's a relief to let everyone know I'm OK so they don't worry.

I say goodbye to the lodge crew and then stop by the office to thank the owners. As I walk down to the dock the lodge pilot who greeted me the first day here is taxiing up in his 206. He's been to Juneau on a grocery run. He's interested in becoming a fire retardant pilot. He strikes me as a very competent fellow. I tell him, however, that being a retardant pilot is probably the most dangerous job in North America. Retardant planes are usually huge, and often decades old. They fly low and slow in smoke and through mountainous terrain with unpredictable winds. They often take great risks to protect homes and lives. It takes a terrible toll. Retardant pilots are the greatest heroes in wild land firefighting.

After saying goodbye, I paddle for the portage leading to Salmon Creek. On the way I listen to some music on my iPod. The mountain scenery is so spectacular today I stop for some self-timer photos of myself with the kayak against the mountains.

After finishing the portage I open a jar of salmon for lunch, with

nice cold water to wash it down. I'm going to make a spike camp tonight. I scout around on an island looking for a good camp spot. There's a nice, flat opening, perfect for a tent. When I look up there are large, dead branches dangling above me. Not a good spot. I walk farther down the ridge and find another flat spot without big trees above it. I lay down to test the flatness and slope. This will do nicely. Before standing up I lay my cap where my head is to mark the spot, then dig my tarptent out of the dry bag. I run a pole through the sleeve at the foot of the tent, then put each end in the grommet to form a hoop. I lay the tent out, using my cap as a guide for placement, then stake the foot end.

I used this shelter for my traverse of the Brooks Range. Normally a hiking pole is used to hold up the peak of the tent, which is at the door. Without a hiking pole I find a straight, strong stick and break it off to the right length. I use my Leatherman to tap a nail, brought for this purpose, into the end of the stick so that the head barely sticks out, then run the head of the nail through the grommet at the tent peak. With the peak raised I stake the front of the tent, pulling it taut against the foot.

After staking out the front corners I stake out the sides for a nice, taut pitch and I'm done.

When I was hiking the Appalachian Trail I would lay under my tarp and think "wouldn't it make sense to sew some bug netting to the edges of the tarp and a floor, so you'd have a bug-proof, lightweight shelter?" Nowadays, several small manufacturers make shelters like that, including this one. I roll out my sleeping pad and sleeping bag. It's nice to give the bag time to "fluff up." As I'm setting up I notice some blueberries right next to my tent. Not for long though, I gobble them up.

Even though I'm so close to Salmon Creek I'm not going to go fishing. I have a good supply of salmon. I'm going to look for some new berry spots. Berries are the biggest challenge now.

I make the short paddle to the mainland. I decided not to wear my waders. Water squirts up through the drain holes of the self-bailing floor and my butt gets splashed with a cold water. Nothing like a nice soggy butt!

Right away I find berries. They are the black ones, the ones I am calling huckleberries. They are bigger, blacker berries and the bushes are sturdier. The berries aren't particularly sweet but I'm glad to find them. I even find a couple salmonberries! It's some thick going here. I find myself crawling over logs and pushing through brush. I sing or talk out loud at times so I don't surprise a bear.

I climb as I pick and end up on a flat "bench" on the mountainside. Like the other bench by Falls Creek, this one has good berry-picking, the best I've found. There are blackberries, and the highbush variety of blueberries, and the most "lowbush blueberries" that I've seen. The blueberries are sweeter so I focus on them. When I quit I've gathered two and a half quarts. A very successful berry picking expedition.

I manage to paddle across to my island camp with a dry butt. I have a good "bear moat" around me on this island. I savor some salt and peppered salmon for supper with berries for dessert.

I relax in my warm sleeping bag, listening to recorded episodes of the radio show "This American Life" on my iPod. I last heard these episodes on my Desert Trail thru-hike which took me from Mexico to Canada. As each story unfolds I'm transported back to where I was hiking when I last enjoyed them: remote desert mountains and across arid, windswept valleys of California and Nevada, places far, far away from this temperate rainforest.

July 17, Day 18

I slept well. I lounge in my tent for while, listening to another *This American Life* episode. This one is about the powerful effect of testosterone, a hormone with an importance far beyond sex drive. It has an enormous effect on our general motivation and confidence and mood as well as things like sleeping and body fat. They interview a fellow who once lost virtually all his testosterone production. He lost his desire for virtually everything, for women, for good food, for competition, for achieving goals or accomplishment of any kind.

I paddle across to the mainland and pick another quart of berries, then return to pack up camp. By 11:15 I'm paddling in shallow water near the place I caught so many crabs by hand, this time armed with a landing net. There is a commotion in the shallows near the creek mouth, bulges of water streak toward deep water. What is going on?! Heads pop up one by one. Sea lions! They were obviously chasing salmon upstream. It made them nervous when I appeared and they couldn't dive into the depths.

When I get to the good spot there isn't a single crab in sight. Strange. It's a minus tide, too. A minus tide is lower than the average low tide. I land the boat on high ground and wade toward the creek without seeing a crab. When I get back to my kayak I paddle around and spot a stray crab here and there. Three times I deploy the landing net but it's much harder working from the boat. The water depth, the moving boat, ripples on the water and clumsiness thwart me. At last I give up.

Salmon jump and cruise the shallows with fins breaking the surface of the water at times. I see a pink salmon or two jump as well, identifiable by their relatively small size, the first pinks I've seen. There must be a dozen sea lions chasing salmon around in the cove, swirling in boils of seawater. A sea lion jumps clear out of the water. And again. Several are successful in their hunting, grabbing a salmon and flinging it around with their teeth like a dog shaking a gopher. It's dramatic and exciting, my own nature show.

I paddle all the way back past my base camp and on for another

mile until I get to my crab trap. It's heavy. When I swing the trap into the boat I have six fine crabs. Four of them are legal, including what is probably the biggest one yet. This is great!

Back at base camp I stash the kayak, grab some supplies and head to cook camp for a feast. With water heating on the stove I make a crude jar brush from green hemlock branch tips and scrub out eight jars. It's a chore. The tide is steadily moving in and I have to keep retreating, setting the jars behind me as I finish them. I should have brought a proper jar brush. Time after time I think I've done a decent job but find little bits of fish skin clinging to the clear glass. At last all eight jars are clean. I carry them up to cook camp and set them top down to drain and dry.

The water is steaming but the fire has started to die down while I was washing jars. I add more wood and it's soon boiling. I drop the crabs in. When they are done the feast commences. I eat my fill and then begin shelling the rest of the meat.

From time to time on this trip the no-see-ums have been annoying. They choose this moment to descend upon me. The bandana hanging from my cap helps, but I'm having to wave the especially aggressive little %&#@!s away. Not good conditions to shell crab meat, when I have to use both hands. With one crab eaten, and one and a half crabs worth of meat shelled and stashed in a quart jar, I gather everything, including the three unshelled crab halves, and head back to camp.

After hanging the crab halves in a tree I flee the no-see-ums by ducking into my tent and zipping the screen door closed. Although daylight is visible in narrow gaps next to the ground around part of the perimeter of my nylon tipi, it still does a remarkable job of keeping flying insects out.

For dinner I clean up what's left of a jar of salmon, and for dessert, a full quart of berries! Before bed I read *The Fifteen Decisive Battles of the World from Marathon to Waterloo*. It's interesting, even if the author's Victorian attitudes on the inherent supremacy of the British Empire are rather amusing.

# CHAPTER 11

# Sea Lions and Orcas and Bears

July 18, Day 19

Every time I woke up last night it was raining. It's still raining this morning. With the patter of rain on the tent and the screaming of eagles overhead I can barely hear the weather radio! I'm planning an easy day today.

About 9 AM the sun comes out. The winds are calm. The sea is smooth. Many species of birds are calling loudly and enthusiastically: numerous eagles, scores of seagulls, a dozen or more crows. I leisurely lay out the solar chargers. Most of my stuff is dry but I hang things that are a little damp, like socks and boots, to bake in the sun.

I eat crab meat from the jar as I read. It's amazing how good it is with no seasoning at all, lightly salty and rich.

It's a nice day for repairs. My boot repair has been a failure. The boat glue didn't hold very well, despite what I thought was careful preparation. Is there something about the boot that prevented the glue from sticking, residual silicone or something on them? Looking over my repair kit I decide to try duct tape next. It won't last the rest of the trip, but even if I have to replace it periodically it would be nice to have dry feet. I carefully sand and clean the area to make the tape stick better, then cut duct tape patches that extend well beyond the holes, rounding the corners to help prevent peeling. I firmly rub the tape down onto the boot, taking special care all along the edges. Lastly I set the boots in the sun. Maybe it will help the tape glue set.

I'm reminded of a collapsible plastic water bottle I repaired on my Alaska traverse. A sharp rock had punctured it. I simply dried the outside and covered the hole with duct tape with rounded corners. Years later I was bragging about that repair to a friend as the bottle sat on a rock, full of water.

"I repaired that in 2006, and it hasn't leaked a drop since," I pointed out.

"It's leaking right now, isn't it?" she said, pointing to a tiny trickle of water. I had to laugh. She was right. Still, that repair lasted for years. I'll be happy if this repair works for a fraction of the time.

The calm winds are holding. The tide tables show a 12:22 low tide. Slack tide occurs near high or low tide when the tidal currents slow as they switch between coming in or going out. Slack tides are supposed to be good for halibut fishing because it's easier to keep bait on or near the bottom.

On a map of the bay there is hump of higher ocean floor shown. It is about nine fathoms, or 54 feet deep, with surrounding bottom considerably deeper. Humps like this are said to be good halibut fishing spots. Twice in past years I've been halibut fishing with good success, but they were guided trips and I have no experience on finding good fishing spots on my own. I'll try this spot.

Serious halibut fisherman have specific set-ups for halibut. They'd never use what I'm using, a spinning setup that I bought for king salmon. The pros wouldn't use a spinning reel, they'd use a level-wind reel. They wouldn't use a pole as long as I'm using, they'd use a shorter, beefier pole. And they wouldn't use 40 pound test; they'd use 100 pound test, maybe heavier. The thing is, I couldn't justify buying a whole new setup just for halibut. Who knows when I'll go halibut fishing again? Anyway, I've got what I've got.

I tie on a one pound jig head with a huge hook. The size and weight seem ludicrous. I look at the huge hook bend and my inflatable kayak and promise myself that I'll do my best to avoid puncturing my boat! I take an enormous soft-plastic jig, white and scented, and skewer it with the hook. When I lower it over the boat and give it a test jig the tail swims enticingly. It looks alive.

After I launch the wind, predictably, begins to rise. When I am just upwind of the "hump" I lower the heavy jig over the side until I feel it hit the bottom, then begin to jig it up and down, bouncing it off the bottom and raising it three or four feet each jig. It just feels right. A bite seems imminent. THERE! I set the hook. Nothing. I get a snag briefly but it comes loose. Good thing because I only have two of the big jig heads. I have tackle to fish with bait if I lose both jigs, though. I drift over the hump and far downwind, letting out more line as it gets deeper, then paddle upwind of the hump and jig as I drift once more.

The wind increases and it begins to rain. Am I doing something wrong or are they not biting? Or both? Regardless, I've given it a good go. I'm heading back to camp.

After successfully fighting the wind and rain all the way home I carry the kayak up to the trees then flop it down in the grass and drag it under the low branches into the edge of the open timber. As I lean the rod against a tree I notice teeth marks on the jig. Are they halibut teeth marks? Or maybe crab-claw marks? I'm not sure, but something was grabbing at it, that's for sure.

The headwind drove rain in around my hood. My face and neck and collar area are wet as are the cuffs of my shirt.

I change and lie back on my cot wearing dry long underwear and dry socks, tucked in my sleeping bag. I read with my head propped up with spare clothes. You only really feel dry after you've been wet, especially after you've been chilled and wet. I am ridiculously comfortable.

Lunch is all-I-can-eat crab, finishing off the last of the crab I got yesterday. It's blueberries and huckleberries for dessert.

The rain stops and sunlight floods the tent. I take my chair and set it up down by the water where I sit, writing in my journal, looking up at the magnificent scenery when I need inspiration. It becomes very, very still. Somewhere, far off, something is blowing and splashing. *There!* Sea lions, chasing salmon, seagulls hovering over them watching for scraps.

July 19, Day 20

When I wake up I lie there, taking stock of how things are going on the trip so far. Pretty darn good, I've got to say. The greatest challenge on this adventure was food. Right now I have good reserves, canned salmon and trout and two jars of canned crab along with several jars of fresh berries. My morale is excellent. I'm not lonely, I don't really get lonely, it's how I'm wired. I'm rarely craving "town food." One of my biggest fears, getting tired of fish, has not been an issue. Deer season starts in less than two weeks. Once I have a deer, I'll really be set. I can almost taste the venison already. When I first got here I still thought deer season started August 10, but when reading the hunting regs I was happy to see that a "bucks only" season starts August 1.

I bring a trowel and head up into the timber to dig a little "cat hole" latrine. Later I do a little exploring around the area. A few yards from high tide there is an old river otter skull. I'm also keeping an eye out for something to prop up the legs of my cot. In the current camp spot the ground is covered with soft, uneven moss and the cot is wobbly. I find a tree has broken off about twenty feet high. From its side flat "planks" have split off. They should work. I tote a couple back to camp and experiment on how best to place them.

I finish the *Great Battles* book and write in my journal. I hear the rumble of a crab boat tending trap across the still waters of the bay.

It's a hassle not having a watch on my wrist. I experiment with methods to keep it handy and finally settle on tying a loop of cord through the buckle on the remaining side of the wrist band, then looping the cord through the buttonhole of my left shirt pocket. That should work well. I'm always wearing this shirt.

While I'm in a repairing mood I check the duct tape patches of my boots. Knowing the peeling edges will be the demise of my repairs, I run a tiny bead of Super Glue all along the edges. Seems like that should hold for while. My rain pants have small holes on each cuff where the legs rub together as I walk. I put a duct tape patch on each hole, rounding the edges as usual, then sew down the edges with a needle and dental floss. That should hold.

At my kayak I check the knots on my paddle lanyard, then tape the paddle end of the lanyard to keep the knot from untying or slipping down the paddle. I also check the knots on the crab caliper lanyard.

What else needs to be done? I should do something about the food cache block and tackle. The way I have it set up it's only a 2:1 mechanical advantage. It's a pretty hard pull with all those heavy jars and I'm a little concerned that the cord will break from the hard pulling. Experimenting around I find that I have enough unknotted rope to use four pulleys rather than the two pulleys I was using recently, so now I have a 4:1 mechanical advantage. It makes a big difference. I started out with six pulleys, but it didn't extend far enough that way. Two pulleys was too hard to pull, but four seems perfect.

During the course of the day I pick and eat some raw sea asparagus, something I do often without thinking about it. The thimbleberries around camp are just starting to ripen and I eat several. They will be a real bonus once they start ripening in earnest.

During a long break back at the tent I finish reading *WILDFIRE: Memories of a Wildland Firefighter*, a book about smokejumping. I know the author and many of the people and events so I especially enjoy it. It's clear that smokejumping had an enormous impact on the author's life, his experiences largely defining his self-identity. I think the same is true for many old smokejumpers.

Late in the afternoon I hear a float plane circle. I walk down to the water with binoculars and watch as it sets down on the ocean across the bay, beaching on a steep point of land a mile or so away. Three occupants stack a pile of gear on the shore. Soon the plane roars off. I last see the tiny figures carrying gear along the shore and into the trees. It's strange to have other people camping in Wild Bay, even if they are a mile away. I have blueberries and salmon for dinner, then read a little bit more and call it a day.

July 20, Day 21

What was that? A big animal is breathing outside my tent! *A huge animal!* There is splashing. It's out in the bay. I slip on my boots on and walk down to the water. Tall black fins slice through the water. Orcas! I quickly put on my life jacket, grab my kayak and carry it down to the water. Because I'm not wearing waders I sit on the bucket cover to avoid getting a wet butt, then launch, hoping to get a better look at the whales that are disappearing around the point. They surface, breathe and disappear, unpredictably changing directions underwater.

The stark contrast of their black on white skin is striking. They aren't making the big "blows" that I usually associate with whales, rather they are simply exhaling, taking a quick breath and then diving. Why no big blows? Maybe because they are mostly cruising on the surface rather than taking huge breaths for long dives. Regardless, it's impressive, and thrilling.

I head back to camp, reoutfit, then paddle across the glassy smooth water for some halibut fishing. Over the same nine fathom hump in the seafloor I add some fresh fish oil scent to the plastic bait, then start jigging, barely drifting in the calm wind and minimal tide. Again, it just feels right. It seems like I'm going to hook a big one at any minute. Twice I can feel a gentle bite and I'm still mystified as to what it is: crab, sculpins maybe, or is it actually halibut that I'm not hooking? I've got a marine chart app on my iPhone, and use it to pinpoint another hump a few hundred yards away where I try my luck again. Because I'm barely drifting, I get a lot of fishing time in before I've drifted back over deep water.

From time to time I hear whales. A mound of water rises a stone's throw away. A tall black dorsal fin and glistening back of a killer whale appear. With a loud exhalation and a plume of steam, its warm breath condenses in the cool air. The monstrous animal gasps a new breath then plunges into the churning water. Wow! That was really cool.

My whale luck has been great, but my halibut luck or maybe skill, has not been so impressive. I reel in my jig and find some new teeth marks on the plastic grub. Hmm.

I decide to check out My Creek to see if any salmon are in. Ahead is a grassy island that gets flooded at the highest tides. I grab the lanyard attached to the breast pocket of my shirt and pull out my watch. 8 AM! Yikes, it's already been a big day. Consulting the tide tables retrieved from the other breast pocket I see high tide is at 8:46 and that it's a 12.1' high tide. That's compared to the 19.4 foot high tide the night I walked back to camp at 1 AM. Big difference. I carry the kayak and stash it on the highest ground of the island. It's easy to read the charts wrong, at least it is for me, and the consequences of a mistake could be huge. So I check and double check: today is the 20th, I'm looking at July, and I'm looking at AM, not PM. Check, check and check. I'm good. The tide will soon be falling, then I'll be doubly good.

I walk across the flats. When I hit the creek channel I follow it upstream until I reach a brackish pool with ghostly dead jellyfish on the bottom. Many tiger-striped fish are cruising in three or four feet of water. Salmon! The first salmon at My Creek. This is exciting. It's even more exciting when I look up to see a brown bear walking the bank towards me, scanning the water for fish!

"Hey!" I yell. He glances up and freezes, then rises to his hind feet, a tower of brown fur, trying to see what I am. He drops down, turns and lopes for the timber. I can tell he's gone for good.

I drop my pack and cautiously approach the pool to avoid spooking the fish. I begin to false cast, extending the fly line each time before sending the purple egg-sucking leech far across the pool. After allowing it to sink to the level of the fish I begin stripping the fly through the pool. BANG! I have one on but after a brief struggle I lose it. No matter, it was a female, and I'd prefer to catch males. I hold my breath as the leech pulses past the main part of the school. A big male swings his head and the fly stops dead. Fish on! He rushes upstream, scattering his neighbors. I slowly fight him towards the tail of the pool. When he is tired I slide him onto the gravel bar, rap him on the head to stun him, then bleed him. Nice!

It seems to me that brackish water shouldn't be the best place to fish, but if so, the fish don't seem to know that. In no time I hook another fish, a big, striped male. Cool! I work him towards the tail of the pool, taking a good look around for bears as I do. This is great. I don't want any more fish right now, though. It's funny how fishing can be boom or bust. Today I could have caught barrels of salmon by the looks of things. I clean my catch, put them in a bucket and head back to the kayak.

The crab trap is on my way home so I stop to check it. It feels particularly heavy. Holy smokes, there's a bunch of them. 1,2,3,4....8 eight crabs! What a haul! Some beauties, too. Although I've often reached through one of the trap-doors to grab crabs, this time I open a whole side of the trap and cautiously pull out the first one, who does his best to reach back and pinch the dickens out of my fingers. He fails. I put the caliper on him. Legal! He goes in the bucket. Another legal one, this one over 7". I end up with six legal crabs! Two big salmon and six legal crabs. And it's not 10 AM yet! What an epic day it's been.

I paddle over to a nearby rocky spit for photos, laying the six fine crabs on their backs to keep them immobile. I put my camera on a tripod and set the timer. With one salmon lying behind the crabs I hold the biggest fish up. The flash goes off. The moment is frozen in time. My smile is genuine. It is a far cry from the first hungry days.

A friend once told the story of climbing in the mountains. He stopped to take a photo. His climbing partner scolded him by tapping his head and saying "The best camera is right here, in your head." That fellow was full of baloney. The best camera is a camera.

On the way back to camp I drop the crab trap in the same spot, then continue home.

I fillet the salmon. Plan A had been to grill a meal's worth of salmon and to can the rest, but this is going to be a time-consuming operation and I don't have the patience to add to the complexity. Instead, I fill six jars with salmon fillets. Next I get a nice hot fire going and start heating water in the canner, and when it boils throw in the cleaned crabs. When they are done I shell the biggest pieces of meat: the meat from the body, claws and upper legs. It fills two quart jars. I stack the six jars of fish and the two jars of crab in the canner, tighten the canner lid, and start

heating it. After it vents for a while and the weight is on and chattering I eat my lunch, the lower legs of the crabs.

This was a good strategy I muse, It takes 110 minutes once it gets to pressure. Eating crab legs is time consuming. I can eat while I wait. When I'm done I have eight more jars of canned seafood. As they cool, five jars seal with a "ping" as the lids are drawn down, but three don't. Bummer. I tried reusing some lids, just to make sure I wouldn't run short of new ones. Probably that caused it. You're not supposed to reuse this kind of lids. I'll have to eat the unsealed ones ASAP. I hang up the five sealed jars in my food cache and carry the rest back to camp where I set them just inside the electric fence. It's nearly 8 PM. This day went nothing like I expected when I woke up. There were a whole string of awesome surprises with the three unsealed jars being the only negative event. Any day where you can see whales, face a towering brown bear and catch a bunch of salmon and Dungeness crabs is a day to remember!

# CHAPTER 12

## Nature's Garden

July 21, Day 22

I remember the sound I heard last night, some kind of small animal screeching. Probably a mink. I bet a couple of mink ran into each other feeding along the beach and they were fighting it out over territory. There are so many mink it seems like the best explanation. It sounded something like cats fighting.

It's an absolutely beautiful morning, sunny and clear. It was a typically cloudy day yesterday so this is a treat. For breakfast I eat as much salmon as I can comfortably hold, most of a quart!

I hang things to dry: sleeping bag, waders, pack, damp socks, on tree boughs or dead branches sticking up on shoreline logs. I set up the solar chargers. I aim them so the moving sun will strike them squarely in an hour or so.

Another crack is appearing on the side of my rubber boots. I fear it's going to end up being a losing battle, but I take the time to make another careful duct tape repair and hope for the best.

I'm going to explore a different area for berries, a new area of the peninsula I'm camped on. I check the contents of my daypack. I have a jar of good fire-starting materials: paper, dry twigs, dry splinters, candle, lighter and matches. Other items I've packed include a space blanket, rain jacket, fleece jacket, knife, water, DEET, bandana, LED light, rain pants, balaclava and two empty jars.

I follow a low ridge towards the mainland. At first the walking is fairly easy, with a few stray berries. I'm forced to cross a brushy ravine scattered with Devil's club, crowned by their large leaves and bristling with wicked thorns. I slow to a crawl climbing over giant, half rotten logs. Deer trails snake through the area. I'm not far from camp yet. I haven't seen a deer this close to camp, but they must see or smell me fairly often.

There aren't many brown bears out on this peninsula, but I still don't want to take the chance of surprising one, so I clink a berry jar or talk out loud now and then to give them advance warning. When I was planning this trip I thought I'd carry my 30-06 for bear protection on occasion, but I haven't yet, and I have a feeling that I won't. I'm focusing more on preventing a surprise close-range encounter and in selecting my camp sites. It would be so much handier to camp near my best food sources, the creeks. But that's where bears concentrate. I purposely picked out a camping area far from salmon streams. An ounce of prevention is worth a pound of cure. Bear spray would be better than a gun for bear protection anyway, in my opinion. It's so much easier to carry and have handy. Bear spray is also less likely to escalate a bluff charge into a wounded bear situation. In any case, an actual bear attack is very, very unlikely.

When I regain the ridge, the brush thins. There are a few more berries, but it's slow picking, a few huckleberries or blueberries here and there. I'm enjoying the big timber, though, as well as the fine weather, calm and fairly warm.

With the berry picking marginal, I angle towards the bay. It's nice to get out to easy, sunny walking, with good mountain views. As I walk I see something interesting.

Pea pods! Some kind of wild peas. I find two or three pods and watch all the way back to camp, finding maybe a half dozen more.

This should be good. Something different. Better check the

guidebooks first, though. They say some wild peas are considered poisonous.

I've got a couple of foraging guidebooks, and an iPhone app. I look up peas and find "Beach Pea." The pod photos look identical to the ones I've found. The description is matching, too. "Beach pea is a clambering plant." Check. "Smooth, hairless pea pods." Check. "Branching tendrils at the tips." Check. "Arrowhead shaped stipules." Hmm, looks like it to me. There aren't any flowers, so the flower description is no help.

The leaves look similar but a little different, narrower. I know plant leaves often vary quite a bit, though. The biggest catch is that the one guide says beach peas have three to twelve pairs of leaflets. Some of these have about 14, maybe more. One guidebook though, pretty much settles it. It's a list of flowers of Alaska. I look at every legume listed: Is this Milk Vetch? Nope. Black Oxytrope? Nope. Scammon's Oxytrope? Lupine? Eskimo potato? Hedysarum Mackenzii? Nope. According to the plants listed in this Alaska guidebook, that leaves only beach pea.

I'm pretty confident, but only confident enough to eat a few to see how I feel. This is a time where data coverage for my smartphone would be extremely useful. I could look up a bunch more information, see more photos.

I walk around the end of the point checking the thimbleberry patches. A red, ripe berry is waiting for me. It falls off as I grab it but I catch it in the cup of my hand. It's really sweet. I find about two handfuls. They are the best, sweetest berries of the whole trip. I also find the mother lode of beach pea plants, many with multiple ripe pods. I'd chow down but I don't dare yet.

Boats have been sparse in the upper bay where my camp is, but today is an exception. At least three crab boats come to the head of the bay, checking traps. When I cross the spit I see a yacht, a huge, freaking *yacht*, anchored at the head of the bay near my crab buoy. Man, does that seem out of place, out here in my wilderness. I guess it shouldn't be that surprising though, this is a bay of the ocean. There's going to be fisherman and sight-seers. The yacht, I'm guessing, came to the head of the bay to do a little exploring, perhaps to see some brown bears, and to anchor for the evening in water largely protected from wind.

I'm kicking it in camp, just finishing up the classic book, *The Time Machine*. It's a good book, even though it was first published in 1895. I work on a crossword puzzle for awhile.

I pick up my rubber boots. Two huge cracks are opening up. These boots are done for. They are name-brand boots, too, only about eighteen months old. That is really lousy quality control. There's no hope of keeping them waterproof now. I guess I can wear them around camp until they fall apart completely. Not having good rubber boots is going to be a bummer. I can't run to the boot store or order another pair online.

This evening is exceptionally pleasant, calm and sunny. I sit on a beach log and watch the sun set over the mountains. I can smell the sea. No bugs hassle me. The boats are gone. Salmon are jumping here and there. Ravens and gulls call raucously. Shorebirds feed along the water's edge, twittering busily. A seal pokes his head out of the calm water and cruises past, studying me curiously. The flaming yellow orb of the sun touches a mountaintop and slowly sinks, leaving a halo of orange light, the rugged peak becoming a black silhouette.

July 22, Day 23

This morning, I'm trolling a halibut jig across the bay to the steepest shore near Falls Creek. I'd like to catch a halibut, or cod or some other edible fish, but what I do catch is nothing. With my rubber boots shot to pieces I peel off my waders, slide plastic shopping bags over my thick wool socks, then put my wet wading boots on over them, lacing them tightly. Not as good as proper rubber boots, for sure, but it will be much easier walking than with waders, and I won't have to worry about wader punctures. If I don't step in water over ankle deep my feet should stay fairly dry. We'll see.

It's almost a routine now, picking a few berries on my way to the bench, where the real picking begins. I even know the best spots for berries in that area, the opening near the creek. By the time I get there

I've already filled the first jar with black huckleberries mixed with blueberries. There is good blueberry picking near the far corner. When I look at my second jar, now three quarters full, I notice alternating layers of black and blue berries. Just for fun I search around for some nice, black blueberries to finish off the pattern of layers. On a little knob I top off the jar and pause to admire the affect.

There are a few plants of Labrador tea growing here on the bench. Labrador tea is common in the Interior of Alaska, around Fairbanks and in the taiga where I usually fought forest fires. I have on occasion drank tea made with their leaves. I was intrigued reading their description in the guidebooks. They are a member of the Rhododendron genus. It makes sense, they look like tiny Rhododendrons, but I'd never thought about it before. Rhododendrons seem out of place in Alaska. It reminds me of the tiny sagebrush plants growing on south-facing slopes above Fort Wainwright where we would often make practice parachute jumps. There weren't many sage plants there. They were so small they were hardly recognizable as sage. I liked to pick a few leaves and crush them between my fingers so I could smell the faraway West as I looked out over the Alaska Range.

I pick a few Labrador tea leaves and flip them over and see the usual brownish fuzz on the bottom. The guidebook warned about confusing this plant with the toxic bog rosemary which lacks the brown fuzz. That was news to me, a toxic lookalike. They look quite similar. I crush the leaves and note the distinctive resinous odor. Maybe I'll make some tea. The guidebooks also warn to drink Labrador tea only in moderate amounts. On rare occasions excessive amounts have been fatal! I suppose that's true with a whole lot of things.

Near the kayak I find a nice wooden plank, about two inches thick and eight inches wide and four feet long. Might be good to hold up my still-wobbly cot. I tuck one end under the kayak seat then paddle towards the head of the bay. After rounding a point I land and stash the kayak.

I follow the shoreline watching for salmonberry bushes. I soon spot a nice patch of bushes. A large, orangish-red berry peeks out from the green leaves. Upon closer inspection, I see several more and add them to a jar. As I walk along the shore I notice some salmonberry patches with an orange shade of berry, while other patches have more red berries. The berries are good but not particularly sweet, some are quite tart. It's fun picking them, though, because they are so big the jar fills rapidly, and because it's been so difficult finding this berry that I'd expected to be a mainstay.

Where there are ripe berries I find it's worthwhile to part the bushes to look for more.

It seems like these bushes should have stickers. They look so much like raspberries. *They must be related.* When I look closer I see that some bushes do in fact have thorns. Good thing I didn't rip my Gore-Tex waders.

When I have a quart of salmonberries I hike back to the kayak. Three quarts of berries today, my best berry day yet! I paddle for my crab trap, not far away. It's starting to rain. A seal trails me. I swing the dripping trap over the side of the boat and find... nothing. That's strange.

I'll try another spot closer to camp. At least it will save me some paddling, and maybe it will be a better spot. The one sea floor hump I've been fishing is nearly sixty feet deep, that's a good depth. When I get there, half way to camp, I lower the trap down. Fortunately I hang onto the buoy because I run out of rope. I am over a spot marked as nine fathoms (fifty-four feet,) verified by my nautical chart app on my iPhone. How is this possible? The map must just generalize the depth of a vicinity maybe? It's a long haul pulling the trap up a hundred feet. I load the trap and paddle nearer to shore. A reasonable distance from a commercial trapper buoy I drop the trap again. This time there is only five feet of rope left. And it's near low tide! #$ %&! I pull the trap all the way up for the third time. Defeated, I paddle through the dreary rain nearly back to where I first pulled the trap. This time when I drop it there is rope to spare. Whew!

At base camp I walk around the point, picking as many thimbleberries as I can find. They are ripening rapidly and I get a half quart of the sweetest berries I've found out here. I also find lots more peas and pick a whole quart of pods in no time. I really got ahead of the curve today on berries: two quarts of huckleberries and blueberries, a quart of salmon berries, half quart of thimbleberries, with the bonus quart of pea pods.

It's good to get back to the tent and out of the wet. Rain blew in around my hood and water ran up my sleeves while I was pulling the crab trap over and over. I sling off my daypack and fling it on the floor with a wet plop, right on top of my nice dry camp shoes. Crap! I quickly move it. I slide out of my dripping raincoat and lay it in a corner, then sit down and take off my soaked wading boots and peel off my wet waders.

It's so great to crawl into my dry sleeping bag. I pull out my watch. 6 PM. Other than a few berries and peas I've eaten nothing all day. I open a jar of salmon. Rolling over, I find the salt, pepper and fork and dive into the salmon. That's some good stuff. Hunger does wonders for your appetite! I devour the whole jar. I suppose I should probably put the empty jar outside the tent. I look at my 30-06, and think about the electric fence. I've slept with game meat in camp many, many times before. To hell with the bears. I read until I'm sleepy then call it a day.

In the middle of the night I wake up to the sound of pattering rain. After a while I fall back asleep.

# CHAPTER 13

## Life in the Wilderness

July 23, Day 24

It's still raining in early morning. When it lets up I get up to stretch my legs and pee. While I'm at it I pick a few peas which I shell and eat.

The sun is struggling to burn through the clouds. I lay out the solar chargers to charge up the radio which I use daily to check the weather. I also charge up my iPhone, which I'm using as a camera, for the nautical charts, and more. I'm surprised to see some gain in charge even when the sun is partially veiled by clouds.

With the sun winning its battle with the clouds I hang up my wet stuff to dry: waders, jacket, shoes, pack socks, hat, bandana. It's about noon before the clouds sweep in again. By that time everything is dry and charged. I stash everything back in the tent. I pour the berries out on some foil and clean all the debris out. I get a kick out of the colorful jars, for the variety of food they represent and for the beauty of the contrasting colors. I line them up on the gravelly shore and take a photo.

Maybe they'd look better on a green background. I carry them up the hill and lay them in a row on the green moss, delicate ferns around them: first a jar of green pea pods, the next jar with alternating layers of

black huckleberries and blueberries, the center jar filled with bright orange and red salmonberries, then another jar of layered blueberries, and lastly a jar of red thimbleberries. I love the variety and the cheerful, contrasting colors of my own little cornucopia.

Back at the tent I put duct tape on the newest and biggest holes in my rubber boots. These repairs are now just delaying the inevitable total failure.

Pondering chores I should do today, I decide to make a better buoy tag. I'd written the info on my buoy with a pen but it has partially worn off. I find a beefy tag used to mark my air cargo and write the information on that. I'll wire it to the buoy next visit. I also scout for a good rock to use for a trap weight. I'm concerned that the one I have now may move and hold a trap door open. I find a long rock that will be easy to wire in place. It's about two inches square and a ten inches long.

I walk around The Point picking and eating newly ripened thimbleberries. In the distance there is a larger fishing boat. What are they doing, some kind of netting? They are too far away to tell. Sea lions are cruising around, making a racket at times, splashing after salmon and taking gasping breaths on the surface, one of them even barks.

My main food of the day has been salmon. I eat some whenever I'm in the mood. Along with the thimbleberries I also eat some of the goose tongue plant I discovered some time back. It's another one of those plants I've been stepping over. It grows in what looks something like clumps of quackgrass with heavy blades. It's pretty good raw, just pluck it and eat it. Goose tongue and sea asparagus have been my main green plant foods.

I have a book on Dungeness crabbing. I flip through it again to see if I can pick up any tips. The author says lots of bait types will work, but shad is the best. I don't even know if shad live around here. He says fresh bait has been proven to be better. Maybe I'll try to switch the bait out more often. It was from this book that I got the tip to not leave crabs in a bucket full of water. That's exactly what I *would* have done! Nothing like getting advice from an experienced hand. The author recommends minus tides for dipnetting, something I'd already considered, but he also recommends checking out areas with eelgrass, something I didn't know.

I go through all my guidebooks to cross reference beach peas again, and again come to the same conclusion: they have the smooth pods, the round peas, the tendrils, and they grow along the beach. It's the leaves that don't look quite right. Sure wish I had some more photos to compare them to, or had access to the internet. I'll "increase my dosage" of peas and see how it goes and try to check on them online when I get back to the lodge.

Before I fall asleep I turn on my Kindle and read *Extraordinary Popular Delusions & the Madness of Crowds*. It's a fascinating book. One of the topics is "Tulipmania." Tulipmania was centered primarily in what is now the Netherlands and involved wild speculation in the buying and selling of the recently introduced tulip bulb. As prices spiraled upward, more and more people saw trading tulip bulbs as a way to get rich quickly and easily. Some tulip bulbs were selling for the equivalent of several year's wages. As is typical of speculative bubbles, the whole mania collapsed precipitously, with fortunes vanishing as quickly as they had been made.

July 24, Day 25

The clock on my weather radio says it's 5:40 AM. The weather report is calling for a mostly cloudy day, light winds, probably no significant rain. I consult the tide tables. Let's see, today is July 24, low tide is...6:29. I'm pretty well packed up already so I grab my fishing and crabbing gear and head to "the Hump" to jig for halibut. Once again, I feel a bite of some kind, a crab or a small fish or a halibut. Whatever it is I don't hook it. I'm losing faith in my halibut catching skills.

My luck isn't any better with crabs today. The trap is empty. Bummer. I really wanted the fresh meat. With the buoy and rope on the floor of the kayak I set the trap across the tubes in front of me and paddle to the nearest island. When I land, several clams spit streams of water out of the sandy beach, a comical site.

When I was planning this trip I thought I'd eat a lot of clams. When I researched the topic I soon found that eating clams from untested beaches is not recommended because of the risk of Paralytic Shellfish Poisoning (PSP.) That was a huge surprise. Haven't people been eating clams for thousands of years? I find this quote: *The Alaska Division of Public Health strongly recommends against eating noncommercial shellfish from Alaska Waters. However, if people choose to do so they should never eat alone, know what the symptoms of PSP are, and seek medical help immediately if symptoms develop.* I find some examples of reported cases in Southeast Alaska in certain years. But does it actually *kill* people? People often fear the wrong things. So I look for examples of actual deaths and find this quote: *Alaskans have been fortunate in recent years in that those who have been as severely poisoned as the index case in this outbreak have been close enough to medical life support systems to sustain them through their period of respiratory paralysis. Less fortunate were over 100 Russians and Aleuts who died in Alaska's worst PSP outbreak in Peril Straights in 1799. PSP deaths along the Pacific coast continue to occur on a regular basis.* I also find out that there was a case of PSP from clams dug right here on Admiralty Island in 2012. OK. That's good enough for me. It's a chance I don't have to take, so I won't.

It's a shame though. Clams would be an easy, delicious food source, a good way to vary my diet, too. Although I can't eat them, I can use them for crab bait. I untie my kayak paddle and walk along the beach until I see a clam squirt. I dig there in the sandy shore and soon flip up a nice butter clam. I dig a couple more then grab a few black mussels which grow in profusion on the nearby rocks.

One day I found a plastic bait cage a commercial crabber lost overboard some time back. It's pretty weather-beaten, but fully serviceable. I crush the shells of the clams to release scent, fill the bait cage and wire it to the top of the trap. I remove the ballast rock from the trap, then fetch the long rock from the bucket and wire it to the bottom of the trap. Lastly I wire the new name tag to the buoy.

I paddle out to a new spot, off the point of this island and not far from the mouth of My Creek, and drop the trap. Looks like about sixty feet deep. Maybe the fresh clam bait and a new location will do the trick.

In the distance I see the big fishing boat I'd seen yesterday. It was anchored in the same spot for at least twelve hours. That seems strange. Did it have nets set out or something? Maybe it was making repairs? In any case it is now heading out for the main Sound.

Back at base camp I read for a while. There are some interesting parts in the book about witch burnings way back when. Fearful mobs can be an irrational, dangerous, evil, force. Reading some of the angry, irrational political hyperbole on the internet sometimes, I have no doubt something similar could happen again.

What's that outside? *Whoosh*! Whales! I put on my PFD and a bucket cover to sit on and paddle out to see them. Two hundred yards away broad gray backs with short dorsal fins rise from the water, each releasing a gush of steam and sinking again with a flip of their tail. Humpbacks! I watch as they grow smaller each time they surface, heading towards the Sound.

I eat some salmon and berries then gather up all the empty jars. I make another crude jar brush, this time by wiring the tips of a spruce bough to a stick. It works OK, but not great. It falls off after a while, and it is soon tattered and falling apart. I do manage to get all the jars clean though, and tip them upside down in the moss to drain and dry.

Organizing camp I notice my surviving drinking water jug. There are still nearly two gallons left of the original ten gallons. Amazing.

July 25, Day 26

This morning the radio calls for wind and rain. It's still calm now. It's often calm in the morning. Although it's not quite 5 AM I am moving, hoping to check my crab trap before the wind and rain hit. I climb the slope behind my tent to dig my morning cat hole latrine. Through the trees I see *two* boats anchored in My Cove. *That's* a surprise! One is a nice little sailboat. The other boat, also small, must be a crab boat.

The wind hits as I paddle round The Point, and although there is some chop, it's not raining. There are new colors of crab buoys showing up, meaning new boats are fishing the bay. Most buoys have contrasting colors, green and white, yellow and red, blue and white. I suspect some of these new boats don't know the bay very well, with traps set in seemingly random spots. Or maybe they know something that the first crab boat or two don't. It takes a while to spot my red and white crab buoy as I approach, but when I find it and haul the trap aboard. It holds two crabs, one too small and one well over seven inches, easily legal.

There's a mystery I'm pondering: All the crabs I've caught so far have been males. Now why would that be? Is it because females are so much smaller? The escape rings let crabs smaller than about 6 ¼ inches escape. Maybe that's why it's all males.

I've had a little trouble with water running down my kayak paddle, ending up in my boat, sometimes on my head or even up my sleeves. There are rubber drip rings on the paddle to prevent that from happening. I've had them pretty close to my hand, figuring that would work the best. To change things up I slide them down almost to the blade. As I head back working against the wind, I find that moving the rings makes a noticeable difference.

As I clean the crab back at base camp it starts to rain. It looks like it might rain for a while. I put the crab in the bucket then retreat to the tent.

It's a good time for reading. I pick up the *Madness of Crowds* book. One topic is alchemy. Alchemists struggled for centuries to make gold out of base metals. It is remarkable how some charlatans would live lavish lifestyles, having duped kings and emperors. They would often string them along with tricks "proving" that they had figured out the process, perhaps by concealing a small amount of gold dust in a hollow stirring rod thus "creating gold out of nothing." People are often easily convinced to believe what they want to believe. Richard P. Feynman said,

"The first principle is that you must not fool yourself and you are the easiest person to fool."

Although it's still raining, I'm hungry and want to get the crab cooked while it's still fresh. I don rain gear, pull on my tattered, duct taped rubber boots, grab the bucket and head for cook camp. It's nice to have the tarp up. I start the fire and walk down to fill the frying pan with salt water. When it's boiling, I pull it off the fire and put the crab halves in, arranging them to lie as flat as possible, letting excess water run over the top and pouring out a bit more. I cover the pan with foil. When thick steam starts billowing out from under the foil I hit the timer button of my stopwatch. In eleven minutes I pull the pan off the fire, pour off the water and set the pan on the moss to cool.

A minute later I break off one leg and juggle it, steaming, from hand before biting the upper leg to crack the shell and extracting the meat.

"Mmm. That is sooooo good!" I say out loud. It's especially nice to be sitting here eating this hot food in a dry spot, rain streaming off the tarp, immersed in the scent of wet forest and the sea. The big crab is the perfect amount of food. It is a fine, simple meal.

With the rain still pouring down I return to the tent where I change into nice dry clothes, including a warm fleece jacket and balaclava.

My radio receives AM, FM, shortwave, and weather band. I am really, really fortunate that out of all those options the weather band is the one that works out here. I try, again, scanning for stations on AM and FM. Nothing. On nice clear days I can sometimes pick up snippets of music or a few words before I lose the signal, but it's not enough to merit listening too. I know some people might think it's blasphemy to want to listen to the radio out in the wilderness, but I think being out long enough on your own tends to change people's minds. I think it's fair to say that most trappers in remote cabins in Alaska listen to the radio if they have reception. That is how Trapline Chatter came about. Trapline Chatter is a radio program on KJNP out of North Pole, Alaska. (Back home, I have a North Pole telephone number but a Fairbanks address.) People can call in messages to the radio station and have them broadcast out to "the bush" where they can be heard by listeners. People in remote cabins might learn of a resupply flight coming in, a birth or family emergency, or even be wished a happy birthday!

I can't blame my radio for the lack of reception out here. It's primarily the fault of my being so far up Wild Bay, with tall mountains blocking the radio signals. It's a handy little radio, though. The LED shows the time. It's got an LED flashlight I rarely use. It's got a little solar charging panel on it but apparently it's not quite enough to keep the radio charged on its own. It can be charged with a hand crank if you want to do a whole lot of cranking. The rechargeable batteries can be charged from a wall socket as well, or by USB as I did today. It's even got a siren! It's a cool and useful gadget.

The forecast, according to the radio, is rain through Tuesday. Today is Friday. Ouch! Already I can see the effects of 100 per cent humidity. Book covers are curling. When the weather turns for the better I'm going to want to do laundry, get cleaned up and head to the lodge to update my website. I should gather a whole bunch more wood and store it out of the rain under the tarp, too.

It's nice to have this big tent to hang out in. I'm accustomed to backpacking with tiny tents. With no chance for solar charging the next few days, I switch from the Kindle to a paperback book. When I was packing I dug around my bookshelves to find paperback books that I'd never read. I begin to read *Gone With the Wind.*

My beard has grown enough so I can really feel it, and it's a little itchy at times. Out here shaving would be a big hassle so I'm just going to let it grow until I get back home.

After a few hours I need a break and despite the rain put on my rain gear for a walk along the shore. With long views out at the end of the point I can see three crab boats. It's practically a traffic jam! Those guys need to work, rain or no rain. Guess I'm lucky in that respect, spending most of the day in my tent, reading. But when they are kicking back this evening with a hot shower, a good hot meal, and a beer with their buddies, they probably wouldn't want to trade places with me.

Sea lions are chasing salmon around. I see a salmon get flipped into the air before it is chomped again by the successful hunter. Whales spout in the distance. They are far enough away that they look like humpbacks, but I can't be certain.

I've been eating off and on all day, whenever I'm in the mood. In addition to the fresh crab I have some salmon, salmonberries, peas, and blueberries, a pretty good variety of food!

It's 7:08 PM according to the radio LED. It's gray outside, and still raining. The air is heavy and damp. I am, however, well fed, dry, warm and comfortable. I might just snooze. And I might just sleep straight through the night if I feel like it. With days of rain I expect I'll be doing lots of hunkering like this. I check that my rifle is at hand and put my headlamp in the same place I always put it, where I can find it in a moment even in total darkness.

# CHAPTER 14

## Rain Forest

July 26, Day 27

It rained all night. As far as I know, anyway. It's still raining and according to the radio it's going to keep raining. For a while I hang around the tent, but I need to go out and relieve myself. It doesn't sound fun in the cold rain. Rounding up a tarp, cord and the trowel, I put on my rain gear and leave the 100 per cent humidity of the tent for the 100 per cent humidity and pouring rain outside. Rain squishes in the moss, drips off the trees and sweeps the bay.

I scout around for a good place to hang a latrine tarp. I should have done this when it was sunny. It's not easy finding a big enough opening. Finally I decide to hang the tarp over the roots of a downed tree, tying off the corners to bushes. The tarp looks sloppy, misshapen and wrinkled, but when I step under it I'm out of the rain. I use the trowel to dig a hole. It's nice to not have cold rain running down my butt.

After washing my hands I walk around the end of the peninsula checking the thimbleberry bushes and manage to get a partial jar of ripe berries. I pick a few pea pods, too, while I'm at it, maybe a quarter jar.

Back in the tent I notice an occasional drop of condensation. Up until now condensation hadn't been an issue. Whenever there was enough to form a drop it just ran down the inside of the tent wall and dripped on the ground. It's just too humid now, for too long. I hadn't put up the tent liner when I moved camp. Like the main tent body, the liner is held up with the tent pole. When I move the pole to position the liner there is a general shower of cold droplets. Bummer. I should have anticipated that. I should have wiped down the tent walls or tapped the walls first to make most of the water slide down onto the ground. Committed now, I center the liner then raise it and the tent body back up. I still have to attach the loops all around the perimeter of the liner, which of course matches the tipi shape of the tent with a slight gap between the two. I'm trying to loop the bungees around the tent stakes from the inside. It's not going well. The stakes are driven in deep enough that the bungee keeps popping off. So I put on my rain gear, go outside and pull each of the dozen or so stakes an inch out of the ground. Back inside it's much easier to loop the bungees over the top of the stake but I still have to crawl around on the ground to reach them. When I have that accomplished I go back outside and push each stake back down flush with the ground.

It's tempting to just hang out and read and avoid the rain, but I'm already in my rain gear. I'm going to look for more salmonberries and check the crab trap on the way home.

It's about a mile to my salmonberry spot. When I land it's a portage of several hundred yards to get above high tide. I find a few more berries in the old areas. The bushes are soaked now. When I reach up to grab the higher berries rainwater runs down my arms. There are a few currants which I eat as fast as I pick them. I scout beyond the area where I've picked salmonberries before and find the best patch yet. Most of these are the red variety. They seem sweeter than the yellow ones. Once I find this good patch it's not long before I've topped off the quart, not including the ones I was eating as I picked. At the edge of the trees there is a patch of Devil's club with striking, bright red leaves. Is this its fall colors, or is it caused by something else?

When I pull up the crab trap there is a crab frantically trying to squeeze through one of the round escape rings. I feel sorry for him, trying so hard to live. He was trying so hard he was jammed. When I get him out I'm happy to find he's too small. I drop him in the ocean and watch him kick as swims and sinks out of sight. The other though, is not so lucky, he's a keeper. I drop him in the bucket and paddle for home. On the way, it's still raining hard and the wind is blowing rain in around my hood. I am wearing my balaclava, a foolish mistake. I should have kept it dry for sleeping. I would have been plenty warm with just my hood.

I'm grateful to have the cook camp tarp waiting for me. It's nice to get out of the rain, and even more importantly, to have dry wood stored and ready to go. This time I try cooking the crab a little longer, fourteen minutes of boiling time. It turns out even better. It could use some salt, though. Why isn't this one as salty as the others? Because of all the rain! It's rained many inches. I scooped seawater up off the surface of the sea for cooking, and there was enough fresh water in it to make a noticeable difference.

On the way back to camp I pick some goose tongue and sea asparagus, both of which grow in profusion in this area. They are handy plants to pluck and eat. Sea asparagus is a bit salty, goose tongue less so. One of my guidebooks has some interesting nutrition information. It says that both goose tongue and sea asparagus contain vitamin C, niacin, calcium and iron, while sea asparagus also has vitamin A, thiamine and riboflavin. I don't really think about the specifics like this much, but I do think about trying to eat a variety of foods. It seems like both plants would be good for roughage as well.

I'm soon back at camp in nice dry clothes. In this humidity I'm not even trying to dry anything except maybe a little drying with body heat. If I had a whole bunch of dry firewood in the tent I suppose I'd set up the wood stove to dry stuff, but I don't have dry firewood here. Some wet clothes and gear isn't so bad if I can be dry in camp.

Before I turn in for the night I put on my Micro Puff jacket with its good warm hood. That will keep my head warm in the absence of my balaclava. I will dry it tonight in the pocket of my jacket. It's easier to *keep* things dry than *get* things dry that's for sure. Sleeping clothes should be kept dry.

July 27, Day 28, Sunday

I've slept in relatively late. It's still raining. Not particularly wanting to go outside, I nonetheless swap my nice dry camp clothes for my wet rain gear, then head up to the latrine. While I'm up here I modify the tarp a bit for better coverage.

Checking out cook camp I notice that it's near low tide and quite calm as well. I pull out the tide book from my shirt pocket: low tide is in half an hour. I launch the kayak and paddle in shallow water near cook camp looking for crabs, but I don't see any. A small dark animal is darting through the tall grass. A mink! He follows along, curious. Finally he runs across the shore towards my boat, approaching within ten feet, staring me in the eye with beady black eyes. He loses his nerve and bolts, but then comes down to the water again. He jumps into the water, swims out a few yards then dives headfirst into the water, kicking furiously. It's comical. He seems so buoyant compared to a seal. His dive is marked by tiny bubbles rising to the surface. Suddenly he bobs to the surface, looks around and sploosh! He's gone again. Very amusing. He actually seemed gleeful in the water.

I next paddle past my crab trap to the mouth of My Creek which has become a small river, an amazing transformation. Looking down into the shallows I see some flat fish zipping away in a swirl of sand. Are they small halibut, or flounder maybe? There's a crab. I reach behind me for the landing net and scoop him up. While he's still tangled in the net I measure him. A keeper! My faith in dipnetting crabs is somewhat restored. Still, I have definitely been humbled since my first effort where I easily caught eight keepers at low tide.

I manage to net a another crab, this one with a tiny claw growing back after having lost it in accident, no doubt. He's too small though. So is the next one. I fail to net the following crab. When I check my trap I find another legal crab. I add crab shells I brought with to the bait cage, then drop the trap back into the depths.

I land near the grassy narrows of the peninsula which is near to both cook camp and main camp. I swing my kayak off my shoulder and it lands with a bounce. I hear a distant, muffled rifle shot. When I hear it again I recognize what it is, a whale! I run up over the top of the peninsula. A humpback whale is only 100 yards from camp! That is really cool! I watch for him to spout again, but he's gone.

Fresh crab for lunch. I stop by cook camp to get the pressure canner cover. I've been storing it in camp. A bear could easily break it's fragile pressure gauge so I store it inside the electric fence. I'm using part of the airline magazine for tinder. It will barely light. Is it the humidity or is it possible inflight magazines have fire retardant properties? The wimpy flames of the paper finally light the twigs though, and the fire is soon blazing.

It is really nice to have the hot, fresh crab to alternate with fish. As I eat, I notice the sounds of roaring water. Countless mountainside brooks have turned into raging torrents. Judging by containers I've left outside, it must have rained five inches since the rain started. Maybe more! There have been some lulls in the rain today, but these last three days have been by far the rainiest stretch of the trip. It has a big impact on the experience.

With the remaining cooked crab and the canner cover I head back to base camp. I rolled up my shirt sleeves before putting on my raincoat this morning. I should have thought of that before. When I roll down the sleeves they are nice and dry. I live in this shirt.

Getting into dry clothes is a luxury I enjoy and appreciate every time. And now my balaclava is dry, too. Warm and cozy, I soon fall asleep.

Man, I slept for three hours. That's a good nap! Something about getting out of the rain does that, when you're slightly chilled and wet around the edges, it makes you sleepy. I eat some blueberries and salmonberries while I read. A quart of berries a day, that's the goal. My diet sure has changed from what it was back home. Fish, berries, crab, and some coastal greens. I pinch the fat on my belly. Not much left. It would be interesting to step on the scale. I must have lost at least ten pounds.

# CHAPTER 15

---

# Humpbacks at Camp!

July 28, Day 29

It's raining again. I think my first three weeks here were drier than normal, but that's changed. I'm in no hurry to get out into the rain. There's no need. I read *Gone With the Wind.* There's an inscription on the title page in a beautiful, feminine hand:

"Hanukkah 1967

Dear Sharon,

I hope you love the book as much as the movie.

Love Always,

Michelle."

That was 47 years ago. Where are they today? What would they think if they knew that their book was being read here on this trip in 2014? Who were the people that have read this book since then, and what were the paths that delivered this book to my possession? I can't even recall when and where I got it.

My down bag is a little fluffier this morning. There was no noticeable loss of warmth before, but it was looking a little saggy. The greater loft is likely because of several factors: I wasn't drying out my damp socks or balaclava inside my bag last night, and I prevented my sleeves from getting wet yesterday. Body heat can do a remarkable amount of drying. I have no doubt this bag will keep me warm the whole trip.

I'd anticipated spending considerable time in camp, waiting out rain. The preparation is paying off now, 10:22 AM by my watch. I'm sitting in my camp chair, legs in my sleeping bag and my feet propped up on the cot. Comfy! As I read I munch on salmonberries, eating the last of them.

For lunch I finish off a jar of salmon. I'm getting antsy. I need to go out and do something, an expedition. I put on my waders and wet rain gear and step out into the soggy forest.

The wind is light. I'm going to try for some rockfish. I put some fishing gear in my pack, grab my spinning rod, and paddle upwind several hundred yards before dropping the double-tailed white jig overboard, letting it sink until I can feel it bump the bottom. This has been a great trip, but I've really struck out on the saltwater fishing. Maybe today is my day. The wind is slowly pushing me along. Only occasionally do I need to paddle a few strokes to bring the kayak closer or farther from shore. It's a fairly steep drop-off here, and rocky. Seems like there should be some fish here. I get a snag, but manage to pull it loose. When there's a bump I set the hook and immediately feel a fish struggling.

"Hey, I got a fish!" I say out loud. This is exciting. What's it going to be? Man, I want to land him. I want to have caught a rockfish and I want to eat one for supper. When he breaks the surface my enthusiasm wanes. It's a sculpin. At least I think that's what they're called. Maybe two pounds. It's brown and has a huge head with spikes along its dorsal fin and with pectoral fins (the ones that correspond to "arms") sticking straight out and also bristling with spines. I don't even know if they're edible. The spines look dangerous so I carefully grab it behind the pectoral fins, back the hook out and drop it into the water. Oh well, maybe the fish are biting and I'll catch an actual rockfish. Alas, I jig all the way back to camp with no further excitement.

Back at camp I pick a quart of beach peas and then nearly a quart of thimbleberries. The thimbleberries are really ripening fast now. It's so nice having these, my favorite berries of all, growing right next to camp.

Was that a whale I just heard? I launch the kayak to see if I can spot it. Where is it? I round the point into My Cove. Suddenly the broad gray back of a humpback whale arches out of the water, maybe a hundred yards away. It takes a quiet gasp of air and then sinks headfirst back out of sight. Wow! We're a stone's throw from cook camp! I'm surprised it's even deep enough for a whale to want to swim here.

Now where did it go? The water bulges and there is an exhalation of breath. It surfaces only fifty feet away! Then a much bigger whale appears, it's mama, covered with barnacles. Her twin blow-holes barely clear the surface and she exhales then inhales, w*hoosh-whoosh*, and sinks. The giant calf is swimming along with its back and stubby dorsal fin out of water. It angles towards me and then circles, closer. It's passing only twenty feet away! Holy smokes! This huge animal is hardly disturbing the water as it gently swims past. I can *feel* that it's looking at me from underwater. *Whoosh*-whoosh. Finally it just rests, floating there. It's curious. It's checking me out! I drift, barely breathing. Suddenly a giant bumpy head of the adult punches out of the water just beyond the calf, then lands with a crash. *Wow!* She leads the calf away, her enormous tail fluke barely clearing the surface before powerfully propelling her into the depths.

Next time they surface they are about 200 yards away. Just when I think the excitement is over, mama punches out of the water, her giant mouth agape, with long, striking grooves in the skin beneath her chin. She lands with a crash. She is feeding. Spectacular! Each subsequent surfacing they are farther away until they are gone for good. That was incredible!

Back at camp, I shell and eat cold crab for supper. I'm still buzzing with excitement. Those whales! That was so cool. I will never forget it. Never.

July 29, Day 30

I had that dream again last night, the recurring dream. A happy dream. I am in my padded smokejumper suit, parachute on my back, in a plane flying over some remote mountain range in Alaska, watching the wilderness roll by below us. We are laughing and joking, the Bros and I, excited to be jumping a fire in this splendid country. I am back for one more year of smokejumping. It feels just as natural as can be. This is who I am.

"It's great to be back," I tell them, "I thought my smokejumper days were gone forever." The other smokejumpers reflect my big smile. We know we are living the dream.

It's raining again today. I've been listening to the weather radio often the last few days, waiting to see when the weather will break. It's entertaining. The short-term forecast, within three days or so, often changes a little. It might go from cloudy to mostly cloudy, or rain to showers. But several days out? That's where it's interesting. It can change a lot. I've taken to jotting down the forecast for the next week. It's fun to have it handy for planning purposes, and just to see how the forecast evolves.

Tomorrow they are calling for a mostly cloudy day with scattered showers, followed by some partly cloudy days. It looks like there are at least two days next week where it won't rain. Yessir!

It's foggy this morning. Good thing the tent liner is up because the condensation would be extreme. When I walk down to check out the fog lying over the water a mink is scampering along, hunting. I squeak at him and he freezes, looking for the mouse he's about to catch. I squeak again and he bounds towards me, approaching to within about fifteen feet. He can't figure out what I am, but he's pretty sure I'm not a mouse! He dashes into the high grass.

Deer season starts in three days! That's really exciting. It will be a new chapter in the adventure. I want to check out the high knob at the head of the bay, the one with long views of the tidal flats and the grass along the edge of the timber. It is easy to imagine seeing deer there. In fact, I've already seen deer there while fishing nearby My Creek. Just as I paddle around the Point, another mink darts among the rocks searching for food. When he spots me he leaps into the water and swims straight towards me! He cruises nearly up to the kayak, boldly looking me in the eye, then paddles for shore where he runs among the rocks and kelp left by the low tide. I suspect he is the resident mink, or at least one of the resident mink, and familiarity with seeing me has made him more curious than cautious.

I want to try some more halibut fishing on the way to My Creek. I notice a distinct line in the tide currents. If this were a river, this should be a good fishing spot, this seam with faster current on one side, still water on the other, and floating debris spinning in between. I drop my heavy, white halibut jig overboard and begin jigging it. Suddenly it stops dead. I set the hook. There is a heavy weight on the end, but it's not moving. I pull a little harder, then wait. Nope. Nothing. Snag. I let out a little line and pull from "upstream." Doesn't work. I let out way more line and go farther upstream. No. I tug it and bounce it and pull from all directions but it will not budge. Finally I get some slack and wrap a loop of line several times around my paddle and pull. It will either pull loose or break. It breaks. Oh well. I'm headed to "the Knob."

The ocean is blanketed with fog. I navigate by glimpses of recognized islands. But now the fog is starting to recede. The head of Wild Bay appears as the fog begins to climb the mountains until only a layer of fog is left above the treetops. I paddle towards a reflected world: above is the overcast sky, just below is the mountains, the clouds and the big timber. Below the water line is the same scene in reverse, the watery world identifiable only by the slight ripples.

Finding a place to climb the Knob is challenging. It's mostly steep rock, partially shrouded by brush. Finally I find an angled cleft. I scramble up, grabbing berry bushes and tree branches for with the assistance. On top is a flat, mossy opening. There is a 90 degree opening in the trees, to the left, with long views across the tidal flats and along the grassy forest edges where I expect to see deer. It's a great view. Suspiciously good. On the trunk of a big tree I see where someone has cut branches long ago to open up a larger "window." Most likely bear hunters decades ago. There are smaller openings on the right towards My Creek, perhaps 150 yards away, and another view straight ahead, to the closest forest edge, only fifty yards away. I'll have to pick my shots up here. I could see a deer a mile away!

One other thing I see, a pile of bear scat. Now how did a big bear get up here? That must have taken some scrambling. And WHY did he take the trouble? Maybe just to check it out. He is a hunter, like me.

When I clamber down I notice a nice thicket of red, ripe thimbleberries. Each one falls off into my hand with the slightest tug. There are also some currants, and a red berry that I haven't identified yet. I taste one, it's OK, but I spit it out just in case. It looks kind of like a red blueberry.

Not far from the Knob a foot-square piece of plywood lies at the edge of high tide. This will make a good, flat stove stand. I pick it up and carry it back to the kayak.

When I get back to my kayak I check my watch. 9:19. It's just before low tide. I wanted to be here now to look for crabs. It's started to rain pretty hard. Nevertheless I manage to spot a crab, half-buried in the mud. When I scoop it up I'm surprised to see it's a female, the first I've caught this whole trip. Although I haven't gotten a female before, I easily identify her by the rounded pattern of the plates on her belly. I wade around in thigh deep water, trying to peer through the rain-dappled water at the bottom. Finally I give up.

On the way home I stop to check the crab trap. When I swing it onto the kayak in front of me something isn't right. One whole side of the trap is open. The cotton cord holding it shut is broken. The trap is bent as well. Sea lions! Or seals. So maybe they weren't just being curious when they'd watch me set the trap. They stole my crabs!

The cotton cord used to hold the side of the trap shut is a great idea. Cotton rots, so if a trap is lost or abandoned or gets snagged on something on the ocean bottom the cord will rot after a few weeks and the door will open. It's easy to see how bad it would be without that precaution. Crabs would be trapped, and then other crabs would enter to eat their remains, and so on.

Other than the theft of the crabs, not much harm was done. I easily unbend the trap. The hardest part is piecing together shreds of cotton cord to hold the trap shut in a legal manner.

Back at camp I visit my cook camp tarp and modify the pitch to catch rainwater, then set a bucket beneath it. Immediately a steady trickle pours in. Catching rainwater is way easier than carrying it from the spring, or treating or filtering water for drinking.

After gearing up I paddle towards the Sound to try rockfishing again. I go farther than I've fished on the bay before, past several rocky points. There are some good-looking spots. The water drops off steeply with big rocks sticking out of the water and disappearing out of sight below the surface. A doe and two fawns are feeding in the green grass along the edge of the forest, still brown in their summer coats. They are the first deer I've seen for days.

I've got my lighter rod now, and a smaller, double-tailed white jig. I actually feel a bite or two, a least I think I do.

I'm keeping my eyes peeled for more deer or good berry picking or other food sources. There is a thick patch of thimbleberry bushes and I land to see if there are any ripe berries. There are. It's a slightly different variety of thimbleberry, with smaller leaves and ripe berries that cling a little tighter to the bush. There are a lot of them though, and I eat steadily in the falling rain.

Twenty minutes later I'm back on the water. Hey, I've got a bite. *I've got a fish!* Excited to see what I've got I reel him in. A sculpin. Drat. It was exciting though. That was fun.

With the rain still falling I head back to camp, then head over to cook camp to see how much water has collected. The bucket is already full! That's an easy way to get water. I replace it with another bucket. It's already filling as I walk away.

I'll try to get to the lodge in a few days to let people know I'm OK. I want to look up the beach peas to make sure of their ID. I've certainly been eating some of them but I don't dare go "whole hog" until I get the ID completely nailed down. I can easily gather lots more than I've been eating. I get out my iPhone and take several photos of the plants, and also a similar plant with no peas. Or is it a subspecies of the same plant, like the two varieties of thimbleberries?

Back in the tent I swap to dry clothes. I was wearing my fleece hooded sweatshirt/jacket. It is wet around the hood and cuffs. No biggie, though. I have dry camp clothes. I wring out water from the cuffs and around the hood. It will be fine to wear outside. I'll dry it when there is some sun again. I think that's what they call that warm, yellow object that appeared in the sky in a bygone era!

# CHAPTER 16

## Glorious Sunshine

July 30 Day 31

I've been out here for a month today. A month! That's a long time to be out here alone. To live completely off the land. It's satisfying to mark this milestone.

Apparently the weather didn't hear the forecast for today because it's still raining.

On the way to my crab trap I'm jigging the smaller twin-tailed jig. I hook a fish but quickly lose it. There is another identical bite and struggle but this one stays on. When it nears the surface I see another sculpin, the biggest one yet. If I knew for sure they were edible I'd probably cook him up. I soon land another, then another. I gotta admit, it's kind of fun. And each time I think maybe this time it might be a different species, a halibut or rockfish or *something* I want to keep.

The crab trap is empty. With My Creek running ten times it's normal flow, maybe the water here is too fresh? I paddle the trap over to what has been the best spot before. The water here should be less affected by the creek, and therefore saltier.

I land on the biggest island to look for berries. I'm happy to see plentiful thimbleberries, red gems among the green leaves. I follow a nearly continuous patch of bushes, grazing on the sweet berries as I go. I cross the gravelly "causeway," that runs over to the mainland, now exposed by the low tide, and explore a new area along the forest. Here there is hardly a berry, only a single, wary spotted fawn. He stands up in the tall grass then bounds away into the timber. Walking back along the causeway I notice many crunched-up clam shells. What animals have been eating them? Bears? Otters? I don't know.

Not long after my return to base camp the sun comes out. Glorious sunshine pours over the beach. Rocks and logs steam, drying in the sun. As I sort through gear that I want to launder today I find my good ball cap. It is covered with patches of green mold. Bummer. I gather up my dirty clothes and a bottle of shampoo and head for cook camp. I heat up a canner full of water then pour half in a bucket and carry it down to the beach. Much of the beach is in the shadows of the big timber, but I find a warm, bright patch of sunlight and set the bucket down. Stripping down I dunk my head, then shampoo my head and scrub my face and neck with the suds and warm water. Then I stand in the bucket. For a few glorious moments I simply enjoy the pleasure of the hot water and the warm sunshine on my body and face.

After scrubbing off the rest of my body I rinse off in the bucket. With a little shampoo on the dirty spots on my pants, I scrub the spots together briskly for a while before tossing the pants in the bucket. I do the same with my shirt, underwear, cap and socks. Once in there I squish the warm, sudsy water through the clothes over and over with my hands, until I'm tired of bending over, and then by stomping on them with my feet. I then wring them out and dump out the dirty water. With clean, hot water in the bucket I rinse myself down, then squish clean water through my clothing. I call it good and carry everything back to camp to hang in the sun.

After all those days of rain and with all that humidity, I want to get everything dried out and baking in the sun. Soon, most of the contents of the tent are outside, turned to face the sun, and placed to maximize air circulation: cot, sleeping bag, waders, packs, books, spare clothing, guns. My books are laid out on the cot to dry. Boulders, branches and chair are draped with drying gear.

I lean the big, foldable solar charger up against a leaning boulder, at a good angle to maximize sun exposure. I hold it it place by putting a stone on the top flap. Nearby I lean the other smaller foldable charger and my sCharger. Yup, I have *three* chargers. Why? Because sometimes the sun doesn't come out for days, and I might have to do a lot of charging in short period of time. Make hay while the sun shines. Plus, electronics often fail so I want a spare charger.

There's muffled boom. What was that? *Whoosh!* Whales! I see them spout a few hundred yards out, their giant tail flukes flipping up in the air is the dive. Humpbacks! A while later I hear them again and look up to see their plumes of steamy breath drifting in the breeze.

Today is the 30th, deer season starts August 1. Two days! Time to check the zero of my rifle. I gather my rifle, ammo, ear plugs, chair, another old five-gallon bucket I found in the grass at high tide (cracked and unusable) and my GPS and walk to a straight stretch of beach. I set down the chair and use the GPS to measure off 100 yards, and there set the bucket down. It is white with a piece of black duct tape on it for a bullseye. Bullets will hit the beach behind it and any ricochet will go into the timber.

Back at the chair I put in my earplugs and sit down on the gravelly beach, finding a good solid lean on the chair in front of me. Not exactly a shooting bench, but pretty darn solid. I squeeze the trigger and... nothing. I see the reason why, my Ruger's safety is in the middle position, not on "Fire." Doh! My bad. I am happy I didn't flinch when I pulled the trigger and it didn't fire, though.

Flipping the lever to "Fire," I get settled again. When the rifle fires, the crosshairs are on the tape. I walk down and take a quick look. Pretty good, a little high. I want it two or three inches high at 100 yards. I fire a second shot. Looks good, but a bit to the right. I use the GPS to measure off 200 yards. Man, good thing I have the GPS. I was way off on guessing the distance. When I squeeze off the next shot I know I had a good sight picture. The bullet hole is about 3" to the right. I adjust the scope a few clicks and the next shot looks great. Darn near a bullseye. This is a good rifle. It will shoot as straight as I do when I see my buck.

Back at camp, I tend to the drying and charging operation. It's all solar powered! I fluff things up, flip them over, turn them around, and re-aim them at the sun. As I work around camp I am grazing: a few thimbleberries, some goose tongue, a few sprigs of sea asparagus. I also finished a jar of salmon and started a jar of crab meat today.

*Whoosh! Whoosh!* A pod of humpbacks arch above the water and then back out of sight, just out from camp. I grab my iPhone and run to the end of The Point, hoping for an even closer look. *Whoosh! Whoosh!* They surface out from The Point, heading for the middle of the bay. That was so cool! I'm liking whales at camp!

July 31, Day 32

It looks like a beautiful day. I woke up about 3 AM. I don't think I really fell back asleep again. I think I just dozed. It's early but I'm half awake anyway. It will be good to get an early start for the camp move day.

There's hardly a cloud in the sky. The morning sun glitters on the snow-capped mountains across Wild Bay while my camp still lies in the shadows.

I'm going to take advantage of this good weather to combine this camp move with drying everything thoroughly again. I'm packing my camp down the beach again on this move. On the way, I hang up and lay out most of my clothing and gear. By mid-morning it's all soaking up the sun, even the solar chargers.

I take down the tent and carry it down the beach. A mink lopes by me. It's the third one to pass me today! When he passes, only about ten feet away, he glances up at me with an expression displaying no more fear or interest than a pet dog. We make eye contact and he doesn't even break stride.

"Hey, show some respect!" I say to him. He glances over his shoulder and keeps on going. He has places to go and things to eat.

At the new camp site I set up the tent again, lifting up the center with the pole and staking out all the loops. This leaves the liner still dangling from the pole. Since I'll be using the liner every time, I ponder ways to make setting up the tent and liner easier. The liner has bungees at each stake-out point that naturally correspond to the tent stake-out loops. Each bungee has a Cord Lock. From inside the tent, I take one end of the bungee out of the Cord Lock and run it through the corresponding tent stake-out loop. Then I run it back through the Cord Lock. Crawling around the periphery of the tent I do the same at each stake. When I'm done, I go outside and put each bungee over a stake.

The tent pitch turns out great and there's a nice breeze coming through the trees. I zip the screen door shut, then open both halves of the Silnylon tent door wide open so everything can air out. One thing I've learned is to keep the screen doors zipped shut. Even if there are no visible bugs flying around there often are quite a few that a person doesn't notice. Several times I've left the door open for a while and returned to find varied and numerous flying insects gathered near the tent's peak. I usually handle that by opening the stove pipe hole and unzipping the top of the screen door, shooing the bugs until they've flown out. As usual, an ounce of prevention is worth a pound of cure.

Out in the direct sunlight, I see my old shotgun is speckled with rust again. I've got to admit, I'm surprised it's been this difficult to fight rust. I haven't gotten any salt water on it and I wiped it down with oil again on the last cleaning. Obviously it's really tough to prevent rust with the salt air and the humidity. Once again I sit down to clean both guns.

I hear a whale blow and see the spout drifting away far out in the bay. I've seen several whales today, all of them in the distance.

I partially disassemble both guns, being careful to put each part in the gun case so I don't lose anything. My rifle has a custom trigger, which I love, but one disadvantage is that the trigger is held on by a tiny pin, which I have to remove to take the gun apart. It's a piece that would be very easy to lose. I use a safety pin to push out the trigger pin. I clean the bore with Hoppe's and then scrub surface rust. I wish I had brought a bronze scrubbing brush. I use the bore brush instead. I've got to be careful, though. The stiff bristles sometimes poke me in the hands. Next I wipe off dirt and rust with an oily rag, which results in a surprising amount of rust on the rag. Lastly I do a final wipe-down with a clean oily rag. I sure am glad my rifle is almost all stainless and plastic. It sure would save me a lot of work if my shotgun was stainless or had some synthetic surface. I took a look at shotguns like that before I left on this trip, but I couldn't run out and buy all new gear. It's a chore, but finally the guns are cleaned to my satisfaction, both with a nice sheen of oil.

The bear fence move is even easier this time. Winding up and unwinding the wire is the most time-consuming aspect. I changed the batteries a few days ago. They lasted almost a month, not bad!

I walk around and check out my solar charging operation. iPhone, 100 per cent. AA rechargeables, fully charged. Kindle, stuck at 59 per cent. Hmm. I swap cables. I don't think it's the cables, it's the Kindle, but it couldn't hurt. I also restart the Kindle. When I check awhile later it's up to 61 per cent. Excellent. For some reason it simply doesn't want to charge at times.

I empty another salmon jar at lunch. There are several more fish and crab jars to wash as well. I carry them to the bay and scrub them with spruce bough tips and ponder my plan for tomorrow, the opening day of deer season. Yahoo! I'd assumed I would devote opening day to deer hunting, but after checking the forecast it makes sense to make my biweekly lodge trip tomorrow. I'll hunt all the way there and back. I'll get a good early start. Maybe I'll see a buck along the shore. This will be a new kind of deer hunting for me. I read through the applicable sections of the regulations again. It looks like the "bucks only" season runs all the way until September 10 in this area. Across the bay, near the mouth of Falls Creek, I see a large brown object. It's moving. A brown bear. I haven't seen many from camp. I'd see more if I glassed more often. I get my binoculars and watch him forage below high tide.

With more thimbleberries ripening every day, I check all the nearby berry patches and make a good haul of ripe red berries. Warmed by the sun they seem even sweeter.

I walk around gathering everything that was out drying. It takes several trips. I stuff clothing and sleeping bag into a pack, making sure that I haven't missed anything that might have fallen down. And now,

when I gather the solar panels, even the Kindle is nearly fully charged. After everything is toted back to camp, I take a walk back to the old site to check for overlooked gear, and make a final walk around the beach as well. I don't want the tide to carry anything away.

Soon I have everything nicely organized in the tent. It has been a good day. I feel like I've really gotten things done. The camp move was a biggie. Gun cleaning is a chore I'm not too crazy about. I had nice conditions for it, sitting on a chair in the warm sun. It's good to have that done. After all those rainy days and all that humidity, my belongings are fully dry again.

As I drift off to sleep I try to imagine where I might see a buck tomorrow, and how I will get him if I do. What will my strategy be if I get him before I get to the lodge? Dress him out and pick him up on the way back? Bone him out and bring the meat to the lodge and then on home? I'll play it by ear. Grilled venison. I can't wait!

# Chapter 17

# August: Deer Season!

August 1, Day 33

August! I came out here the last day of June. That's getting to be a while. It's pretty cool to "flip another page of the calendar."

Today was long awaited, it's the first day of deer season. I've purposely let my cache of canned salmon and crabs dwindle to save up enough empty jars to can most of a blacktail deer. It is "bucks only" here until September 10. One concern I have is that I haven't seen a single antlered buck since I got here! And I've spent a whole lot of time outside and looking for deer. There are things I can do to increase my chances of seeing a buck, like spending more time in the best deer habitat and glassing more. Hopefully actively hunting deer rather than passively looking for them will make the difference.

I'm mostly packed already, but I run down my gear list, written on a blank piece of cardboard. I am a believer in lists. It's especially important on a day like today, when I'm doing something different. Three items specific to today are deer tags, rifle, and ammunition.

I launch my kayak before 5:30, paddling across the smooth waters of Wild Bay, keeping a close eye on the grassy edges of the forest, still in the morning shadows. These are the places where deer often feed. A mink scampers along the water, stopping to check something out, then loping on. An eagle perches on a towering spruce, guarding a nearby nest.

Off the end of a rocky point the calm water ripples. When I draw closer I see a head pop up, then disappear, then another. A river otter swims to shore and clambers up on the rocks to eat a fish, I hear the crunching as it enjoys its catch. Another otter swims to shore with a fish in its mouth. The water is dappled by small fish who are themselves feeding. The hunters become the hunted.

The largest otter on shore looks up and sees me gliding along, too close for comfort. It gives an alarm call and several heads pop up. After spotting me they all scramble for shore and bound through the rocks and into the forest.

There is an island ahead. I pull ashore at a nice landing spot to check it out. It's an easy climb, twenty feet up to a flat mossy bench under huge hemlocks. It's an absolutely beautiful campsite with a great view over the bay. This would also be a strategic place to move next time. It's much closer to Salmon Creek, my best food source. Bear proof, too, being an island. Above me I hear the chatter call of a circling bald eagle. A short distance away, on the mainland, I see an adult bald eagle watching me from a high perch. I catch brief glimpses of the chattering eagle circling overhead, round and round. There's a nest here. I can't camp here. Bummer.

Back in the kayak, I'm watching something mysterious up ahead. There is movement on the water, something big, or a bunch of... something. Is it resting whales maybe? As I draw closer it sort of looks like seals, some of them half out of the water. What? OK, it IS seals. They are on a rocky island being flooded by rising tide. The commotion, I think, is probably seals jockeying for position on the remaining "high ground," their guttural calls, sounding like a crowd of grumbling old men, rises rapidly in volume. As I pass, one seal jumps in the water, which triggers a mad rush for the others, a tremendous plunging and splashing. Once in the water they scatter in all directions. Soon there are dozens of seal heads popping up all around, looking at me curiously.

Still cruising at a steady paddle, about a dozen seals follow me, behind and to the side, each leaving a tiny "V" of ripples. One by one they fall away, diving away into the deep.

Here is another island, this one with trees on it. To the west, the morning sunlight is hitting the timbered shore of the bay and the mountains rising above, still partially blanketed with last winter's snow. All is reflected beautifully on the glassy water, colors rich in the morning light. I stop to get a good self-timer photo of my kayak and me and the beautiful scenery. I hang the boat up on rocks barely sticking out of the water, then set up the mini tripod and camera on a wet rock and hustle back to the boat taking care not to take that extra step into ten feet of cold seawater. I turn to face the camera with a genuine smile. I'm happy to be here. Before leaving the boat again I double check it's hung up solid. This is another situation where it would be a real bummer if my boat got away. I then retrieve the camera and tripod and return them to their dry box.

Looking towards the near shore, the low morning sun is blinding, so I paddle until the sun is blocked by tall timber. That's much, much better. I'm in an arm of the bay that I can explore later for deer, no time right now. I pass a rocky point at the mouth of the bay...

Deer! Right there, disappearing around the corner towards the arm of the bay. It didn't see me. Don't know if it was a buck. I paddle towards shore and quietly land and secure the boat. I grab my rifle, chamber a round and sneak through the edge of the trees until I can see around the corner. I thought I'd see it here, but it must have walked into the trees. I have a great view about three hundred yards up the arm, though, and I'm in the shade. It's a perfect place to glass. I walk quietly through the shaded trees until I get to a point where the view is even better, then sneak out to a patch of shady bushes and begin glassing.

Immediately I spot a deer feeding in the shady grass along the opposite side of the cove, maybe two hundred yards away. It's a doe. I slowly scan the shoreline. There are ears! A small deer, probably her fawn, is bedded nearby. Another doe is barely visible, feeding near a wooded point farther away. This is great! Looking along my side of the

arm I don't see any deer, so I swing the binos back to the deer I've already spotted and glass back towards the mouth of the arm. There's another doe! And two fawns! Man, there's got to be a buck here somewhere. There's another deer. No antlers on that one, either. I know most bucks are supposed to be up high, but there's always a few bucks down low. So I've been told. Usually they are smaller bucks, but I'm not going to be picky. I want the meat. What if I see a buck across the arm? Could I hit it? Probably. As long as I sneaked until I was straight across from it and got a good lean and really squeezed the trigger. Now I spot yet another deer, closer than the others, and it's a... doe. For sure. I glass for ten more minutes but keep seeing the same deer. Time to move on. Man, that was awesome. I've seen nine deer already today and it's not even 8 AM!

The ocean is so smooth right now, it's easy paddling, and fun, watching for deer and not having to fight the wind. Except for some ripples from swimming seals and sea ducks the water is glassy. I take a couple of photos of the reflected mountains with the front of my kayak in the foreground. The sky is blue with wisps of clouds. With the sky and mountains properly exposed, the kayak is dark, and my wading boots appear nearly black. Between my feet the stainless barrel of the rifle reflects the sky. This is fun.

A few minutes later my heart jumps and adrenaline pours into my bloodstream. A buck! A *big* buck! He's only about 75 yards away, feeding along the shore. Judging from his body language, he spotted me at the same instant I spotted him. I don't move. My kayak is still gliding slowly and quietly, water dripping off my paddle. He turns and slowly disappears behind a rocky point. He's not spooked, I can tell. If I can land quietly I bet he'll be within sight.

I paddle quietly to shore and gently ground the bow of my kayak a foot out of the water. Picking up my rifle I walk quietly over the wet rocks, my heart pounding, my gaze sweeping back and forth over each foot of ground appearing over the point as I climb. There! I can see the top of a bush wiggling. A deer is feeding on it, just out of sight, only about forty yards away. This is it! Creeping forward I see... a fawn. Where's the buck? In the thick brush a few yards away a fawn scrambles away into the timber, the other fawn joining it. No other deer are in sight. What happened to my buck? I watch intently, then sneak into the big timber where I can see about fifty yards. A bush makes a zipping sound when it rubs on my life jacket. There's another zipping sound when a branch slips along my waders. I cringe each time. I'm not dressed for sneaking through brush, that's for sure. I don't see the buck. I don't hear him run. He must have been heading into the timber when he first turned. Oh well! I climb to the top of the open ridge but there's no sign of him.

Here is an island I haven't explored yet. An old map showed a cabin on the opposite side. I'd like to check it out if it isn't long gone. I land on a gravelly beach. Bringing my daypack with emergency supplies I go exploring. There are beautiful giant trees. I keep having to navigate around Devil's club and fallen logs. When I finally reach the general area where I expect to find a cabin, or its remains, there is no sign of it, just a profusion of Devil's club. I'm wearing my waders. I don't want to risk them. I head back to the kayak.

It's already been an adventurous day by the time I get to the Lodge. After a quick chat with the owners I head over to the main Lodge. Bubbly Anna greets me again. It's a treat to talk to people, especially one's so good-natured. The rest of the crew files in for their lunch break. The young fellows working here are good guys on a grand adventure, in remote Alaska for their summer jobs. They work at the dock, fuel boats, clean fish, and carry out numerous other duties. Like all young guys, they give each other a hard time.

I've written up my online journal entry already, saving lots of time. I also have to check my email for critical news, and try to verify that I've found beach peas.

Jody, one of the owners, has come in and is working around in the kitchen. She heads my way with a plate with two huge burritos and a fork, holding it out for me to take. She knows I'm out here for a couple of months, but she doesn't know I'm "living off the land."

"Wow. Thanks Jody. I really appreciate it. But I'm good. I've got my own food. I really, really appreciate the offer though."

"OK. Let me know if you change your mind."

There's an email from my brother. He's found the new duck hunting regs online. Duck season doesn't open in this area until September 15. Ouch! Bad news. I'd looked forward to hunting and eating ducks and geese.

I am trying to limit my internet usage to one hour as I'd originally agreed. I've burned up lots of time already and still need to research beach peas. Each page loads in slow motion as I try to make small talk with the crew. My armpits are sweating, the kind of stress sweat I don't have to deal with when I'm out there on my own.

I'm looking up descriptions of beach peas and find this quote.

*Similar Species*

*Giant vetch can be confused for beach pea, as it is a purple flowering plant that may be found on beaches as well. However, the flowers of giant vetch are narrower, and the leaves (leaflets) are generally longer and there are more on each stem (18-26 versus 6-12 on beach pea stems).*

*Uh oh.* My guidebooks made no mention of giant vetch. It looks mighty suspicious that I've found giant vetch peas, not beach peas. When I do an image search for "giant vetch," Bang! There's a photo that's an exact match for my plant.

So now what? I mean, I've eaten at least a quart of whole pods, and maybe a half quart of shelled peas. I enjoyed them. If I'm poisoned, I haven't noticed! Should I eat more? I do another search for "Giant vetch edible." One Google preview snippet says *"Edible parts of Giant Vetch: Young seed - raw or cooked."* That's good news! A preview of another page says *"Some native North American Indian tribes regarded the seeds as poisonous."* A third says *the seeds of this vetch are edible and used by the Indians, but no such use was found here.*

I don't have much time to read through these pages, but it's clear that some peoples ate giant vetch peas and some tribes didn't. I can't find any mention, pro or con, on eating the pods. Some legumes are perfectly fine in moderate amounts, but can become poisonous if eaten in large amounts under starvation conditions. Maybe that's why some tribes consider them poisonous. I don't know. I'm not going to push my luck. I won't eat any more on this trip unless I can get more definitive info.

After saying goodbye to the young folks in the main lodge, I stop to thank the owners in the office. They tell me it rained *eight inches* during the last rainy spell! No wonder it seemed so rainy!

It's nice to be paddling across the bay, away from the busy lodge and back to the soothing calm of the wilderness. I cruise the coast, watching for berry bushes and deer. There aren't many berry bushes and I've yet to see a deer on this shore during the whole trip.

Behind me, somewhere in the distance, I hear a loud noise. Was that a whale? I look back for awhile, see nothing, and continue paddling. There it is again! But again I see nothing. A third time I hear something and turn around. Then I spot it.

Several hundred yards away a giant humpback whale rockets out of the water, hangs for a moment, then falls, slowly turning before crashing to the sea in a thunderous cannonball, sending cascades of whitewater shooting up in the air all around. *AMAZING!* I hear the booming of his landing moments later. I turn the kayak around. In seconds, his dark head shoots out of the water again and, in what seems like slow motion, he rises to the peak of his jump, his long pectoral fins waving as he slowly spins on his way down. *Kabloooooosh,* the sound reaches me moments later. Is it the same whale each time? I don't know, but there it is again, and again, and again. I start counting. Finally the sea is calm again. *Eighteen* successive jumps. What a breathtaking experience!

Ahead I see a large flock of seagulls along a sandy spit. It looks like it might be the mouth of a stream. When I beach my boat and walk over, rifle in hand, I find a nice little stream and in it are dozens of pink salmon and a few chum salmon! There are lots of bear tracks and salmon carcasses stripped of meat. I watch carefully for both deer and bears as I head upstream. It's not until I reach a rock outcropping that I recognize where I am: Falls Creek! That's funny. I arrived from a different angle and somehow that threw me. There are plentiful salmon here. If I want any pinks this is much closer than Salmon Creek.

I'd been planning to continue hunting up the bay and then check my crab trap, but I suddenly realize how tired I am. Nope, I'm headed home.

At camp I relax, finishing off the jar of salmon I've been eating today. It's thimbleberries and blueberries for dessert. This has been a big day. I'm going to sleep well tonight.

August 2, Day 34

I'm going to hunt hard today. It's 4 AM. I'm up and packing, and by 4:30 I'm paddling towards the head of Wild Bay. I arrive just before high tide so it's a short portage to the treeline. With my daypack on my back, my rifle in one hand and my folded up camp chair slung over one shoulder by its strap, I follow My Creek and watch for salmon on my way to the Knob. There are a few chum salmon in the lower pools, but it is loaded with pink salmon! Amazing. It's like flipping a switch. Last time there were no pinks here. How do they do it? How do they travel far out to sea and not only find their way back to their home stream, but do it at exactly the right time?

I scramble up onto the Knob and set up my chair in the most strategic spot. Following my rule of adding clothes before I get cold, and removing them before I sweat, I put on my fleece hooded sweatshirt and then my rain jacket and rain pants for warmth and wind protection. Since I don't have to worry about it getting wet today, I put on my balaclava.

The air is chilly here under the big trees, but the warm light of the morning sun slowly flows across the flats. In some places saltwater nearly reaches the timber, and in others there are two hundred yards or more of grass above high tide. The grass is a beautiful light green in the low sun, with the forest a dark green with black shadows cast by the giant canopies, some trees rising well over one hundred feet tall. Around the mouth of a small creek are the round tops of cottonwoods.

From this vantage point I can see at least a mile of grass along the edge of the forest. With all the many points and indentations, with the depth of the grass and the thick forest, a deer can appear at any moment. I sit down and glass all along the shore. *There!* A deer, the sun almost glowing on its shiny brown hair. There's another nearby. A doe and fawn I bet. No antlers, anyway. I see two more brown dots with my naked eye, dots that become deer in the binos. With these good binos and in this good light I think I could see antlers, certainly big antlers, even though they are hundreds of yards away. It's fun to see deer. Hopefully I'll see something closer. And something with antlers! It would be great to get one this morning so I have all day to cut it up and pressure-can it.

I've been glassing for maybe two hours but I'm not seeing any more deer. That's the way hunting is, though. Before season I was really confident this would be a great spot. And I guess it is a decent spot, I've already seen four deer, haven't I?

Time for breakfast. From my pack I retrieve a jar of salmon, a fork and salt and pepper. I'm still not sick of salmon!

*Splash!* What was that? Sploosh, *Sploosh!* It came from over by My Creek. It's less than two hundred yards away. It's a bear. A bear is chasing salmon in the creek. Cool! There is more splashing over the next few minutes. I'm going to sneak over there and try to watch him fish. I'll stay out in the grass where I should be able to see him before he gets too close.

Normally I'd make noise to spook a bear at a distance, but this time it's a calculated risk, and well, I'm deer hunting! I don't want to scare everything away. I walk slowly, watching for any movement or noise, deer or bear. Near the creek, it's clear where bears have walked through the grass, looking for salmon. A mature bald eagle flies up and lands on a dead tree not far away. He was eating the remains of a bear-killed salmon.

Out on a wide gravel bar I stand, watching up and down stream. Salmon are swirling in the creek, lots of them, mostly pinks. There's a brown bear! Crossing the stream below me. He immediately disappears behind a grassy bank. My camera is in hand, ready to go.

Come on, come back out to the gravel bar. He suddenly rushes back out into the stream, fountains of water flying upwards in all directions, ten feet over his head. No time for a photo. He walks behind the grassy bank but whirls back and charges into the water again, nearly disappearing in a glittering curtain of water. Wow! Disheartened, or more likely, already full from the fish he caught earlier, he ambles into the trees and is gone. I didn't get a single photo! Maybe I should have set my camera to video and just let it roll. That was really cool either way.

Back on top of the Knob, I glass the long views and occasionally turn around to watch along My Creek for more bears or feeding deer. I have a feeling feeding bears may be spooking deer out of the area near the creek. They'd spook me, if I were a deer! Bears are so fast. It must be dangerous business for a deer, wandering through the brush and high grass. Bears must catch them once in a while in a quick, mad rush.

There's some deer! Three of them, running, a quarter mile away. Through the binos I can see it's a doe and two fawns. Spooked by a bear maybe.

I unzip my rain jacket and grab the lanyard of my watch and pull it out of my shirt pocket. 10:45. It's going to be low tide soon. I've been sitting here for over five hours. I'm going to go check for crabs at the creek mouth. At the base of the Knob, I gather some thimbleberries and currants for brunch.

When I get to the edge of the saltwater, it doesn't look like low tide. Did I read the table wrong? No. The difference is that this is a 2.5' PLUS tide. Usually I'm trying to net crabs during a minus tide. It must be four feet deeper this time. A wind is blowing up Wild Bay now, too, and the rough surface makes it hard to see. To heck with it. I'll check the crab trap.

When I pull it up there are two crabs. One is huge. Acting fast so the wind doesn't blow me too far, I quickly measure the smaller one and toss him back in the ocean, then put the biggest one in the crab bucket. I don't even have to measure him.

I paddle against a brisk wind to drop the trap, then paddle steady and hard to fight my way back to camp. There are new crab buoys in places, in water that seems too deep. But what do I know? I'd be curious to watch them pull the traps, see if they are catching anything out here. Maybe it's not even Dungeness crabs they are after?

The wind dies noticeably when I get to the lee side of the timber near camp. I'm due for a break. After stashing the kayak I kick it in the tent for a while. It's really nice to relax and finish off that jar of salmon.

Although it's breezy, it's sunny. I unzip the silnylon tent door and let the wind blow through the bug netting. Nice to keep things aired out. After laying out the solar chargers I head to cook camp and clean and cook the crab. He really is a big one, the biggest yet, I think. I hang his shell up next to the shell of the next biggest crab. Not only is he big, he is mighty good eating. I save half for later.

This being such a nice day I'm going to collect some firewood. I bring my biggest pack, the hatchet and the saw and head into the forest. I'm looking for some poles to cut, poles that I can saw to a good length to burn in my tipi stove. I still haven't set that stove up, but I'm going to be here for five or six more weeks and it will be cooling off with the approach of fall. It's not easy finding dry poles. I find a small tree, dead and barkless, usually a sign of good wood. I thuds dully when I rap it with the hatchet. Nice dry wood "rings" when you rap it. This stuff is wet. Must be a little punky.

Finally, I find a reasonably dry pole, about three inches thick. I saw it off flush with the ground so as to not leave a stump (leave no trace!) It takes another hour or so to find and cut two more good poles. One pole I carry to the beach and lay it on the rocks to bake in the sun and get a little drier. Another I saw up and put in my pack. The third I realize is too wet and heavy when I pick it up. I wasted my time with that one. With my pack on my back I wander around determined to load it full of firewood. It's a huge pack, maybe double the size of a standard duffel bag, so it takes a while. There's dead wood everywhere, it's the dry wood that's hard to come by. I manage it though, mostly dry branches. I take them, twigs and all, for kindling, most of which I get from the base of big spruce or hemlock. When I'm done I carry the whole shebang and put the pack, wood and all, under the center of the tarp. That will hold me for at least two weeks, probably more.

There's a mink. This is the third time a mink has run by me today. My tame mink, maybe! This is the minkiest place I've ever seen, that's for sure.

Over at the food cache, I untie the paracord from a nearby tree and lower it to the ground, pulling the jar box out of the bag. Only seven jars left. I pull out four then slide the jarbox back in the bag and pull it up into the tree. I've let my canned food stash dwindle on purpose. A whole deer will take up lots of jars. If I've got seven jars, that will last me about a week if I supplement it with the usual plants and berries and a few crabs. So I'm good for a while yet.

The solar panels came through again, everything is charged, so I gather them up. At the far side of My Cove I see a brown dot. Is that a deer? Raising my binos I see it is, a doe, feeding in the spot where I most commonly see deer, a nice patch of grass near a brook, right on the edge of the trees. No antlers though. Bagging a buck would have been a good way to end the day.

When I walk up to my tent I glance at the electric fence energizer to make sure its power light is blinking. It isn't. What's the matter with it? The batteries can't be dead yet. The last set lasted three times as long. I fiddle around with it a bit. *Maybe I put one good and one dead battery back in it when I changed them by mistake?* Finally I notice the cover isn't snapped on solid. When it clicks in place the light begins blinking. I'm glad it's something simple.

I finally unzip my tent, step inside and zip the door shut again, sitting heavily in my camp chair.

"Man, I am a tired puppy," I say aloud with a big sigh. I didn't get my deer, but I made a good effort. the Knob didn't work out. I had high hopes for it. Maybe tomorrow I'll head back to where I saw all the deer yesterday. Make a spike camp so I can hunt that area really early in the morning and late in the day. Save me a whole lot of paddling. That'll be the plan. Unless I think of a better plan before I leave.

August 3, Day 35

It's 5 AM and I'm paddling to "Deer Cove", the place I saw the most deer on opening day. I've got enough gear to spike out a day or two. The landmarks are familiar now: the island with the eagle's nest and the island where seals rest until it's flooded out at high tide. There are seals there again.

I land at the mouth of Deer Cove, the near side this time so I can use trees and rocks to stay out of sight while I sneak around the corner and look for deer. Soon after landing I spot a deer, a doe. She wanders off into the forest. My timing should be good. I'm earlier than last time. Most deer should still be feeding. I sneak along the edge of the forest watching the grassy fringes of the cove. A deer snorts inland but I don't see it, I don't even hear it run off. I can see far down the cove to where a forested peninsula blocks the upper cove from view. I return to the kayak and paddle until I can begin to see around the peninsula. I spot a piece of brown out in the green meadow. A deer raises its head and takes a step forward away from me. I quietly paddle to shore.

With my rifle and pack, I carefully sneak round the end of the peninsula, ducking under low-hanging branches, careful to move slowly and stay in the shade. On a sunny day, shade is the best camo you can have. This is exciting. With any luck at all there should be an unspooked deer or two out in the meadow within easy range. If I'm really lucky, there'll be a buck!

A deer raises its head out of the tall grass to look around. I freeze. When it puts its head down I slowly sit down and raise my binos. Another deer appears from a low swale, a fawn. The other deer looks up again. It's the doe. Man, if one of them had antlers! After a while they wander away into the timber. I walk around the corner towards the head of the cove. This is awesome looking habitat. I can see nearly all the way around the head of the cove. There could still be deer here. Probably are. There are more swales, more tall grass where deer could be bedded. There's brush on the edges of thick timber that might hold more deer. I sneak cautiously, stopping frequently to glass.

Numerous pink salmon are jumping out in the cove. I expect to find a spawning stream but there is nothing but a tiny trickle of a brook, definitely not a spawning stream. There is a stand of small cedar growing in low ground not too far off the meadow. There are many small, barkless dead cedars. This would be a good place to saw up a bunch of dry wood for the tent stove. There is also a nice camp spot, flat and dry in the short grass and a short walk from the water. The big disadvantage though, is that every deer at this end of the cove would immediately spot the tent.

There is another cove farther down Wild Bay. I think I will hunt that cove and set up a spike camp there so I can hunt this whole area. I launch the kayak and paddle along, keeping my eyes peeled for deer, watching for twitching ears, or patches of deer-colored brown or a leg stepping forward.

What's that along the shore? Is that a boat? I paddle closer, until, sure enough, it IS a boat, washed up into the rocks. Why didn't I spot it last time? Because of shadows, I guess. Must have looked like another rock. I can't imagine not going over there, seeing what kind of shape it's in, if it's been there a while, and if it has, if there's anything that might be useful in it. It looks like it's in good shape at first, but as I draw up I see a big hole in the side, like "The Minnow" in *Gilligan's Island*. There are a few bullet holes in it as well. Guess I'm not the first one to notice it! If there was anything of interest to be found inside, it's long gone. I wonder where this boat came from? Did it hit a barely submerged rock nearby? Break its mooring lines during a storm somewhere and end up aground and battered here?

As I paddle onward the beauty of the scenery across the bay catches my eye. I reach for my camera to capture the moment. Above is a light blue, nearly cloudless sky. Rocky peaks and alpine tundra are frosted with white snow. Below are light green bands of alder brush. Next is dark timber, spruce and hemlock. Nearly all of this beautiful scene is bathed in the rich colors of sunrise. The centerpiece of this natural painting is an island in the foreground, capped with two hemispheres of timber, side by side, still black in the shadow of the mountains behind me. I drift until these black hemispheres lie in a wide, deep notch of sunlit mountains.

The smooth ocean reflects the whole scene nearly perfectly, except for the head of a seal who is leaving a tiny wake behind him. This is perhaps the most splendid landscape I've seen on the whole trip. The colors are wonderful, the angles of the mountains dramatic. The contrast of the dark island timber and the brightly lit mountains is

striking. But what really stands out, what really makes this scene so enchanting is its extraordinary symmetry. Not only is there a nearly perfect reflection, above and below, but a striking symmetry left and right as well, from the bookend mountains to the two nearly identical halves of the black island timber. I think it's important to notice moments like these. To recognize and appreciate them. That's what gives the beauty its magic.

Finally I turn the corner into the next cove. It was farther than I'd remembered. There is a low, grassy peninsula three hundred yards ahead, on the left. I think I see a deer. It's sure the right color, anyway. My binos are hanging from their harness. I lift them up and see... yup, a deer. And another little one bedded. A fawn. Guess the other one's a doe. Then another fawn walks over the top of the peninsula. The boat is moving just enough so it's hard to hold the binos steady enough to see if there are antlers but at last I can see there aren't. It's a doe and two fawns. I angle across the cove to hug the shady shore, paddling slowly along, trying to spot any nearby deer before it spots me.

A deer! Close! A stone's throw away a deer is feeding in a patch of grass in an opening in the brush. Our eyes meet. It studies me as I drift along from the power of my last paddle strokes. No antlers. No binos needed. It turns, trots a few steps, then bounces away. That was exciting. It would have been more exciting had it been a buck.

It's fun paddling up the long arm of the bay, hugging the shore. As I round each point a new vista opens up. I spot a doe feeding in the sunny grass on the edge of the timber. Nearby is her spotted fawn. He flops down in the grass to take a nap. I am still in the shade, on the other side of the arm. I ease the boat over to shore until it rests on the bottom. The deer haven't spotted me yet. I'm going to call this long, narrow cove "Blacktail Arm." It must be at least a mile long.

When the deer wander away into the forest I paddle until I can see the head of the Arm, there's lots of grass there, much of it in the shade. I land and carry the kayak above high tide near a fallen tree for some cover. I set my rifle where it's handy, then get half the crab I saved from yesterday and a bottle of water. I sit down on the bucket and crack the first crab leg with my teeth while watching for deer. This is living! It feels good to relax. The crab is excellent and it's a good vantage point to see deer. If I see a buck I should be able to get a shot, too. It's not hard to imagine a buck walking out of the trees to cross the head of the arm through shade of the grassy opening. I'd have a good shooting rest on the boat or tree.

There's a deer! Crossing right where I was watching! With my binos I see it's another doe. She stops to feed and then a spotted fawn walks out to join her. They meander around eating a little here and there before disappearing back the same way they came. It's fun seeing deer, even when they aren't bucks. It's only a matter of time until I see antlers.

When the crab is finished I toss the shells into the water, then grab my rifle and pack and still-hunt the edge of the timber to the head of the Arm. When I get there the meadow narrows, but I can see sun shining through thin timber ahead. I'm hoping to see a series of meadows that I can still-hunt, or at least some open timber. There are a few chest-high berries so I stop to pick and eat them, one or two at a time. Many of them aren't sweet, in fact some taste bad and I spit them out. I start noticing how many are like that, it's nearly one in five. Now why would that be? I've got to admit, the mixture of huckleberries and blueberries I've been eating on this trip have sometimes been just OK, not great. Is it possible that insects have eaten the sugars in many of the berries? I've definitely noticed some berry worms.

I pick my way along a marshy brook, stepping among large-leafed skunk cabbage plants and weaving through patches of Devil's club and berry bushes. There are fresh deer tracks here and there but the view never really opens up. It will be hard to see deer before they see me. I turn back, picking some berries as I go.

My heart jumps when I spot another deer, back at the grassy meadow at the head of the bay. There's her spotted fawn. I bet it's the same ones I saw an hour ago. When they are gone I walk back to the kayak and paddle back down Blacktail Arm, watching for deer and good campsites.

A doe and fawn walk out of the trees following the shore. I watch with interest when they reach a spot where a low cliff reaches the water. How will they get around? Will they swim or climb up and around? The doe stops, considering her options, then heads back and into the trees, taking the fawn with her. On the next peninsula I watch three deer through my binos. Perhaps the ones I first spotted in this arm.

When I reach a point where I can see up and down the Arm I land and look for campsites. Here and there yellow leaves stand out among the green. A very few stray bushes are mostly yellow. I'm calling it: these are the first colors of autumn.

I'd like to camp here where there is such a good view but it's thick getting through the alders lining the beach. When I get through there are mossy openings in the timber but they are either too small for a tent, too wet, too steep or too uneven. I meander about considering the pros and cons of each spot until I give up.

Farther along there is a flat spot, a couple of feet above high tide but mostly covered by sparse alder brush. Scouting around I find a grassy opening, plenty long but just a little wider than my tarptent. It's a few steps from my beached boat but is protected from wind by a screen of relatively open brush all the way around.

I take the time to switch from waders to camp shoes, then shuttle camp gear. I pull out my tent and center it in the best spot, laying down on top of it to test it out. This will work nicely. I install the hoop pole at the foot of the tent, then stake out that end. I break off a stout stick the proper length then tap a nail in the end until it sticks out a half inch, then run it through the grommet at the peak of the tent. With the pole in place I pull out each loop and stake it. It's a nice pitch.

It's not long before my pad is rolled out, my sleeping bag is fluffed up, dry socks are donned, and I'm kicking it in my sunny tent, my head propped up with spare clothes and reading an old issue of Backpacker Magazine. The sun shines warmly on the fly.

"I wonder what the poor people are doing today?" I say aloud, making myself smile. It's what we used to say when smokejumping, during exceptionally cool experiences. Of course, we weren't rich in money, but we were rich in experiences and freedom and lives full-lived. Someone might say it on a patrol flight, looking down over the spectacular Arrigetch Peaks of the Brooks Range. It might be while fighting an especially hot fire and pausing to watch the drama of a giant retardant plane come thundering in, a hundred and fifty feet high and a stone's throw away, dropping a red cascade of thousands of gallons of fire retardant. It might be shouted by a young smokejumper to his jump partner over the roar of turbine engines, just before leaping out into the screaming wind to a wildfire in rugged mountains three thousand feet below. Or it might be sitting on a mountaintop, the fire out, in the joy of being alive and knowing you are living the life you were meant to live.

I read until I'm sleepy, then lay down the magazine, close my eyes and drift off to sleep.

When I wake up it's about 4:30. I've napped nearly two hours. That was great. I'm going to hunt Deer Cove this evening, and try to get back here to Blacktail Arm in time to glass it before dark. On the way to Deer Cove a family of four otters are feeding in shallow water. An adult spots me and coughs, sending all of them clambering clumsily through the rocks and out of sight into the forest. At Deer Cove I find a spot where I can sit on a boulder with another in front of me for a good rifle rest should a buck walk out. The weather is still holding. Suddenly I hear a raucous bird call. A cobalt blue Steller's jay lands on a branch above me, soon joined by a second and a third. They hop around, calling harshly, seeming very peeved to see me sitting there, obviously hiding and up to no good.

"Hey!" I want to tell them. "Shut your beaks and maybe I'll get a deer and guess what you'll get to eat? Deer scraps!" Luckily they soon lose interest and fly away.

After a long sit, no deer have appeared. I get up, put my daypack on and sneak along the edge of the trees towards the head of the cove, keeping a sharp eye ahead of me as well as to the sides. When I pass the last point where I can see to the end I see the head and neck of a deer. Although I can't see any antlers, there are likely other deer out there. When she is out of sight I walk forward, crouched over, watching for ears or a whole head sticking up. As I get closer I crawl on all fours, then belly crawl. My heart speeds up. I'm going to see deer pretty soon. Probably close. There! I take a look through my rifle scope. It's a doe. She turns and looks back. I follow her gaze. A fawn walks out. Together they feed. The doe looks at me, lying flat in the grass. She can't tell what I am. They feed their way away from me, the doe occasionally looking back to see if I move.

I walk back to the kayak without seeing any more deer, then paddle back to spike camp, watching for deer in the failing light. I'm glad I took a good look back before I left camp so I'd recognize landmarks. Now, as I approach my camp I spot the log and boulders near the tent. It is nearly 9:30 and almost full dark. I didn't get a deer, but it was a good day. Allowing for repeat sightings, I likely saw fifteen different deer today. That's a success in itself.

# CHAPTER 18

## Avenue of the Giants

August 4, Day 36

I'm awake early and lie here listening. It's sprinkling. I hear a bald eagle, two of them. A pine squirrel. Ravens. And a kingfisher. There have been quite a few kingfishers around here.

I start packing up spike camp. It's a darker day, overcast with rain predicted. It's holding off pretty good now. It's not fun packing or setting up if it's raining very hard.

When I take the first load to the kayak, two deer are barely visible across the Arm. I sit down and glass them. It's the usual, a doe and fawn.

I paddle down Blacktail Arm and into the main bay all the way to Deer Cove without seeing any more deer. I'm going to sit and watch the head of Deer Cove. I paddle half way down the cove until I get to the peninsula and stash my kayak in the trees. I spot a deer feeding across the cove, a doe, and spot another on the other side of the peninsula, on my side of the cove. I sneak through the trees. I don't think it saw or smelled me, but when I get to where I expect to see it, it's gone.

Staying inside the treeline I follow a path until it comes out at the large meadow at the head of Deer Cove. I carefully sneak down to the edge, watching for deer, then sit beneath a spruce tree and lean back against my daypack in a steady, light rain. The spruce is shedding the rain quite well. Wearing my raincoat with the hood up and with my lightweight waders I'm nice and dry, and with my fleece jacket on I'm warm, too. This spot just feels right, so do the conditions, a light rain or mist is often a plus.

What's the rumbling noise? Two deer are bounding through the open trees a hundred yards away. The fawn comes scrambling out, then runs in a big circle, disappearing the way it came. Minutes later it comes bounding back out, stopping fifty yards away. It stops and shakes like a dog, surrounded in a thick mist of flying water. It looks around and bounds back into the woods from where it started. It's just playing!

I sit for a long time. It's easy to be patient in this good spot. There's a deer! Sneaking along the edge of the meadow. As hard as I try I cannot see any antlers. After a while without seeing anything more I sneak back towards the boat on the very edge of the meadow. Deer! Walking right towards me! I freeze until I see it's another doe. When it heads into the woods I walk all the way back to the kayak.

There's another grassy cove on my way to base camp. I'm going to check it out. I land my kayak, planning to hunt along the brook that runs in here. I step out of the boat and a deer suddenly stands up in the grass only thirty yards away! It's a doe. We both freeze until she loses her nerve and trots away into the trees. In a light rain like this it's common to see deer at close range. It only takes one buck and one good shot!

With the kayak stashed I sling my pack and sneak along the edge of the meadow, looking for deer as far ahead as I can see as well as to my right and left. I catch movement of the corner of my eye on the nearby hillside. A deer is trotting through the trees. There's another one, trotting just ahead.

I think it's a buck! I'm slipping my scope covers off as I sit down and lean against my pack. I slip the safety off, my heart pounding. When I look through the scope all I see is the blur of fog. *Dammit!* I've got my cotton handkerchief handy but by the time I grab it it's too late. When did my scope lenses get wet? As I gently dry them I wish that I had my other rifle scope that beads any water up, so you can see through it even if it's rain spattered or the conditions are foggy. I don't think I could have gotten a good shot anyway though. It looked like a forkhorn. That was exciting. I darn near got a shot at a buck!

I walk to the end of the meadow and into the big timber. Even the twigs are too wet to snap. A light rain falls steadily and drips off the trees. Ahead is a park-like corridor of giant spruce and hemlock with patches of brush here and there. I'm going to call this "The Avenue of the Giants." It's nearly ideal still-hunting conditions. Deer seem to like to move in a light rain, mist or fog, I can see well in this open timber. It is a little foggy and extremely quiet walking on the mossy ground. Is that a deer chest? Yup. It takes a few steps and a bush wiggles as the deer browses on it. I watch as it meanders around feeding. It's a fawn, but I don't want to spook it.

When it moves on, I continue and another deer bounds off. It must have been looking in my direction. It didn't hear or smell me. Hopefully it wasn't a buck. I can see another meadow ahead. I'll sit on the edge for a while. There's *another* deer! It's a doe. She walks towards me a few steps, suspicious, trying to see what I am, then thinks the better of it and walks away.

I reach the edge of the prettiest meadow I've seen yet. It's large and round with a small pond in the middle, brush around the perimeter and big timber beyond. The middle is lush green grass. I sit down under a cottonwood tree. What a beautiful spot. I'm going to call this "Magic Meadow." A deer is sneaking through the brush on the opposite side but I can't see if it's a buck. After thirty minutes or so I sneak along the edge of the meadow. There's another doe, feeding nearby. And another! Wow, there sure are a lot of deer around here! I pick a few huckleberries then start back towards the kayak.

A little spotted fawn is feeding only thirty yards away. He has no idea I'm watching him. He is sampling a little bit of everything, herbs, brush, plants of all kinds. He steps ahead and poses with both feet up on a little hump of moss as if pretending to be a mighty buck. I get my camera out. He feeds my way and suddenly notices me and freezes. He obviously has no idea what I am. Full of curiosity, he daintily steps my way past glistening skunk cabbage and dripping ferns. He walks closer and closer, raising and lowering his head as deer often do, trying to get a new perspective to puzzle me out. He's extremely cute with his spotted coat, short nose and dark eyes. He's so close that I'm pointing my camera down at an angle. He's studying my knees, only ten feet away! I'm trying not to laugh. Finally he smells me and trots off. That was great!

Near the water I think I see a deer's head. Is it? Maybe not. Then it lays its ears back. Yup! In a few steps I see it's a fawn bedded beneath a tree. There's a nice game trail in open timber along the cove so I follow it along. When it fizzles out I beeline for the boat. On the way I find not one, but two orange commercial crab bait cages, maybe five inches long. Unfortunately they are both missing their covers. I also find a small buoy with a tag. Might be useful for something.

On the way back to base camp, I pass some lounging seals. Twice I stop at nice thimbleberry patches to eat some of their sweet berries.

It's not quite 1 PM when I get back to base camp. Man, it's been a big day already! It's calm and nearly low tide. I'm going to halibut fish. I put on a new leader and lure, then paddle out to deep water and start jigging. I feel several bites but don't hook anything. There's a bigger bite! I set the hook. He's on! This is something bigger. Come on, halibut! It's not a huge fish, but a ten pounder would be awesome. I lift the rod tip, then reel as I lower it. Over and over. He was pretty deep. I look down and see white. Halibut bellies are white! But it's a jellyfish drifting by. When I can finally see the fish it's a... sculpin. Rats. It's a big one, though! It was exciting for while. He has a crab in his mouth.

I try a different spot and jig until 2:30. I'm hungry. I open a jar of char and chow down. It's still raining. To heck with it, I'm heading in.

I change into dry stuff and take a nap. When I wake up the sun is peeking out. I turn my rain jacket inside out and hang it up in the sun along with my shirt. I wander along the beach, picking and eating goose tongue and sea asparagus. After cleaning my rifle I read for a while and call it a day. A very full day. I saw about eighteen deer. Despite not getting a buck, it was one of the most fun deer hunting days I've ever had.

## August 5, Day 37

It's barely 6 AM and I'm sitting on my bucket atop the Knob, waiting for a buck to walk out. I felt strong paddling over here. Maybe today's the day. Hungry for breakfast I open the last jar of Dollies and sprinkle it with salt and pepper. It's good stuff.

There's splashing over at the creek. Must be a bear fishing. There's water flying up! He's hidden behind the creek bank and grass. I can see stretches of gravel bar. There he is! He's got a fish! It's a medium sized brown bear. He carries his prize up the opposite bank and flops down in the grass, chowing down. Pretty cool!

Ten minutes later he gets up and walks down into the creek. A mature bald eagle swoops in to clean up the remains of his fish. Several gulls land nearby, waiting their chance. The bear is busy chasing salmon around in the shallows. I catch glimpses of him as well as the geysers of water he sends shooting up. He's not particularly efficient at catching fish! He's got another salmon now. He climbs the bank again, flushing the eagle and gulls. He looks content lying there eating his prize, pinned down by his front paws as he pulls off strips of meat and skin. He is making good progress at fattening up for the winter. When he's finished, the eagle swoops in and ravens and squabbling gulls claim the other fish.

Water flies and fish splash frantically through the shallows as the brownie rushes back into the school. He gets one pinned to the bottom and instantly ducks his head to chomp it in his huge teeth. He triumphantly climbs the bank with the flopping fish, scaring away a growing flock of ravens, crows, gulls and two eagles. The fish is the big loser and the bear is the big winner, but plenty of other wildlife is scoring a windfall of food. One eagle is boldly feeding on the scraps of a salmon near the bear. The bear, disrespected, makes a rush for him but the eagle launches with powerful wing-beats and lands a short distance up in a nearby tree. Gulls hop in to snatch up scraps when the bear returns to his fish. It's my very own Nature program!

What's missing is deer. I think I'll still-hunt for awhile. The farthest north arm of Wild Bay is just out of sight. I'll sneak around the corner and hunt the edges and into the timber if it's fairly open.

It's easy walking overall. There are deer tracks in muddy spots. At the end of the grassy flats, I continue hunting into open timber but don't see or jump a single deer. If you can't find what you want to harvest, harvest what you find. Huckleberries and blueberries in this case. They aren't very thick, but they make a good brunch.

As I'm passing the Knob on my way back to the kayak I stop to look over the flats once more. Three or four dark animals are moving along the edge of the timber several hundred yards away. Otters I bet. When I lift the binos up they are gone, hidden in a low spot or behind high grass. Wish I'd gotten a better look. Finally I spot a bear's head sticking up. It walks into shorter grass followed by two cubs. They look black! There are no black bears here on Admiralty. So I've been told. Burning with curiosity I scramble up the Knob and sit down to glass, my elbows braced on my knees. Mom is feeding in the grass, the cubs alternate between feeding and romping. The mom, now that I have a better view, looks dark brown. The cubs still look nearly black but in low light dark brown can look black. They are brown bears in any case, not black bears.

At the base of the Knob I notice numerous nice red thimbleberries and proceed to gobble them up. It's official, I'm voting these the best, sweetest berries of the whole trip! Black currants are also hanging from bushes clinging to the hillside. I enjoy a handful of them as well.

Deer hunting hasn't worked out but I've brought my fishing gear along. Having just seen a bear here an hour ago, I sing loudly as I near the stream. When I look upstream I'm startled to see "my bear," or at least "a bear," walking down the stream. I quickly reach for my camera but when I look up he's gone. Somehow he hadn't heard me, but he must have smelled me just as I looked away for my camera.

My Creek is loaded with hundreds of pink salmon! It's exciting just to see them. In places, scores of fish hold in place, noses upstream. In other spots the main school of salmon holds while smaller groups patrol up and down stream with individuals often charging at another.

Water levels in My Creek have fallen to near normal levels. I walk down to a rocky ledge where the creek runs over two small falls, each only a foot high and a foot or two wide. It would be interesting to stand here and watch salmon navigate the narrow passages. I wonder if bears ambush salmon here? I observe for a few minutes but don't see any salmon make the climb. Upstream though, are countless fish. I tie on a purple egg-sucking leech and, standing on the rocky ledge, make a few false casts before allowing the fly line to curl out ahead and settle to the water. The fly sinks at the head of the pool and I strip the fly back towards me through dozens of fish. It still amazes me to witness a fly moving through a big school like this without a single fish showing any interest! Several follow-up casts also fail to trigger a strike.

Twenty steps upstream I have a better view of the pool. It will be difficult *not* to catch fish with hundreds of fish in sight! I cast to the opposite bank and begin stripping the fly back, inadvertently hooking one in the dorsal fin. Snagged fish usually fight much harder than mouth-hooked fish, it gives them more leverage. This one is no exception. Fish scatter as my fish races up and down the pool. I get him into the shallows, grab the hook and twist it out. The fish rockets back into deep water, unharmed. It's his lucky day. Well, except for the part where he got hooked!

This is fun fishing. It's always fun to know there are plenty of fish around, but it's especially enjoyable to be able to sight fish. I can usually see my fly from the time it hits my water until the time I lift it from the pool for the next cast. I can see how the fish react. A big male swings his head and the fly disappears in his mouth. I set the hook and he rushes upstream, the line zipping through the water. I keep steady pressure on him and each run gets shorter. Looking behind me I spot a stick and holding the rod and line in my right hand, step on the stick and break it off with my left. When it's time, I slide my salmon up on the low gravel bar and grab his tail to rap him on the head. He flops wildly. I miss the first time but succeed the second. I reach for my daypack, grab my knife and slash his gills. Dark red blood squirts out and sinks into the gravel. Out of respect, I carry him to the water and wash him clean.

I lay him on the dark gray gravel bar atop a clump of short green plants. My fly rod lies above him, the purple and pink fly still in his mouth. He's a beautiful fish. The classic hump, the source of the Humpies nickname, is just starting to develop. His jaws have a slight hook. His skin is still smooth and healthy looking, his tail and dark back are sprinkled with trout-like black spots, his belly sleek and white.

With all these fish, I've learned to strip the fly slowly to avoid snagging them. I often see fish make a swing at the fly without taking it, and even grab the fly and instantly spit it out before I hook them. But I also see another grab the fly and get hooked solidly. After successfully landing him I keep him as well.

Soon I hook and land a female. I've decided to keep only three fish, so I let her go. I want to have as many empty jars as possible for when I get a deer, but I need a few fish to carry me over until then. It only takes a few more minutes to land another female, which I release as quickly and gently as possible, without taking her out of the water. At the head

of the pool are a few fish that likely haven't seen my fly yet. A big male grabs the leech and I fight him the length of the pool until he's tired, then beach him. There, I line my three prizes up and take a moment to admire them.

With all three fish head-first in my bucket, I hike to my kayak and paddle out to the crab trap. It holds two crabs, including a real dandy. I release the small crab and lay the big one on his back in the kayak. With the trap across the bow I paddle to the closest island, a little one which henceforth I'll think of as "Small Island."

I've brought the fillet board. I clamp the fish to the board, one by one, and drop the fillets into the rinsed bucket. I dump out all the old bait from the crab trap. Some of it was getting stinky. I fill the small bait cage with fish guts and the big bait cage with a fish skeleton, then wire two heads to the top of the trap. That should do it!

From the front pocket of my pack I retrieve the plastic buoy tag I found yesterday. I cut off the bottom part of it and on the blank upper half I've written my contact information with permanent marker. I tie that tightly to the buoy. My other buoy tagging hasn't lasted, this one will.

After dropping the trap I paddle for home into a hard wind. A crab boat is motoring across the bay. We are on course to cross paths. Two crewman are standing on the deck looking at me. We pass close enough so I catch a single snippet of conversation over the boat's engines.

"...you have to be pretty hardcore to..." I suppose paddling around in a kayak pulling up crab traps might look hard compared to using a motorized puller from a power boat, but I usually only do it once every day or two. I'd say you have to be pretty hardcore to be a commercial fisherman!

At cook camp, I slice up the fillets and put them in jars. The rapidly rising tide keeps pushing me towards the trees. I notice a bunch of tiny eel-like fish eating fish scraps, maybe they ARE eels. There is also a tiny, mottled sculpin. His coloration and pattern are nearly identical to the bottom. It's amazing, and beautiful.

I cook up the crab and enjoy it while heating up the pressure canner. After I'm done eating I hustle back to camp. The sun isn't really out, it's just soaking through the clouds, but I lay out two solar chargers anyway, along with the tarptent, waders and socks to dry in the breeze. It's a treat to put on my running shoes.

I hurry back to the canner to find that the cover is leaking steam along one side and the pressure is down to zero. On closer inspection, it looks like the cover isn't level. Bummer. I don't know how much time I lost, so I restart the clock just to be safe.

After successfully completing the operation I carry the hot jars back and set them just inside the electric fence. I pluck and eat some goose tongue from the beach near the tent. I'm pleased to find the Kindle and iPhone have charged to 100 per cent. I don't think the sun ever came fully out although the disk of the sun was visible through the clouds. Guess that's all it took!

Light is failing and I'm happy to call it a day. Didn't see a single deer, but caught all the salmon I wanted to catch, and also got a crab and all those berries. Not too bad! I'm sleepy. I drift off.

I'm startled awake. *A big animal is breathing just outside my tent!* I grab my headlamp, turn it on, then quickly pick up my rifle and chamber a round. I listen. Nothing. I step outside, rifle at ready, and sweep the light around. I don't see anything. I don't hear anything either. That was almost certainly a brown bear. Whatever it is, it's gone. That got my heart going! I wait a few more minutes but hear nothing but the wind in the trees.

Back in the tent I put my headlamp in its usual spot and unchamber the cartridge, leaving the magazine full. For a few minutes I lie awake looking upward into the darkness, then fall back into a sound sleep.

August 6, Day 38

I'm going to take it slow today and won't do any deer hunting unless I happen to spot a buck. I lounge in the tent, reading *Still Wild: Short Fiction of the American West, 1950 to Present*. I really like it. Short stories are nearly perfect for a trip like this. As a matter of fact, I enjoy well written short stories almost any time. Distilling a story to its essence is an admirable skill. There is something special about the American West to me as well. The West represents wide open spaces and adventure and the pioneering spirit. I'll never forget heading West to work for the first time. The long drive to Wyoming, twenty years old and the excitement and promise of the unknown ahead of me. Crossing the plains and driving through a snowy storm and then breaking out into the sun at Powder River Pass in the Bighorn Mountains. It was absolutely thrilling! A few miles later I stopped to fish in Tensleep Canyon, hooking and landing a fine brown trout. I was in the West. I was a part of it.

At 10 AM I paddle to the center of the bay, angling towards the Sound. I'm soon jigging for halibut in time for the slack tide that will occur around 10:30. When it comes down to it, wind is a bigger factor here, near the head of the bay. In general winds push me much faster than tides.

There is no particular bottom structure shown on my maps in this area, but my plan is to let the wind slowly carry me towards the head of the bay. Maybe I'll stumble across a halibut hotspot. I'm getting a stray bite here and there, sculpins likely. I end up drifting along a "seam" in the current. What causes the sea to move at different speeds at this particular spot is a mystery to me, yet the seam is plainly visible. After drifting a good mile I find it's getting shallower. I keep reeling in a little line at a time. I must be coming up on one of the rock piles that emerge at lower tides. Just when I decide to reel in my heavy jig it's too late, I'm snagged. I let out line and paddle upwind of the snag and give it a good tug. No luck. I paddle even farther upwind and tug even harder. Still no dice. I really don't want to lose my last big jig head. I drift until I'm directly over the snag and wrap the line around my paddle and pull as hard as I dare. It works! Very satisfying.

Thwarted once again from catching a halibut, I paddle over to a peninsula that I haven't explored before. There I find a new thimbleberry patch. They are numerous and sweet. I pick the edges of the patch, eating as I go, then carefully weave my way through little corridors to find even more. I bet I've eaten a quart already! I walk along the shore and around a point, headed to the salmonberry patches I found before. Numerous pink salmon are jumping in the shallow water of the bay.

The salmonberries have already peaked, there are less than before. I watch for good photo opportunities of especially nice berries. I take a shot and admire the result, bright red, pebbled berries against the richly green and delicately veined, serrated leaves of the salmonberry bushes. Again, I find the berries only moderately sweet. They have a strange aftertaste, a mild taste of orange peels, perhaps. I eat a few currants as well. I should have brought my rifle. It's a mistake not having a rifle handy during deer season.

The wind has risen. I have to paddle at an angle to get to the crab trap, blowing sideways across the water as I go. Hey, I'm crabbing to the crab trap! It starts to rain, hard. I zip up my rain jacket. When I swing the trap onboard it holds a nice crab and a... halibut! Well I finally got my halibut, a ten incher. I quickly open the trap and toss him overboard. I never considered I might catch a halibut in a crab trap. The crab, I'm happy to find, is a legal one.

Heading home I paddle into an ornery wind and relentless rain.

It's about 3 PM. Under the protection of the cook camp tarp I start

a fire in the rocket stove and cook the crab. It's fun to watch the rain pour off the tarp. It feels like a victory somehow. Like always, I enjoy the hot crab meat and the process of cracking the shells to retrieve it. I've been lucky so far, not craving "real world" foods much. When I do it tends to be things like hot, fresh bread. I'm not much of a cook, and even less of a baker, but I make a lot of fresh bread with a bread machine. That's what I most often think of, shaking out a perfect loaf of hot bread, then spreading butter on a steaming slice, savoring every bite.

When I'm done eating I untie the center cord at one end of the tarp, letting it fall to funnel water into a bucket. It won't take long to fill it!

Back at camp and in dry clothes I listen to the weather. Sounds like plenty of rain in coming days.

# CHAPTER 19

## Day of Days

August 7, Day 39

It's early and I'm paddling to Deer Cove. Just short of the point that marks the mouth of the cove I secure the kayak and climb the hill, planning to still-hunt to the cove and then along the edge to the head of the cove, where I'll sit and watch for deer.

Reality immediately thwarts my plan. I must have landed too early because I've hit an unclimbable cliff. I hike back down to the shore and look for another way. When I try again I hit alder brush so thick it's unhuntable, too noisy and too dense to see. Again I scramble back down the hill to the beach, following it, looking for a workable route. I round a point that I mistook for the mouth of the cove and at last follow deer trails to the top of the ridge. Eagles are wheeling and screaming overhead.

I reach the edge of the cove without spotting or spooking any deer. When I step out of the timber and look down the grassy shore there isn't a deer in sight-this at the spot I saw so many deer just a few days ago.

When I'm halfway down, I spot two deer on my side. I check for antlers with my binos-nope-then I scan all along the shore and find two more deer near the head of the cove. If they have any antlers, I can't see them. With four deer ahead of me, and likely more hidden behind the point of trees ahead, I sneak back into the timber to use the cover of the trees to get to a place where I can sit and watch the upper half of Deer Cove. There's a nice trail inside the tree line, with numerous deer tracks in muddy spots. When I see nice bunches of blueberries, I take a few moments to add them to my breakfast.

The trail swings towards the meadow, just where I wanted to come out. I crouch down and slowly and quietly creep out, stopping periodically to glass. There are several deer within sight! Still in the shadows and largely hidden by brush, I slowly sink down and take off my daypack, pushing it ahead of me and then leaning back against it. Starting on the left I methodically scan the grassy meadow with my binos. One, two, three, four...eight. Eight deer! Man, *one* of these must be a buck, a spike or a little forkhorn maybe? My binos disagree, however. There are several spotted fawns and adult does and what looks like-I can't quite see but I think-a very small buck from last year, it looks like tiny nubbins of antlers. Any male deer is legal but I'm not ready to shoot one that small yet.

It's entertaining watching so many deer grazing, lying down, chasing each other. At any moment a buck could walk out! After a couple of hours I skooch out on my butt about ten more feet so I can see farther down the cove. It's a good spot with a great view and I'm still under overhanging willow branches and hard to see. In a half reclining position like this I should be able to get a good shot at almost any buck I spot. It's raining, steadily but lightly, but the willow is thick enough that most of the rain is deflected. My raincoat and waders take care of the rest.

The suspected small buck comes trotting my way but at about twenty yards he veers away and heads into the timber, unspooked. That was fun! It looks like the deer are heading into the timber to bed. A big doe comes trotting my way, busily shooing flies away by flopping her big ears. Holy smokes, she's headed for the trail I'm sitting on! I barely breathe, waiting to see what will happen. She approaches so close I can see the long hairs on her muzzle and her dark eyes glistening. At twenty feet she notices me, a low dark shape beneath the brush. She's suspicious, but doesn't know what I am, and can't smell me. Instead of running she slowly turns and walks steadily and quickly away into the brush farther up the meadow.

With the deer all gone, I hunt my way along the inland trail, back towards the raft. I just saw an estimated fourteen different deer. Not too shabby! No longer in any hurry, I pick a bunch of huckleberries and blueberries. When the trail comes back out to the cove I graze on fresh goose tongue and sea asparagus.

As I near base camp on the paddle home I see a humpback whale jumping! There's another one! They soar out of the water, their great size creating the illusion of slow motion, their long front fins waving as they hang at the top of their jump. They fall with a booming crash sending a crown of white water shooting up. One giant whale is on the surface, lying on his side and waving a long front fin. I'm not sure if he is just having fun or what, but it looks like fun to me!

I think I'll check the crab trap and jig for halibut on the way. At base camp I pick up my heavy rod and spare fishing tackle. I hang onto my rifle, just in case. Just short of the Hump I lower the heavy jig to the bottom and jig as the wind blows me across the hump. The jig stops dead. Halibut? Naw, it's a snag. I give it a sharp tug but it doesn't budge. Paddling back upwind I give it another sharp yank and it comes loose. *Yes!* I start to float over the snag area before dropping the jig again, but remember the quote from *A River Runs Through It* "there are no flying fish in Montana," meaning that you can't catch a fish if you don't have a hook in the water.

I drop the heavy jig back into the water. It sinks rapidly with the white tail waving enticingly. It stops dead when I try to jig it. Drat. Another snag. Wait. It moved! Far below a big fish shakes its head. I hooked one, I got a halibut! The rod bows in a steep arc when I try to lift him. The line shudders. Lowering the rod tip I pull as hard as I dare. Slowly the tip rises above the water. I lower it again, quickly reeling up the line, then pull hard again, the rod bending and the line singing under the strain. He dives for the bottom. The drag slips, barely. I reach down with my left hand and loosen the drag slightly. The line throbs heavily. This is a fish. A very big fish. *The biggest fish I've hooked in my whole life!* It's incredibly exciting. After all this effort I want to succeed in catching a halibut. I want to fill up my jars, which are nearly empty. Most of all I want to land this giant fish because I'm a fisherman.

His strength is thrilling. The fight is straight up and down. The halibut powers for the bottom, the drag screaming. Then I slowly work him up fifteen or twenty feet before the pattern is repeated. We slowly drift towards the head of Wild Bay and Big Island. Between my kayak and the unseen fish and the shore to which we are drifting, I see at least four crab buoys, each with at least 100 feet of rope. If I lose him on a snag, it will be on one of those ropes. It will be a while before we get there. Let's see what happens. As the fight goes on and on, I think about the knots I've tied. The heavy nylon leader to the hook should be good. It's the knot tying the leader to the braided line that I'm more concerned about. It's held so far but I winged it in tying the knot, trying to tie it in such a way that the braided line wouldn't cut the nylon leader. I guess I'll see.

I still haven't seen the fish. We are headed straight for the first buoy. Holding the rod with one hand I paddle with the other, perpendicular to the wind line until it looks like we will clear the buoy rope. Nearly an hour has gone by. I've gained considerable line and I start looking down into the water, hoping to catch a glimpse of him. Fifteen feet down there is a broad white flash. *There he is!* He spots the boat and strips out all the hard gained line. But this time I gain line much more quickly. Another buoy is looming. Again I paddle with one hand until we are clear.

Time passes and Big Island is getting closer. The big halibut is tiring, although I still haven't gotten him to the surface. Now he's mostly staying in sight though. I'm keeping steady pressure on the rod, as much as I dare. I want him tired out. I want him so tired that I can land him like a salmon, to drag him quickly up on the shore. There's the bottom: starfish and shells and sand and stones. The halibut fight becomes horizontal as he tries to get to deeper water. I see his broad, flat, brown topside as he fights with powerful kicks of his tail. He's enormous. He's weakening fast though. I think it's going to work. I think I'm going to get him. I'm holding him pretty close to the boat now. He doesn't have much left. I glance ahead. Almost to shore. I reel him even closer. This part is critical. Does he have a major run left in him? The bow crunches to shore. I glance at a big rock. That's where I'll set the tripod for the photos. This is unbelievable!

I stand up and turn around and pull the kayak up on shore with one hand. The line goes slack briefly as I bend over. I reel quickly to keep pressure on. He must be headed towards me. There's a flash of white thirty feet out. It's my jig. "Oh no!" He's gone. I lost him! The biggest fish of my life. That's what I call "the thrill of victory to the agony of defeat." Guess there'll be no pictures.

I stand looking out over the cold water of the bay, deflated, shoulders sagging, tired and bummed. You know what though? That was great. That was one of the most exciting fishing experiences of my life. Even if I didn't catch him. Nothing I can do about it now. A gap in the clouds lets the sun flood the bay and the first rainbow of the trip appears. There you go. You take the bad with the good and the good with the bad.

I paddle out to the crab trap but it only holds a huge starfish. I head for home. Man, what a day. What could I have done differently with the halibut? It's traditional in Alaska to shoot big halibut. It would have been nice to have a pistol. Would the 30-06 work? Would it even be legal? I don't know. Next time, I think, next time I hook a big one I'll slash his gills and land him when he's done for. One thing I *do* know is it's really dangerous to try to land a big halibut before it's dead.

I'm mulling all this over when I spot a bedded deer along the edge of My Cove. I lift the binos but it's too far away to tell if there are antlers or not, especially in the bouncing boat. When I get closer I take another look but I still can't see. I paddle for a way and take another look. Is that antlers, or am I just seeing what I want to see? It could possibly be a small buck, or it might be I'm just seeing the inside edges of his ears, looking like horns.

I paddle to about two hundred yards. The deer stands up and turns its head. I lift the binos. Antlers! It's a buck! A fork horn I think. But now what, how am I going to get to shore and get a shot when I'm out in plain sight? I'm still far enough away that he's not spooked, and he's feeding now, too. Maybe. I'll see what happens. I start paddling for shore. The buck glances up from time to time, but keeps feeding.

Somehow it all works out. I don't crowd him and he doesn't run. A few minutes later I'm sitting, elbows on my knees and with my heart pounding. I have to make this shot count. I watch the buck through the crosshairs of the scope. He turns broadside. Letting the crosshairs settle on his chest I pull the trigger. *Boom!* He stumbles forward, turns around and collapses. "I got him!" Three hundred yards away a doe and two fawns are bedded in the grass. They don't even stand up. I've seen this before. I think they know, instinctively, that my target was the buck.

I walk over to him. It was a perfect lung shot and a quick, easy death. I'm thankful for that. His late summer coat is brown and shaggy. His small forked antlers are still fuzzy and velvet covered. I feel sorry looking down at him. I do. The magic spark of life is gone. But living means dying someday. I'm a predator out here. I killed him so I could eat and live. It's sad his life had to end, but I'm happy for this successful hunt. I'm glad to have gotten my buck and ecstatic to get all the fine meat he'll provide.

I pull the boat up as close as I can and set up the tripod to take a few photos. He's about thirty feet from the kayak. I can drag him right up to it and load him in, easy. After taking a few photos I retrieve my knife from my pack and dress him out. I slice open his belly skin then carefully reach in and slice through his diaphragm, warm steam rising up, I reach through to grab his esophagus with my left hand, reaching in with my right hand to cut the esophagus loose, being very careful not to slice open his guts or my left hand. A few no-see-ums try to chew my bloody hands but I crush them. In minutes I'm done. His warm entrails lie on the grass of the beach. I flip him over on his belly to drain the blood.

I wash the knife and my bloody hands in the sea and stand looking

across My Cove to the other side of Wild Bay with the mountains rising above. Patches of blue sky are visible through the clouds. Bugs flit around. Little fish dapple the surface of the smooth ocean. Camp is only about five hundred yards away, maybe less. If not for the trees I could see it.

An hour ago was one of the most crushing disappointments of my fishing life. If I had landed that halibut I wouldn't have gotten this buck. I wanted this venison even more than I wanted the halibut meat, that's for sure. It ain't over 'til it's over. You never know how things will work out.

I drag the kayak out until it's nearly floating, then load the deer in the bow and set my pack and rifle in back, taking a good look around to make sure I haven't left my knife or anything else.

On the short paddle I think about what to do with the deer tonight. It's been too big of a day to skin, butcher and can him tonight. I'll hang him up and do it in the morning. I land next to cook camp and drag him over to my food cache tree. I lower the nearly empty food bag down. If I pull his head up to the branch he'll hang down too far. So I tie his hind feet to his antlers then tie his antlers to the block and tackle. It's nearly 9 PM. The light is failing. I step back and pull the rope until his head is solid against the branch. He's a good ten feet up. That will work fine.

Back at camp I change into my sleep clothes. Man, this was a huge, huge day. I'm going to call this The Day of Days. All those deer I saw this morning. The jumping whales! That monster halibut. I'll never forget that. Not ever. And now the buck this evening. My first blacktail. Venison tomorrow. Real *meat*! That's going to be awesome.

There will be animals mighty happy when they find the deer guts tonight. I think they are above high tide. There might be some little mink that eat until they explode! If the bears don't clean it up tonight, the eagles and ravens and gulls will make short work of it tomorrow.

I'm glad I'm not a worry wart tonight, here in the Fortress of the Bears, my clothes spattered with blood, my arms, though rinsed off, still smelling of deer blood and fat.

My work is cut out for me tomorrow. It will be a day of skinning and butchering and canning and feasting on venison.

August 8, Day 40

It was a restless sleep with wild dreams. I dreamt I was wandering through a big encampment of people in tents and tipis. My gear was scattered all around. I went into an enormous tipi full of partiers. It was too wild and noisy for me so I left. I ran across two people, one playing the piano, the other singing a sad song. I found my own piano from somewhere and said "No, sing this..." I started plunking out a bouncy tune, singing "I'm so happy..." I'm not sure what that dream meant, but I think dreams are often just dreams.

I eat a leisurely breakfast of salmon while I read, then get ready for the day.

On the way to cook camp I eat some goose tongue. My deer is where I left him. I usually like to skin deer with their head down, but he was tied by his antlers so I lower him until his neck is even with the top of my head. Starting at his belly opening, I slip my knife under the hide, blade facing outward, and slice the hide clear up to his chin. And then, once again cutting from the inside to avoid cutting hair (which will stick to the meat) as much as possible, I cut the hide all the way around just below his head. Next I slice up the inside of each front leg, cut the hide free all around each "knee," then skin out each leg the rest of the way. I'm lucky right now. It's nice and cool and the rain is holding off and there are no bugs to harass me.

Back at his head I start skinning down the neck and on down the torso, pulling the hide away as much as possible, cutting only when needed. Once the hide is free to just beyond his front legs, I skin out his hind legs. I peel the hide away from his body and in just a few more minutes I cut the base of his tail and the whole hide comes free.

I gather up all the clean, empty jars and set them nearby. Since I'm going to be canning almost the whole deer, it doesn't really matter how I cut this buck up. So, starting just below his head, I begin slicing off chunks of meat and putting them directly in the jars. I have his hide laid out to the side as a place to throw inedible scraps.

How much fat should I keep? Normally I try to minimize venison fat in the meat, it's the source of much of the "gamey" taste. It also tends to harden in your mouth if, for example, you eat a piece of fatty venison and take a drink of cold milk. I learned that as a kid! Nowadays, we bone out our deer and trim the fat away and it's made a huge difference. This situation is different though. Calories are at a premium. Fat is very calorie dense. Some hunter-gatherer peoples, dependent on wild game for survival, would starve to death with plentiful meat on hand if it was too lean. That happened sometimes to caribou hunting tribes who were eating half starved caribou with hardly any fat on them.

I decide to compromise: I'll leave some fat in the meat and cut off the biggest pieces. I'll can up a couple jars of pure fat to have in reserve, just in case. I'm doing pretty good on calories so far. It's pretty clear that I've lost weight but I'm certainly not starving, nor do I expect to be. This is how I'll hedge my bets. I carefully fillet the backstraps from along the outside of his backbone, and throw them in the bucket, then fillet the tenderloins away from along the backbone on the inside of the deer, throwing them in the bucket as well. I end up with 21 jars of boned out meat, two jars of fat with a bit of meat in it, and one more jar of scraps that I'll save out for crab bait. I carry the bucket of backstraps and tenderloin down to the shore and cover them with saltwater.

I load fourteen jars into the canner, in two layers separated by a rack, along with two or three inches of water already on the bottom. I build a fire in the rocket stove and set the canner on top. It's heavy!

After adding the windscreen around the bottom of the canner I sit down to feed the fire as needed. Once again I'm surprised to see how long it takes to heat up. It must have taken an hour but it's starting to vent now. Once I have the regulator on and it's chattering away, it all goes smoothly. Ninety minutes at pressure (for red meat) and the first batch is done. Nice!

The second canning batch consists of the last seven jars of meat and the jars of fat as well. Since there are fewer jars and the water and canner were already hot it gets to pressure much faster this time and I'm feeling pretty pleased. The cover is leaking steam. Drat. I watch it, hoping the steam is coming from somewhere else, or that it will stop but neither is true. Bummer.

I lift the canner off the fire. This canner has no rubber gasket, which should be an advantage out here, with no rubber gasket to fail. The tolerances are more critical this way though, so I'm thinking maybe a little fleck of bark is the problem. I carefully clean both the cover and the canner where the metal edges seal together, then carefully replace the cover, making sure it's completely level. I start heating the canner once again.

After steam has been coming out of the vent, aka "venting" for ten minutes I put the regulator on and watch for it to climb to ten pounds pressure and see if the cover will leak. Six pounds, looking good, seven, eight, nine... steam begins squirting out from around the cover. *Rats. This is not good.*

As I let the pressure subside I walk back to the tent and get the canner instructions and thumb through it. Metal-To-Metal Seal, Cleaning and Maintenance. It says to clean the seal occasionally. I just did that. It also says *The metal to metal seal must be lubricated periodically... Lack of lubrication...makes it difficult to maintain a steam-tight seal.* I bet that's it. It goes on to say *Lubricate the metal-to-metal seal on the bottom with petroleum jelly or Vaseline.* I have neither. Lip balm might work. How about deer fat?

There is still pressure in the canner. I slice up the backstraps and load the grill with chops, then clamp it shut, setting the grill on the stove. The stove is full of hot coals, it should be perfect. In moments the delicious smell of roasting meat wafts to my nose. My mouth is watering! The chops sizzle and begin to brown around the edges. I ready the salt and pepper and my canteen by my side. I can't wait. I flip the grill over and watch impatiently as the other side cooks. I reach over with my knife blade and make slice in the thickest part of the meat. It's done!

I pull the grill off the fire and spear a chop with my fork, blowing on it. It smells *so good!* I bite off a piece and hold it in my teeth, blowing on it some more. Then I begin to chew. *Wow.* Excellent. The saltwater seasoned it beautifully. This is what I've been waiting for since June! It tastes as good to me as the finest steak ever grilled. In no time the first chop is gone, followed in quick succession by the second and the third.

The pressure on the canner has hit zero. I remove the cover. I get a piece of deer fat off the hide and wipe it all the way around the rim of the canner, leaving it glistening. That oughta work!

With the canner heating, once again, I slowly savor the last two chops. I've got to admit, as the pressure gauge nears ten pounds I'm a little tense. If it leaks now I'm not sure what the next step is. But at ten pounds pressure the regulator starts chattering, and the cover isn't leaking any steam. It worked! That's a relief. I hear rain sprinkling on the tarp.

With everything going smoothly I round up all the remaining jars that need washing. After checking the canner and adding a little wood, I carry the jars down to the water and wash them, checking the canner every few minutes.

Monitoring the canner once again I think about what day I'll fly out. I'm going to give myself more time in Petersburg. Other than the day I landed I've never been there. It's always good to have a buffer on commercial flights as well-bush flights are often delayed by weather. I'll email my air taxi and ask for a pickup on September 8. That will give me a full day to check out Petersburg and plenty of time to clean, dry and pack things. Hey, I'll be flying out one month from today!

The second batch of canning is finally done. What a victory. I set the canner to the side to cool, then slice up the rest of the backstraps and tenderloin, barely fitting them on the grill. I set the grill on the coals and watch the meat sizzle and brown. When it's done I save it for later.

I carry the hide, scraps and deer skeleton down to the water. I roll a couple of rocks inside the hide along with the scraps and then load the hide and skeleton in the kayak. I paddle out into the middle of the cove and throw the skeleton overboard. It is strange and spooky and a little sad to watch it sink out of sight. Next I throw the hide overboard and I'm pleased to see it sink despite the hollow deer hair. I pick up the kayak paddle and spin the boat around. As I take the first stroke the hide suddenly bobs to the surface! It must have tumbled on the way to the bottom, letting the rocks fall out. I guess I'll let the tide carry it away.

I round up all my gear at cook camp and load it and all the jars in the kayak. I'll hang them tomorrow when they've finished cooling. I carry my knives to the water and wash them off and throw them in the bucket then paddle to base camp. I set the jars just inside the electric fence and bring the chops inside for supper.

That turned out to be a long day! It's 9:45, nearly dark.

In my tent I turn on my headlamp and enjoy some more chops. Where did the time go today? Good thing I didn't try to get all that done last night by headlamp. It's so nice to have that big project done, to have this big cache of food. I can eat venison every other meal for the rest of the trip. What a luxury!

# Chapter 20

## Down Comes the Rain

August 9, Day 41

I wake up to a steady rain on the tent fly. I roll over and turn on the weather radio. They are predicting rain every day for the next week and "rain, heavy at times" today, which is Saturday, and on through tomorrow or Monday. They are even calling for possible flooding in some areas. This is good timing. I'll barely have to leave the tent today if I want to be lazy. I've got days' worth of food and water right here. The tent seems brighter and airier than the last big rainy spell. At least so far! It is a little breezier at this camp spot, with a thinner tree canopy letting more light in. And of course I have the tent liner up now, too, which will reduce condensation. I think those factors will all add up to make this a more cheerful place in heavy rain.

I'm reading my copy of *Still Wild*. I've been randomly reading the short stories so this morning I'm flipping through the book reading ones I've missed. I'm down to the last story, "The Pedersen Kid." I've enjoyed the other stories, but this one strikes me as pretentious and hard to follow. Maybe I'm too dense to follow it so it just seems pretentious.

At 10 AM, I put on my rain gear and what's left of my crumbling rubber boots and step outside to take a look at things. One of the tent's guylines isn't tied out so I tie it to a hemlock branch. That will keep the fly from touching the liner and help prevent condensation.

Things look good in cook camp. I take the leaky plastic collapsible water jug and flip it over so the hole is up, then cut a three inch hole all the way around it. I drop one end of the cook camp tarp, centering the jug so the rain water streams into the hole. Good thing I have a nice stack of firewood under the tarp and out of the rain.

I climb the trail to the latrine. Once again I'm thankful for the protection of the tarp because it's raining hard. Not wanting to go back to the tent yet I walk the shore all the way around to where I killed the deer to see what's left of it, which is nothing. I pull out my phone and look at the photos to make sure I have the right spot. I can see crushed-down grass where I walked around dressing the buck, but his remains have been eaten or dragged away. It must have been a real feast for some beast, or more likely beasts.

On the way back to camp I watch the shoreline for berries but don't spot a single one until I get to The Point. There are plenty of ripe thimbleberries in these good, dependable patches. I pick and eat every one I find. Once I've covered all the best patches I wander along the beach, picking and eating some fresh, green, goose tongue. I bet deer like goose tongue.

Snug in my dry clothes I flip through an old Backpacker magazine while I eat grilled deer chops. They are incredibly good! I relish every bite until the whole grill-full has disappeared. The rain can't get me. I've got lots of food, food I've harvested myself. It's a good feeling to be in this position six weeks into this adventure.

*What time is it, anyway?* I haven't a clue. There has been no sun to help judge time, just a steady rain. When I pull my watch out I'm amazed that it's already 4:20 in the afternoon. Wow, I wouldn't have been surprised if it was 11 AM!

August 10, Day 42, Sunday

It's raining again today, a steady rain, the kind that adds up to many inches a day. I roll over and turn on the weather radio and listen until it gets to the part that applies to this area:

"...INNER CHANNELS FROM KUPREANOF ISLAND TO ETOLIN ISLAND, INCLUDING... PETERSBURG... WRANGELL... KAKE ISSUED AT 4 PM SATURDAY.

TONIGHT, RAIN, HEAVY AT TIMES, LOWS AROUND 55. SOUTHEAST WINDS 15-25...

SUNDAY, RAIN, HEAVY AT TIMES. HIGHS AROUND 60. SOUTHEAST WINDS 15-25...

MONDAY, RAIN. HIGHS AROUND 64. SOUTHEAST WIND 10 MILES AN HOUR...

FOR TUESDAY AND TUESDAY NIGHT, RAIN. HIGHS AROUND 65, LOWS AROUND 56...

FOR WEDNESDAY AND WEDNESDAY NIGHT, CLOUDY, CHANCE OF RAIN...

FOR THURSDAY AND THURSDAY NIGHT THROUGH FRIDAY NIGHT, RAIN LIKELY...

FOR SATURDAY...CHANCE OF RAIN.

I eat a great breakfast of canned venison then putter around for a while. Finally I suck it up and put on my rain gear and head outside to have a look around. I inspect each jar of canned deer, pushing down the lids one by one, and one by one they are silent until one pushes down with a click and rebounds with a dull "clink." It didn't seal. I pick it up and have a look. It's a jar of scraps/fat. Not a big surprise. For the scraps I took a chance and reused lids to save on my supply of new lids. Used lids, the standard kind anyway, are not dependable. The failure is not really a problem in this case. It was a worthwhile experiment.

At cook camp anything beyond the protection of the tarp is completely and utterly soaked. Good thing the tarp is up or the firewood would be waterlogged by now. Big time. I'm surprised to see gusts of wind have blown some sprinkles of water nearly to the center of the covered area though.

The jug that was catching rainwater is overflowing but full of spruce needles. I'm prepared though. From my rain jacket pocket I pull a head net which I poke down into the mouth of the good jug. I carefully pick up the overflowing jug and begin to pour. At first the cascade is wide and much of the water slops over onto the ground, but soon there is a concentrated, inch-thick stream flowing into the good jug. After pouring I pull out the net and shake out dozens of needles it has trapped. I cap the full jug and hold I up to the sky. Nice and clear! I open the jug valve and fill a canteen that I had in my other coat pocket, giving it a taste. Very good.

I walk down to the water's edge and look across My Cove. It is a very low tide, a minus tide. There are wet rocks out there, draped with kelp, rocks I haven't seen before. It would ruin your day to hit them with a power boat! The rocky point, barely visible at high tide, is now a rampart of dark stone. At the edge of the water it feels like I'm in a shallow bowl. If, somehow, I stood here without moving I'd be deep underwater at high tide.

Walking inland, weaving through wet bushes, I pick some sparse huckleberries, then wander the beach eating what I can find. A beautiful white boat comes cruising up the bay and begins turning into My Cove where they anchor, three hundreds yards out. Hey, this is my cove! They have every right to be here, of course. It's some kind of tourist boat.

There's quite a bit to eat, I'm enjoying ripe thimbleberries, some goose tongue, sea asparagus and even do some munching on bull kelp. Not bad! I look up and notice people on the deck watching me. I wonder what they think. Somebody out here, no boat in sight, they can't even see my camp I'm sure. I'm wandering along, grazing like an upright bear! After a while a bunch of them crawl down a ladder into a Zodiac boat and go roaring off across the bay. I can barely hear the excited chattering of voices over the engine and the slap of water on the boat. Good for them, cheerful despite the rain. Probably helps to come back to heated rooms in a couple of hours! They must be seeing a ton of whales, some bears, too, no doubt; eagles, mountains, lots of cool stuff.

Outside the tent I notice an empty jar with three inches of rain in it, all fell in the last forty hours or so. It's a narrow mouth jar, too, so it must have rained at least four inches, probably more. And it's still coming down.

It's great to get out of the rain and into camp clothes. I sit on my camp chair, warm and dry, eating canned venison and reading *Gone With The Wind*.

With all this damp air, it's time to do some gun cleaning again. What is this, the fourth time? A buddy of mine goes for years without cleaning his rifle! Climate and salt make a big, big difference.

August 11, Day 43

It's raining again, as predicted. Listening to the rain on the tent fly I ponder my day's plan. From my shirt pocket I pull the tide table booklet. It looks like the next low tide today, August 11 is... 8:09 AM. It's a minus tide too, -4.1 feet. Scanning ahead I see that this will be the lowest tide for the rest of the trip. Some fresh crab meat would be great. I'll look for crabs in the low water near the mouth of My Creek.

It's foggy. Somewhere out on the Sound, the low moan of a fog horn rolls over the water. I get geared up and launch the kayak. I'm early so I've brought my halibut rod along and jig over the Hump without success. Just before 8 AM I near the mouth of My Creek. Little Island and Big Island, straddling My Creek, loom dark in the fog. There are bald eagles everywhere. They must be after fish heading upstream. Several mature eagles are on the shore at the mouth, some on the gravel, some perched on rocks, along with scores of seagulls, ravens and crows. All watch the water for fish, live salmon, dead salmon, or whatever else may come their way. Periodically, one stabs at the water with its beak, sometimes successfully, other times not. It is a cacophony of bird calls mixed with the sound of water rushing over the gravel bars at the mouth of the rain-swollen creek. More eagles are perched in the trees and soaring overhead. I lift up my binoculars to make a rough count. I can see twenty five bald eagles at once! I'm sure there are more that I can't see in the fog. Wow, that's pretty cool.

After securing my kayak I grab the landing net and wade thigh deep, peering down into the clear water. Back and forth I wander. The bottom is covered with shells and starfish and other sea life, but I don't see a single crab. Tiny, silvery fish run up the little rivulets pouring into the bay where My Creek fans out. That's likely what's drawing most of the bird life. If I were starving I could be catching many of these three inch fish with my bare hands. They panic in the shallow water and some partially beach themselves. I'm surprised there aren't gulls right here. Presumably they are doing fine where they are. Another unusual observation is that I spook several small halibut or flounder in shallow water. They are likely after the small mystery fish as well.

Perhaps the water is too fresh here now, with My Creek in flood stage. In any case all the crabs are MIA. The tide is so low there is an unusual amount of colorful sea life visible. I begin gathering some of it into a shallow pool so I can take a photo. There is a large, pinkish-purple multi-armed starfish, smaller, more muted ones as well. There are five-armed, four-armed, even three-armed starfish: orange, tan, brown, green and reddish. There is an empty Dungeness crab shell. You'd never know it was empty, turned right-side up. There are black mussels and butter clams and brown, delicately ribbed cockles. I arrange them into an interesting pattern of shapes and colors and take several photos.

One of the tiny, multi-armed starfish keeps sneaking away to hide under seaweed. Obviously, it's concerned about predators, but most of these starfish must not be very good eating to most predators or they would be easy prey.

The trap holds a single crab. I can usually tell if they are legal, but this one fools me. He falls just shy of the mark. I add some deer fat to a bait cage. Supposedly fat is good bait. Guess this will be a good test.

Although it's been raining, the no-see-ums are swarming during any slight lull. They have become quite annoying. Since it was raining and I was wearing my rain jacket hood, I'd left my hat with its "Foreign Legion" bandana in the tent. Bad move today. For me that is-the bugs love it. I paddle for home to escape the rain and no-see-ums.

Back home and in dry clothes I enjoy some of that fine, salt-and-peppered venison. I hear a "shot" in the distance and realize it's a whale somewhere in the fog. Lying back on my cot I read *Gone With The Wind*.

It transports me one hundred fifty years back in time, and four thousand miles away, to the hot, dusty city of Atlanta at war.

In early afternoon, I realize the rain has stopped. Good news! I'm going to give halibut fishing a shot again. The Hump is usually easy to find, being seventy-five yards off a low, rocky island. Now though, near high tide, the island is completely submerged. With my iPhone I navigate to the right spot and try my luck. It's much harder to stay oriented without the easy reference of the island. The Nautical Chart map is still a great tool, though. The main problem is my inexperience using it.

Taking a break from halibut fishing I check out the berry patches at Big Island. Starting at one end, I do my best to eat every ripe thimbleberry as I go. This is what I call "local foods." I pop them directly in my mouth. Thimbleberries still rank #1 on this trip on the berry/deliciousness scale. I pick around the corner, down the length of the island, and part way across the other end until the bushes disappear. I'm surprised at how many more I find on the way back, seeing the bushes from another angle or just noticing berries I'd somehow overlooked. The sun is visible through the clouds as a round glow. It even peeks through briefly before disappearing again.

The falling tide has exposed the rocky island near my halibut spot. Using it as a guide, I paddle upwind of the Hump and drift over it, allowing the jig to flutter down until I feel the dull thump of the bottom, then lifting it three or four feet before letting it flutter back down. *There's a bite!* But no hookup.

I'm about ready to leave when I get another bite. Seems like I usually get those bites right near where I hooked "The Big One." My reel handle is about ready to fall off. The spring pin holding it on has fallen out. I have to hold the handle in place when I reel. When I finally reel up the heavy jig I find it is covered with teeth marks and the tail has been bitten completely off! I've proven I'm no halibut fishing expert, but that must have been the work of a halibut. Sooner or later I'm going to land one. For now I'm heading home.

Back in the tent I study my reel handle trying to figure out a way to hold it securely in place. The spring pin is long gone and of course I don't have a replacement. How about wire? I have some about the right diameter, but it's pretty soft. I think it would wear out too fast. In my repair kit is a little "possibles bag," a Ziploc with tiny wire, tacks, bobby pins, safety pins, small screws, zip ties, super glue, a P-38, rubber bands, and more. From it I select a nail of about the right diameter. It fits perfectly. There's enough sticking out that I bend it over using my little vice-grip, then I tape over it with duct tape to smooth it out. That will last as long as the reel!

# CHAPTER 21

## Halibut!

August 12, Day 44

It's another gray, damp day, but at least it's not pouring. Outside the tent I take a look at my shotgun leaning against a tree, protected from rain by the thick canopy. My theory was that the humidity might be lower outside the tent, and the gun would "breathe" better so maybe it wouldn't rust. My theory is wrong. It's thoroughly sprinkled with rust. The humidity is high enough apparently, and I'm sure the salt air must be a big factor. I bring it into the tent and wipe it down with an oily rag.

I launch the kayak at about 7:45 in pursuit of halibut. It's only an hour until low tide so I see the rocks near the Hump. I paddle into position where I hooked the big halibut and got some bites before.

The good spot is on the down-bay side of the Hump. As I drift over it, jigging with four-foot bounces, I feel something and try setting the hook. It's on! A sculpin, no doubt. But this is bigger. I got a small halibut! I pull and reel several times, gaining fifteen feet or so, but then the fish makes a powerful dive for the bottom. Maybe it's not so small!

He's strong, that's for sure. Good thing I fixed the reel handle. I'm slowly gaining line, glancing down into the water, trying to get a look at him. Thirty minutes have gone by when I spot the white flash of his belly. It's a nice fish. I want desperately to land him. All of a sudden he heads for the bottom and all I can do is hang on with the drag screaming. I thought he was getting tired but he's not even close.

The rod is tied to the boat, a wise precaution, I think. The lanyard isn't giving me enough slack, though, so I retie it in front of me. The fight goes on. The dramatic arch of the heavy rod makes me smile. It takes a big fish to do that. I feel good about the strength of my knots this time, I double checked them. If I lose this fish, it will be while landing him. My plan is to get him good and tired while he's still in deep water, then slash his gills, waiting until he's bled out and dead, or nearly so, before landing him. I practice how I'm going to do it in my mind. I'll hold the rod in my left hand. With the fillet knife in my right hand I'll reach under a gill cover and cut across all the gills on that side. That should do it. I hope! I'll have to be super careful not to touch the line with the knife blade. If it touches the taut line, the fish will be gone. I'll try to keep the dull edge facing towards the line. I'll try to cut the gills in one quick slice, and be prepared for a violent response!

Fifteen minutes later he's back near the top. Experts say not to lift their head out of the water. That makes them go berserk. With the rod in my left hand I ready the knife and wait my chance. When it comes I aim and make a quick slash. He thrashes wildly, spraying water in all directions. Cold water runs down my neck. I make another cut and a third. Blood swirls in the water around his head. It's really hard to get a good cut with him thrashing around like that but I got him pretty good. Seems like he's bleeding enough that he'll weaken fast.

He's got plenty of fight left in him, though. He's still making some violent splashes. It would be easy to lose him yet. That would *really* be a bummer now that his gills are cut. I can see red clouds of blood around his head. Patience should do it. Don't force it. Give him more time. I glance at my watch. I'll give him ten more minutes, until 9:30.

When it's time, I pull him to the kayak, lift one gill cover up, and slash full across the gills. He thrashes, but less violently. I lift the other gill cover and cut the other side. Now he's really bleeding. A few minutes go by. I pull him towards the boat to see how much life is left.

Amazingly, he still is able to strip some line. How is that possible?! I'd been thinking I'd drag him in the boat when he's dead, but pulling him in while he can still thrash would be a really bad move, with big hooks and knife blade and heavy fish in a small, inflatable boat. I'll leave him in the water. Drag him to shore that way.

After giving him a bunch more time I grab one of his gill covers. There's almost nothing left in him. How can I tie him to the boat? The crab caliper cord. After losing the other halibut I'm still anxious about losing this one at the last minute. I untie the cord, lift the halibut's head and drop one end of the cord into his mouth and pull it out through the gills. Keeping tension on the rod I run the cord through the boat handle on the stern, then tie the ends together, double and triple knotting it. He's mine. I got him!

It's much harder paddling to camp with the big fish swinging from side to side, throwing off the track of my boat and causing a surprising amount of drag. I keep looking back into the water to make sure he's tied securely. Finally the bow of the kayak crunches ashore and I hop out. I grab one gill cover then untie him, hustling him up the beach. He's heavy! I flop him belly down on the gravelly shore. I did it! I got him! *I got my big halibut!* I'm elated and triumphant.

What a beautiful, strange fish. His right side is his top side, a beautiful mottled grayish-brown, with both eyes on this one side. His left side is his bottom side, smooth and a standard fish-belly white. I take a photo of my prize lying on the shore, with my rod and the huge jig and a Swiss Army knife for scale. How big is he, anyway? There is a length-to-weight chart in one of my books. Securing everything well above the water I fetch the chart and a cloth tape. He's forty-eight inches long. Four feet! I run my finger down the column of numbers until I reach 48 inches. Fifty three pounds! Nice! Wow, the one I lost must have weighed somewhere around a hundred pounds! I am absolutely and totally delighted with this one. I will barely have enough empty jars the way it is, if in fact I do.

I set up a camera tripod and take several shots of me holding my prize up. One photo is against the greens of spruce and thimbleberry,

another faced across Wild Bay with low clouds drifting against the mountains. They turn out great. In the photos the big halibut stretches from my lower shins to my chin. In the water fish look smaller than they are, to me anyway. Now, in the photos, he looks even bigger than he is.

With an empty bucket I wander around base camp and cook camp and gather up all my empty jars. That includes the jars I've been using for storage of miscellaneous supplies. I even empty the canned deer scraps out. At the edge of the water I scrub all the jars. It sure would be nice to have a bottle brush and some dishwashing liquid. It's a chore scrubbing the deer fat out. When I'm done I have fourteen jars. Upon close inspection I find the lips of two jars are chipped. One might still work, one definitely won't. Will I have enough? Maybe. It will be close.

The sun was peeking out a bit, but now it's out enough that I'm going to take advantage of it for drying and charging. I lay out the solar panels on a couple of boulders, then invert my sleeping bag and waders and hang them on the dead branches of a beach log. The tide book shows it's almost high tide so things near the water should be safe.

So what's the best way to fillet my halibut? What can I use for a table? The bottom of the kayak should work. I carry my kayak to the high water mark and flip it over. It's a little low, but it's a wide, fairly flat surface. If I can keep the halibut from sliding off it should work well.

I've never filleted a halibut before. This should be interesting! I find it works pretty well to slide the fillet knife under the skin and hold the right pressure and angle for the knife to follow the edge of the skin. I quickly pull off big sheets of skin, wasting almost no meat. Cool! With the top side all skinned, I slice down to the backbone then follow the bones all the way out to the edges. I end up with huge, boneless chunks of white meat. *Awesome!* Obviously, these steaks are too big to go in the jars, so I slice them into strips and pack the jars tightly to within an inch of the top. With the whole top filleted, I cut out the cheek meat. I've got almost six jars of boneless meat!

Now that I have a little experience, the bottom half goes even better. Stepping around the kayak I notice seawater creeping up nearly to my feet. It was at least fifty feet out when I started! What the heck! I sprint over to the solar panels. They are mighty close to the water. I move them above the high tide mark. The sleeping bag and waders are still good, but over the water, so I move them as well in case a gust blows them off the dead branches. Hustling back to the boat I move the empty jars so they don't float away, one has just started floating! I don't get it. It should have been high tide an hour ago. I check the tide table again. No wonder! I looked at JULY 12. That day had a three foot lower tide, an hour earlier! Today is 19.6 high tide, coming up in a few minutes, one of the highest of the whole trip. That kind of mistake can be expensive. No wonder the tide is pushing me up to the trees! Before full high tide I have to move the jars again.

When I'm finished, eleven jars are maxed out and I've filled the grill with halibut steaks. With the two chipped jars, there is only one jar left! That was close. I walk up to the tent and get a box of new jar lids. One by one, I wipe down the lip of the jars, put on the lid, and screw the ring on.

Flipping the kayak over so it's half in the water I load up the jars, the camp chair, the canner lid and other supplies and paddle to cook camp. It's turned out to be a nice day. Much more fun doing all this on a mostly sunny day rather than a pounding rain!

The canning operation is a familiar routine now. All eleven jars will fit in one batch so that will save a ton of time.

When my watch shows the jars have cooked long enough I pull the canner off the stove and set the grill full of halibut steaks on top. I put on a leather glove, open the lid, and pull all the jars out to cool.

The grilling halibut smells great! At first I can see the glow of the fire through the meat, but as it cooks the meat grows opaque. I flip it over and lay a piece of foil on top so the heat fans out and cooks the edges better. The bottom half has browned slightly. This is a good way to do it, taking advantage of the perfect coals that would go to waste otherwise. I slide the grill around a bit because it's bigger than the opening on the stove. I lift up the foil and poke at the meat with a fork. It flakes nicely. I set the grill on the wood pile, flip up the top half and spear a small piece of halibut, salting it lightly. Holding it up I blow on it then try to take a bite but it's still too hot. My mouth is watering. I take a small bite in my teeth, blow on it and the chew. It's crispy, and firm, and delicious. My long struggle to land a halibut makes it doubly good, and the wonderful new taste and texture makes it even better. It's so different than any of the foods I've eaten so far!

When I've eaten my fill I load nine of the still-warm jars in an empty jar-box, then, using the block and tackle, haul the cache fifteen feet up in the tree, saving some jars for short term use. I am incredibly happy and satisfied to have this big supply of halibut and deer meat. Now I *really* have variety. Hopefully there will be no disasters, like the cache rope breaking, a bear going after the tied-off rope, or me letting the rope slip through my fingers. I'll be careful.

August 13, Day 45

I've been out here a month and a half! This area, once a mysterious, unknown place on a map, has become my home and backyard.

It's raining pretty steadily again today. I'm going to hang out for a while and see what happens. Breakfast is an easy choice, there's half a grill of halibut steaks. Boy, does that hit the spot!

The shotgun is speckled with rust again. Amazing. Even the stock is trying to mold. Sitting in the camp chair I take the gun apart and go over it thoroughly, scrubbing the worst spots with the bronze bore brush. The whole gun is glistening with oil when I finish. I set it down, careful not to touch any metal with my hands.

I go through my box of reading stuff and read an article about the attack on the Japanese base of Rabaul during World War II. It's dramatic stuff. Many Japanese leaders had thought that war with the U.S. was inevitable, and that they would win. Of course, none of that was true. What a lot of death and suffering could have been prevented on both sides if all that effort and money had gone to good rather than destruction! Later I'm reading *Gone With the Wind*. It shows that Americans start destructive wars as well.

In the afternoon I paddle for My Creek to catch the 3:58 high tide. Salmon tend to enter creeks and rivers at high tides so I'm hoping to see salmon going over the two tiny falls. I'm early so I land at Big Island to pick thimbleberries. It's my best berry spot of all right now. All the berries are on one side of the island, so I pick the length of that area and then back to the boat. Many berries that were too green only two days ago are perfectly ripe already.

The tide is near the trees on the mainland near My Creek when I beach the kayak. It's another very high tide. The tiny falls I was looking for are inundated, I should have anticipated that I guess. I haven't checked this stretch of shore very carefully for berries before, so I explore the edges of the forest where thimbleberries like to grow, finding some good but smaller patches. I work my way along in the rain, picking and eating blue currants as well as thimbleberries. My hands are getting stiff in the steady, cold rain. That's got to be my biggest physical weakness, my bare hands getting stiff in wet, chilly conditions like this. The day I finished the Pacific Crest Trail I came to the metal monument marking the end of the trail at the Canadian border. It was an emotional moment after walking all the way from Mexico. Like most hikers, I'd been thinking about what I'd write in the final hiker register, hidden there in the monument, a message to my trail friends, meaningful thoughts on the experience of hiking that long, beautiful trail. But when the time came, my hands refused to cooperate. Instead of writing what I wanted to express, I managed only a few, cramped, marginally legible words. It was frustrating and humbling.

Today, though, I manage to get my berries, then put on my neoprene gloves, nice to have in conditions like this. My lower arms are wet. Water ran up my rain jacket sleeves while I was picking. At least I was smart enough to roll up my shirt sleeves to keep them dry. Walking will warm me up. I follow a game trail through big timber, just inside the treeline, the only sound the light thud of my footsteps and dripping rain. What's this? A bear skeleton! Not something a person finds very often. The skull is gone. I wonder if someone found it and kept it, or if this bear might have been killed by a hunter sometime back?

I walk down to My Creek where the fresh water runs into the first brackish pool. There are many dead jellyfish on the bottom, white and ghostly. Countless pink salmon mill about or hold steady in the current, heads upstream. Only one chum salmon is visible, two or three times as big as the pinks. He cruises through the school like a bomber plane amidst fighters.

For the first time on this trip I do some fishing purely for sport. Of course, since I don't care if I catch any, they are in a biting mood. Most salmon I've caught on this trip have been male, but today each one I land is a female. I release them all. The first few "beat-up" salmon of the season are now visible, fish whose bodies have started to decay at the end of their spawning journey. Time is passing. The seasons are changing.

I retrieve the kayak. The tide has already fallen several feet. Most of the commercial crabber buoys are gone. Commercial crabbing season ends in two days. Crab boats haven't been a big issue, but they have accounted for most of the light boat traffic I've seen. It will be nice when it's even quieter out here. How big of an impact did they have on my crab trapping success? The crab size limits are a great idea. Crabbing definitely has an impact on the biggest crabs, but it seems like the crab population in general holds up very well.

The trap holds two crabs. The smaller one, exceptionally aggressive, grabs my finger through the trap grid. I easily shake it off then reach in, pull it out, and drop it into the ocean. The other one is easily legal. There's my supper. I fill one of the bait cages with halibut skin. Seems like one bait cage full of deer fat and the other full of halibut skin should be a real one-two punch of nuclear-good crab bait. I drop the trap back overboard, taking careful note of where it is in relation to Big Island and a rock outcropping.

There's a stiff wind to battle heading back home. As usual, the big trees help me out by blocking the wind when I approach camp. Their shelter reaches surprisingly far out onto the cove.

I cook up the crab. It's great. Every single crab is exquisite. It's been days since I caught a legal crab. It will be interesting to see if I catch more once the crab boats are completely gone.

Back at camp I peel off my waders. The inside of the seat looks wet. I feel my butt. It's damp as well. Oh-oh. A small wader leak. Looking them over it's clear there isn't a hole, it isn't a failing seam, it's simply a slow breakdown of materials. They are slowly becoming delaminated. Waders are a critical piece of gear. I really don't want to have a wet butt every time I use the boat. It won't kill me though. I'll think about some workarounds.

This evening, they are predicting "mostly cloudy, chance of rain" for tomorrow. This morning they predicted the same, but it's rained almost all day without a hint of blue sky. I'm going to go out on a limb and say that it WILL rain tomorrow.

I didn't eat any "jar food" today, only the grilled halibut, fresh-picked berries and fresh crab with goose tongue and sea asparagus.

August 14, Day 46

My prediction of rain was correct. I believe it's rained pretty much steadily since sometime early yesterday. That's why they call it rain forest. I'd been thinking of making a trip to the lodge today but it's not going to happen. That's one advantage of being out here alone: I don't have to run the idea past someone, no need to reach a consensus. I decide not to go? Done! After listening to the weather, I will shoot for Saturday instead.

It's venison for breakfast. No hurry to head afield today, no need, so I putter around the tent. I do a lot of reading, including an article about "The Winter War," when the Finns fought the Russians at the onset of World War II, making a courageous but doomed stand. Often they used skis for fast, surprise, hit-and-run fighting, draped in over-white clothing so they would disappear against the white snow. It's hard to imagine the horror of fighting in extreme cold. It helps me to keep roughing it out here in perspective.

It's good to get out and be physically active, even when it isn't strictly necessary. A berry-picking foray makes the most sense. At about 1:30 I launch the kayak. It's one of the calmest days I've seen. The bay is glassy smooth. Low clouds drift across the dark green mountains and water dogs curl over the islands.

A sea lion startles me by exhaling right behind me! It always gets the heart pumping to have a huge animal appear unexpectedly just a few feet away, especially an animal with big teeth! He sinks away to get on with his business.

Although I'm headed to pick berries at the Knob, one of the best patches around, I decide to check out Small Island. I noticed some thimbleberry bushes there before any were ripe. When I land I find there are ripe berries galore! I pick and eat my way around the edges of the main patch, then thread my way through openings to get more. With that patch exhausted I pick my way around the whole island. As I round the corner I hear a boat engine and soon see a crab boat pulling up the last of the commercial traps. I am master crabber of the upper bay now! Three quarters of the way around the island there is a small patch of ripe black currants, but not for long. I eat all that I can find.

I paddle out to my crab trap. Its red and white buoy is easy to spot now, the only buoy in calm water. Apparently the halibut skin worked. There are two crabs, one a bit too small and the other an unusually big one. Even on this "day off" I've managed to harvest considerable wild foods.

After starting the stove I experiment a bit with feeding it wood. I try using three one-inch-thick pieces laid parallel to each other. That's worked pretty well once there is a boil and the stove is full of hot coals, but I find it's smarter to use more wood until things are boiling well.

The steaming crab meat is, as usual, wonderful. Crabbing has really added to the enjoyment of this trip, as well as to the calorie count. I eat goose tongue as a side salad.

August 15, Day 47

In the pre-dawn darkness, there is a giant, crashing splash in the distance. A jumping whale, no doubt. I listen for a while but don't hear it again. When I reawaken, seagulls are calling and eagles are chattering but something is missing-the sound of rain on my tent. Good news!

After breakfast I walk a considerable distance down the shore, the opposite direction from cook camp, looking for berries. It's sparse picking but I get a few thimbleberries and currants. Next I cover the good patches near camp. There are more berries here, but it's clear that it is past the peak for ripening berries.

I walk down to cook camp to look for my wader belt and, as expected, find it on the wood pile under the tarp. A while back I'd found some mysterious berries that looked remarkably like blueberries or huckleberries, except they were red. I found them in a guidebook. They are red huckleberries! I'd never heard of such a thing before this trip. Here though, I notice a few bushes sprinkled with them. They aren't as sweet as the best blueberries, but one thing I notice is that there are no "clunkers." All of them are pretty good.

It's started to rain and if anything it keeps coming down harder. I'm going to go hunker in my tent and see what happens. On the way back I graze a bit on goose tongue and sea asparagus. A mink comes scampering by. "My mink," likely. I was wondering about him. He's been missing for awhile.

Safely back in the tent I enjoy some salt-and-peppered venison. Venison is definitely NOT going to get tiresome on this trip!

I lie back on the cot, warm and dry, head propped up, reading.

Taking a break from my book, I organize the tent. More mold is already growing on the shotgun stock! Maintenance is definitely an ongoing chore. It sure is nice being able to stand fully upright in this tent, but there is some faint, funky smell. What is it, dirty socks? I found a leg here from one of the baby crows that were hanging around when I first arrived. A hawk or something must have killed it. Perhaps the second leg is spoiling here somewhere. Whatever it is, I can't pinpoint the source.

The weather radio is calling for mostly cloudy tomorrow with no rain. I'll head to the lodge if it's reasonably calm and not pouring. I haven't posted an update since the 1st. I don't want to worry people. I pull out my iPhone and plunk away at a journal update, one that I can cut and paste when I get there. It's nice to be able to write now, unhurried.

I try the scanner function on the weather radio's shortwave band. I'm surprised to pick up a few stations here and there, mostly in foreign languages. I recognize what sounds like Chinese, Russian, Spanish and exotic music of various kinds, not many toe-tappers to my ear. I pick up the BBC briefly but there is static and the signal is weak. I'm not sure I want to hear the news anyway.

August 16, Day 48

It's a nice morning! I'm headed to the lodge. I launch about 6 AM. The sky above is mostly clear but there is heavy fog out towards the main Sound.

Halfway to the lodge I stop and look for berries around one of my spike camps where I've found berries before. There were a few stray salmonberries here before, there are none now. There are some unusually big and sweet blueberries on an especially high bush, though. They become my breakfast.

I wander along the beach. There are no thimbleberries here at all, but numerous currants, including nice bunches of gray-blue "blue currants." If I didn't know better, I'd be afraid to eat them. They look too much like white baneberries, My guidebook says that many people call these skunk currants or stink currants. It's the crushed leaves that are the primary basis for those names. I crush a leaf and give it a sniff. It doesn't smell like a skunk but it does smell weird. If the berries tasted like that no one would eat them. Apparently the taste of the berries varies dramatically, from fairly sweet to quite bitter. I eat several handfuls. They are fairly sweet but have a strange aftertaste. That's probably why they are usually used for jams and pies and things like that. Nearby are similar clumps of shiny black currants. These are better, sweeter and without the funny aftertaste. They are still not as good as the closely related gooseberries that I remember eating as a kid.

I pull out my watch and am surprised to see it's 8 AM. Time to get going. Out in the bay I paddle from calm sunlight towards a wall of fog.

A minute after entering it all the familiar landmarks have disappeared. Things look identical in every direction. I know that if I keep paddling with no references I'll soon veer off and might end up paddling in circles. My iPhone is in a waterproof case hanging from a lanyard around my neck. I fire it up and start the nautical charts app. Once it gets a fix I use it to beeline to my usual shortcut between the mainland and island. Paddling quietly across the smooth water is fun, it feels like gliding through a dense cloud.

A dark, ghostly shape appears ahead and to my right. It's big trees on the shore. They soon disappear but a few minutes later I see more dark trees loom to my left, and then more off to my right. I'm in the right spot! With landmarks to guide me I head towards the portage. It's near low tide, but it's still an easy portage. I shuttle the gear across trying to avoid crushing living sea creatures.

The fog is lifting and the lodge appears ahead. A couple of young guys attend to the chores down around the dock. Up on the cabin walkway two cleaning girls stop, brooms and vacuum cleaners in hand, and watch me approach.

On the dock I run across one of the dock hands.

"Hey, that's quite a beard you've got going there!" he says.

"You too, how's your summer been?"

"Awesome."

"So what's been good, what's the stories you'll tell when you get back home?"

"Well, it sounds funny, but one story is when a water bottle got sucked into our water line. Me and the other guys spent hours digging, trying to find out where it was. It was actually pretty funny." He goes on to tell other stories of fishing and other adventures, but his story of yucking it up with his buddies working on the water line was one of his best memories.

After stowing my gear and changing into shoes I stop by the lodge office to talk to the owners.

"How's it going out there?" Scott asks.

"It's going really good," I say. "I got my buck. I finally got a nice halibut too. How are things here? How's fishing?"

"It's been a good summer. We've gotten some nice halibut."

"How do you land those monster halibut?"

"If we are going to keep them, we harpoon them." He goes on to explain how they harpoon them through the gills with a detachable harpoon head attached to a big float.

"Sounds like a good idea."

Before I leave they mention the first bit of news from the outside world that I've heard since I got out here: Robin Williams died from suicide.

I'm over at the main lodge working on my website journal update when Anna comes through the door.

"Hi Bruce!"

"Hi Anna. Are you still having fun out here?"

"Yes! Hey, you've got to check out this panorama picture." She proudly shows me her smartphone. There's a beautiful photo of the lodge and mountains and cove. Her positive attitude and enthusiasm make me smile.

I'm glad I have pre-written my update. I just cut and paste it to my site. I skim through my email and answer one quick business email, one old friend's email, and verify with my air taxi the September 8 pickup date.

One of the emails is surprising. It's a stranger lambasting me for the whole trip. He strongly feels that what I'm doing is easy, questioning what exactly I'm trying to prove and asking how I can justify the purchase of my gear and the fossil fuels required to fly here and back home. I could be a good influence, he says, but instead I'm being a bad influence on people.

Why would a person feel compelled to reach out here with all that negativity? It makes me angry and defensive and I begin to consider my response, how I'm going for ten weeks without using ANY fossil fuels, how I'm eating 100 per cent local foods and not buying anything the whole time I'm out here. But of course a response is a complete waste of time. I won't respond at all. I delete it but, knowing myself, I'll mull it over for a while anyway.

As I leave the lodge I decide to take the slightly longer way home. I'm soon swallowed by fog again. This time, though, I catch occasional glimpses of sun or shore to help keep me on track. Still, many times I find I'm veering significantly off course. Somewhere in the fog a whale blows. It's otherworldly out here. Halfway home the fog starts to clear and with the assistance of a slight tailwind I beeline for camp.

It's nice to have the lodge trip completed and my update posted. It's the one outside world obligation I have. The sun is bright and warm now, although there is still a fog bank out towards the Sound. I lay out the solar panels and hang up everything to dry: sleeping bag, waders, rain gear, camp shoes. Seeing things drying in the sunny breeze always makes me happy. Sun is the enemy of rust and mold and bad morale. As everything dries I eat half a jar of salmon, salted and peppered, while reading a book. As the afternoon progresses, a shadow falls across the tent. Outside I see clouds are rolling in. Rain clouds. I hustle around, gathering up the now crinkly-dry gear and the solar panels. Just as I finish it starts to rain. Good timing!

The weather radio is predicting heavy rain tomorrow. That's when I was going to check the crab trap, but I think I'll check it this afternoon to avoid the rain.

The lone crab trap buoy is easy to spot. When the slack is out of the rope it feels heavy. When I swing it into the kayak it is loaded with crabs. Nine! My best catch ever! Is it the commercial crab boats being gone, or just chance? And five of them are legal!

When I get back to camp I realize the day is getting late. I was going to fire up the canner but I don't want to be canning into the night. Plan B, the one I'm going with, is boiling them all up, pigging out tonight, then eating cold crab meat tomorrow.

Out in Wild Bay I notice a large, strange object moving slowly along. It reminds me of similar sights I've seen on Alaska rivers, sights that turned out to be antlers of huge bull caribou swimming across. No caribou here, though. I run into the tent and grab the binos. When things are in focus it turns out to be a huge tree floating with the tide, it's branches sticking into the air. That's a new one on this trip! I wonder where it started out? You never know what the tide will bring in. One of the most unusual things that ever happened to me was during the first time I saw the Pacific Ocean. I lived in Minnesota at the time. A fellow Minnesotan and I, working as firefighters in Oregon, had driven to the coast. When we walked down the beach, there was a bottle sticking out of the sand.

"See if there's a note in it!" I joked. He nudged it out with a gentle kick.

"There is! There's a note inside!" I thought he was kidding, but he was right. It had been thrown in the ocean down the coast somewhere by someone studying currents.

I've finished cleaning all the crabs. I throw them in the canner and cover them with water. Rain hammers on the cook camp tarp and beaded curtains of water stream to the ground all around. Safely underneath I tend the fire while the crabs boil. When they are done I eat slowly, enjoying every bite until I'm comfortably full, then carry the rest of the crabs, unshelled, back to camp for tomorrow.

It was another big day with many miles of paddling. It's good to relax. I munch on a few thimbleberries for dessert while I finish *Gone With the Wind*. It sure tied up a lot of loose ends in the last few pages! It was good. I'm glad I read it after all these years.

They are still calling for heavy rains tomorrow, but the report also includes several days of mostly sunny or partly sunny days in the next weeks. That's great news!

August 17, Day 49

It's raining hard this morning and windy. It's nice to have a pee bottle so I don't have to go out in the cold, wind-driven rain! I'm back snuggled in my warm sleeping bag, listening to the rain on the tent and waves rolling ashore. I look up to where I've covered the stove pipe port hole with a piece of clear plastic, watching the raindrops splatter and trickle onto the tent fly. Funny how I haven't used the tent wood stove at all yet.

The sound of a boat motor barely rises over the noisy wind and waves. Who is out on these rough waters so early? Suddenly there's a horrible scraping noise. It makes me cringe. They must have hit a rock. No sign that they got themselves in trouble, though. Must have got their attention!

Breakfast is an easy choice. It's all-I-can-eat crab, and I can eat a lot. Two full crabs vanish.

It's a bad day to be out on the water but a great day for reading. I read several articles from an old *World War II Magazine*, an article about how a German general defied Hitler's orders and refused to destroy Paris as they retreated. That took courage! Another interesting article is about the Bushmasters, an Arizona National Guard unit that was involved in heavy fighting against the Japanese in the Pacific. Regular people, on both sides, forced into nightmarish situations.

Mid-morning I don my rain gear for a foray outside. It's wild weather out here! There are big waves, the sea is the roughest I've seen it this trip. Strong winds sweep the tops of frothing whitecaps. You couldn't pay me enough to get me to paddle across Wild Bay right now.

It's another day where I'm mighty thankful for the latrine tarp! Cook camp is still secure. Anything not near the center of the tarp is soaked. Fortunately, that's where the wood is. On a nice day I should store a bunch of perfect kindling and dry paper in a sealed bucket. The fine kindling under the tarp is soaking up moisture directly from the air on a day like this.

It's great to have a big supply of food so I can hunker out of the rain. I pick up a new book, *Bear Man of Admiralty Island*. It is interesting to read while here on the island. The bear man's real name was Allen E. Hasselborg. Both of us from Chisago County, Minnesota, both ended up here on Admiralty Island. But I'm here for ten weeks. He was here for decades. The book is an interesting insight into the life of this hermit, hunter and amateur naturalist. Imagine the hard-earned knowledge he gathered in all those decades of observing the weather, the ocean, the land, plants, and wildlife.

What is today, the 49th day? I've been out here for seven weeks. That means, assuming the weather cooperates and the plane gets here on time, I have twenty-one more full days out here. Three weeks!

# CHAPTER 22

## Brown Bear

August 18, Day 50

After a venison breakfast I paddle to My Creek to hit a high tide of only 14.3 feet, predicted for 8:22. High tides on this expedition have been running from just over 11 feet to nearly 20 feet. I want to check the two tiny falls on My Creek again and hopefully see salmon jumping them. Last time the falls were flooded but now they are above the tide. I watch them for a while but don't see any fish coming through.

I walk upstream with my fly rod in hand. Above the falls, the clear pools are loaded with countless pink salmon, a few much bigger chums swimming among them. Movement catches my eye and I glance up to see a brown bear coming around the corner a stone's throw away! He's looking at all the salmon but then glances up, directly into my eyes. It's a thrilling, tense moment. The wind swirls and he smells me. His nerve breaks almost immediately. He whirls and runs around the corner. I didn't even have time to grab my camera. There was true magic in that moment, to stand so near a giant, wild predator. It was sudden, unexpected, unscripted, dramatic.

Out on a gravel bar I make several false casts, then shoot the line out, across and upstream. The purple egg-sucking leech sinks for bit, then pulses during each slow and short stripping of the line. I don't see the take, but the fly disappears and the line tightens. I set the hook and my fish races upstream then turns and charges back downstream and past me as I lift the rod tip and frantically strip line. I manage to stop him before he gets to the little falls. After several more strong runs he tires, a nice big male pink salmon. I release him in the shallows without taking him out of the water.

It's fun and relaxed fishing, with no pressure to catch one or any need to hurry back to camp to preserve my catch. I can just enjoy being out here, seeing the school of fish and hearing the swish of the fly line, waiting for the strike, feeling the take and the living fish on the end of the taut line. Today, every fish I catch is a male pink salmon in good condition.

I make the short walk to the Knob and enjoy a batch of thimbleberries and the most black currants I've eaten yet. Canada geese are honking, the wild sound leading my gaze to a small flock feeding out on the tidal flats. More and more geese are showing up, mallards as well. Seeing the geese and ducks triggers the predator in me. When I see a flock near the trees I think about how I could sneak through the trees, then belly-crawl to the edge of the brushy forest edge until I spotted the nearby birds. I'd suddenly jump to my feet. The geese would launch with wild, excited honking. I'd swing my shotgun barrel ahead of a giant black and white head and pull the trigger, the shot pattern making a clean kill, the huge bird landing with a thud.

I graze the thimbleberry bushes of Big Island next. Thimbleberries are waning back near camp but they are still plentiful here. It sprinkles off and on, but so far the rain hasn't amounted to anything.

The day has been fairly calm but a breeze arises as I paddle out to the crab trap. It holds three crabs, all too small by the looks of them. I'm surprised to see the first two are female crabs. Although I netted a female a while back, these are the first females I've trapped in the fifty days I've been out here.

Back at camp I carry the kayak to stash above high tide and notice some deer across the cove. Through my binos I see it's a doe and two fawns. Good thing I got that buck. I don't think I've seen an antler since.

The sun comes out. I open both tent flaps wide and let the breeze blow into the tent. I lie back on my cot, hands behind my head, absentmindedly watching branch shadows wave on the sun-dappled tent-fly above me.

Tonight's weather forecast elevates my already good mood. There is no serious rain predicted over the next week! For Wednesday they are predicting "Sunny." Not partially sunny or mostly sunny but flat-out sunny! I think that is unprecedented on this trip. Tomorrow's also supposed to be nice. I'll do laundry and take a bath. Gather some firewood, too.

Before sleep I finish reading *The Trail Life*, a book about thru-hiking the Pacific Crest Trail, a hike I did four years ago. Someone once told me that they were amazed at how similar were the various accounts of people hiking the long trails. I am more interested in, and more noticing of, how people's experiences differ. I think someone's perspective is often the primary factor in their perceptions. For example, I read an account of one hiker on the Appalachian Trail. It was her first day of a summer-long, 2,000-mile challenge through steep mountains. Her hiking skills and knowledge and stamina were still untested. She was hiking alone and it started to rain. Some people would have started to cry, faced with the enormity of what lay ahead, and the realization that this cold rain was just the first of many discomforts to come. Instead she started to smile, smelling the rain, and soaking in the experience of the forest and mountains around her. "I love this!" she said "I just *love* this!" All the many hard climbs looming in the future didn't represent brutal hills to surmount, but thrilling challenges. The rain wasn't going to dampen her spirits, it would freshen the air. We see things not as they are, but as *we* are.

August 19, Day 51

It's not raining this morning but there's no sign of any sun, yet. I want to gather some firewood today. One place I've seen plentiful small, dead, standing wood is near the Avenue of the Giants. I can get there in half an hour or less and it will be easy to haul the firewood home in the kayak. For this trip I gather together hatchet, saw, my biggest empty pack bag and my daypack of survival gear.

As I pass an island, I hear eagles calling excitedly. I keep my eyes peeled as I round the island, heading into the cove that leads to the Avenue of the Giants. I'm looking for a nest, but I don't spot it until I've passed the island and I'm looking back. Even then I have to use binos. The nest looks like an enormous tangle of sticks. One of the parents eyes me with outstretched neck. The other scolds me from a tree on the mainland, then launches and circles about, still chattering.

Once onshore I soon find some of the two-inch-thick dead trees. I give them a tap with the blunt side of the hatchet and hear a dull thud. That doesn't sound good. I push one over and break it in half. Usually barkless, standing wood is relatively dry. But these pieces are punky on the outside, and the punky wood has been soaking up water like a sponge. The branches though, break off with a satisfying snap. I start gathering a pile of these dry, dead branches. Tapping a few more of the dead trees with the hatchet a couple of them give a good "ring." They are dry. I push them over and break them into four foot lengths, using the hatchet when they refuse to break. I slide the thickest, branch-less pieces into the bag first, then stuff in the smaller branches, big end forward, until the bag is packed. That will hold me for a while!

I leave the bag full of wood leaning against a tree to explore back up through the Avenue. It looks like a park beneath the magnificent, giant trees. The walking, flat and open, is easy and pleasant. As a hunter, places like this are nice because it gives me a better chance to see game animals before they hear or smell me. Perhaps we instinctively feel safer in these places, too. Since prehistory it's been easier to spot our own potential predators in open country like this, animals like saber-tooth tigers or giant bears.

When the timber opens up to grass I stop to appreciate the beauty of Magic Meadow, green and lush. A blacktail walks warily along the meadow's fringe. When it's gone I follow the edge of the meadow,

watching for berries and, just for fun, more deer. Yellowing leaves catch my eye. They are growing on thickets of twelve foot tall trees. The shape of the leaves is familiar, like apple leaves. I walk over to one of the thickets and take a closer look. Whatever it is I've never seen them around Fairbanks. Then I notice a clump of three marble-size fruit. That sure looks like crab apples! Wild crab apples in Alaska? This is a whole different world from Alaska's Interior, though. I pick one of the fruits and take a tiny bite. It tastes like a crab apple, too. When I look closer I see numerous clumps of tiny fruit. I pick a bunch of them to bring back to camp. If I can verify they are apples, I'll have a new food!

On the way back to the boat I look for good opportunities to take photos of the enormous spruce and hemlock trees. At one especially impressive patriarch I lean the hatchet against the base of the trunk for scale and step back for the shot. The sun has peeked through the clouds, sending foggy beams of white light stabbing diagonally across the dark trunk. Delicate green ferns and mossy roots contrast beautifully against the dark brown of damp, fallen bark. The hatchet is dwarfed where it leans against a root buttress of the giant hemlock.

It adds to the experience of living to notice interesting things in the world around us. A smokejumper buddy of mine is an amateur naturalist with an incredibly broad range of knowledge of plants, animals, and nature in general. For example, one day he was working out in the "bone yard" at the smokejumper base and spotted something barely sticking out of the ground. It appeared to be fist-sized stone with closely spaced ridges. He recognized it for what it was, a mammoth tooth! It is really interesting walking around with him-he spots and identifies countless things that I walk right past, flowers, and minerals and so much more.

It's interesting how a train of thought travels. I think back to the day my buddy Marty Meierotto (if you've seen the TV show *Mountain Men*, yup, it's *that* Marty!) was flying me out to the eastern Brooks Range. We were about to land on a big gravel bar of the Porcupine River to refuel from several pre-stashed fuel cans.

"Hey, do you want me to tell you if I spot a mammoth tusk?" I joked. I'd been in Alaska for nearly thirty years and hadn't found one yet.

"Sure!" he said. We carried the fuel cans to the plane and I handed one up to Marty. While he was pouring it in I wandered down the gravel bar. I suddenly froze.

"Hey Marty, come on over here."

"What are you looking at?" he said, walking my way.

"Come a little bit closer."

"A piece of tusk!" Marty said, looking up in disbelief. "Fantastic! Holy @#$%! Mammoth tusk, how'd you spot that?"

"I saw a smaller piece by the plane and I walked upstream. Can you believe that!?"

That was one of the biggest coincidences of my life. The only time I'd found a piece of mammoth tusks, moments after I'd joked about finding one. One in a million.

Fossils are especially fascinating to me. We had parachuted to a fire along the Yukon River. One day we were walking down the river bank. Two of us had fallen behind to discuss fire strategy when one of the smokejumpers ahead yelled back to us.

"Hey, check this out!"

"What have you got?"

"Just come over here and you'll see."

When we walked up they had dug out the base of a foot-thick object from the silty mud.

One of the jumpers looked up, beaming. "It's a mammoth tusk!"

They kept digging and it kept getting bigger. By the time they were done it was six feet long and must have weighed a hundred and fifty pounds. It is now on the wall of the smokejumper base. You can't keep tusks from public lands without permission. [It might sound pretty common to find mammoth fossils, based on these stories, but few people will ever be so lucky in a lifetime in Alaska.]

I'm going to rock fish on the way back to camp. A crowd of seals grumble from some rocks a few hundred yards away. Passing boats must make them nervous. I haven't seen another boat on the upper bay in days.

There are some berry bushes along the shore. I stop and find the best red huckleberry picking I've found the whole trip. In a few minutes I've picked and eaten an impressive amount. There are a few bonus thimbleberries here as well.

It sure does look like good rockfishing around here with all the rugged boulders disappearing into the depths. I drop a four ounce double-tailed jig to the bottom and bounce it along. *Hey, I've got something!* I'm excited to see what it is but when my catch reaches the surface, I'm not surprised to see a sculpin. I catch three more before I get back to camp. Good thing I'm not relying on rockfish for food-I'd have long since starved!

Somewhere in the distance I hear a huge crash. I heard another crash like that last night. That's strange. It doesn't sound like a jumping whale, both sounded like big trees falling. Big trees fall of course, but usually it's during a big wind or after heavy rain or snow. I recall a time I was hunting in northwest Montana. Day after day it snowed. It was thigh deep except under the big timber. That's where many of the deer were concentrated, so that's where I was hunting them. It was extremely quiet in the deep, fluffy powder, except for the occasional thudding from clumps of falling snow. Suddenly I heard a muffled popping and cracking sound. What's going on? Thirty feet away the trunk of a huge pine started shuddering and leaning over. A hump of snow began rising near its base. A huge root, covered in black dirt speared out of the snow. I was ready to run but the giant tree was falling away from me with a groan, broken branches spinning away through the treetops, the massive dark root wad pulling out of the snow as the tree crashed to the ground with a thunderous roar in a cloud of snow.

By the time I get back to the tent I'm hungry. There's a deer across the My Cove. Is that a buck? I don't want another deer yet but bucks have been so rare I'm curious. I launch the kayak again and paddle closer. It's right near where I bagged my buck, but at two hundred yards, it's clear it's a doe.

Out of my waders and changed into dry socks and running shoes, I sit in the camp chair and finish off a jar of halibut. That's some good stuff. I enjoy hours of relaxed reading back issues of magazines and a new book.

Empty jars build up surprisingly quickly, I'm eating about a jar and a half a day. I take a break from reading and carry the accumulated jars down to the water and try a new method of cleaning. I put about an inch of small gravel in the bottom and fill them about halfway, then put the lid on. By swishing the gravel around and shaking the jar up and down it does a pretty good job of cleaning them. It seems easier than using the tips of spruce or hemlock branches. While I work, a raven is calling, sounding remarkably like an amplified drip of water falling into a full sink. Geese are honking loudly as they feed on grass across My Cove.

In the evening I enjoy more reading. When hungry I eat from a jar of venison, nearly finishing the whole jar. The radio is predicting three days of sun! Yahoo! I thought it would be sunny today, but the sun barely made an appearance. I didn't get my laundry and bath, but tomorrow's the day!

August 20, Day 52

It looks like a beautiful, sunny day. On the rocket stove I heat up half a bucket of water until I can barely tolerate leaving my hand in it then carry it down to the edge of the water. I strip down to my underwear and enjoy the feel of the warm, morning sun on my skin. I pinch the remaining fat on my belly. I'm lean. I tense my stomach muscles. This might qualify as six-pack abs! I bet I've lost fifteen pounds. It's fat I've lost, the fat of the easy living of everyday life, where the fridge is just steps away and where grocery stores are stocked with foods formulated with just the right amount of sugar, fat and salt to make them appealing and fattening.

As lean as I am and as beautiful as the morning is, I want a photo to remember the moment. I set up my camera on self-timer. I look at the resulting shot. The sun shines warmly on the gravelly shore. The sky is light blue with wisps of clouds and just a trace of fog, coming off the cool salt water in the distance. The tops of my green rubber boots are barely holding on to the lower half. My body below my neck is pale except for my arms which are tan below the elbows. My hands are deeply tanned. As thin as I am, and with all the exercise of the previous weeks, I could pass for thirty, judging from the photo alone. Until you look above the neck. There, the illusion of youth evaporates. My beard is nearly white, my hair mostly gray, the top of my head nearly bald, the skin around my eyes crinkled from decades of sun. They were good decades, every one of them, the wrinkles well-earned. It's been a good life.

It's delightful getting all scrubbed. The hot water feels great. There's no hurry in the warm sun. After a good bath, head to toe, I do my laundry. I even wash my camp shoes. I tote everything back to the sunny shore near camp and hang my laundry to dry.

I'm going to take advantage of this sunny day to move camp again. I carry my gear part way to the new camp where I hang it or lay it out to dry. I even carry all my firewood out to bake in the sun. Naturally I put out the solar panels as well to get everything fully charged.

Although I am working in beautiful sun, there is a heavy fog bank down towards the Sound, an opaque wall of cottony white. I feel fortunate to be enjoying this sun. If I were camped a few miles away I'd be in a cloud at 100 per cent humidity!

On the other side of My Cove some deer are feeding. What else am I seeing? Boulders? Geese? I fetch my binoculars and see a doe and two fawns and a yearling. Geese waddle nearby, feeding in the same grassy area. The fawns find the huge geese fascinating. Each fawn follows a goose around. That makes the geese uncomfortable. They waddle away from the curious fawns. The doe is annoyed by the geese. She puts her ears back and rushes into the flock. They run out of range honking excitedly, flapping their wings. She must be defending her food source, the seemingly endless supply of grass along the shore.

Every camp move gets easier, especially dealing with the electric bear fence. I wrap each wire in a different place around the plastic cylinder of the bear canister. It makes a pretty good wire spool for temporary usage like this. (I haven't used it for its intended purpose much, mainly as a container for gear organization.) By early afternoon I have the tent set up in the new spot. As usual, I have a separate cook camp established maybe seventy-five yards from camp.

I'm sitting on a chair in the beautiful warm sunlight. I'm reading and observing the world. The wall of fog has finally burned away down towards the Sound. Murrelets are feeding nearby. They are entertaining to watch with the quick movements of their chubby little selves. They must be speedy underwater, too-they often surface with a tiny silver fish.

My cot and sleeping pad and sleeping bag are all dry. I set them up in the tent. By late afternoon I've got most things in the tent and nicely organized, with some clothing still out drying.

Late in the day I paddle over to the crab trap. There are three females. Amazing! I trapped the first female only two days ago. What changed? The good news is there is also one big male in the trap. I head for cook camp with my prize. It really hits the spot for supper.

The sun slipped behind the mountains a few minutes ago but there's still good light. I walk to my new camp. When I pick up my fleece hooded sweatshirt, it feels damp. I hold it to my face: yep, it's wet! As I gather up the rest of my clothes I notice beads of dew on each item. Rats! I was a few minutes late picking everything up. The dew sure fell fast after the sun disappeared! Good thing most of my gear was already stashed in the tent.

# CHAPTER 23

## Fishing the Falls

August 21, Day 53

It's foggy this morning with traces of blue in a sky bright enough that I know the fog will be burning off soon. I walk through the screen of trees down to the bay. (This new camp faces the bay, the last camp faced My Cove.) A big male mink, a dark, glossy brown, is hunting in the rocks along the water's edge. He pounces, successfully, and lopes towards the trees with his catch in his mouth. As chance would have it, another male mink runs out of the tall grass on his way to the wet rocks. As if by mutual agreement each avoids eye contact, thus avoiding a territorial fight.

Mountaintops materialize through the layer of fog. With camera in hand I walk out on a rocky point to experience the morning. One of the mink reappears nearby, looking for prey among the rocks. At first he doesn't notice me. He pops up nearly at my feet. Although I have my camera ready getting a good shot is like trying to capture lighting in a bottle. Mink don't lounge around. I laugh when I look at my best photo, a brown streak, clearly a mink but comically blurry.

As the mountains emerge, their rugged topography is accented by light and shade. I take shot after shot. Every minute the light changes

and there is another beautiful and different landscape. The gray and white and greens of the sunlit mountains are vibrant in the low angle of the morning light. Their image is reflected in a mirroring cove which curves gracefully out to a rocky point, still dark green and black in the early morning shadows. Even the narrowing layer of fog is beautiful, reflected and blue and wispy. Ravens croak as they head off on their morning mission.

I think about my morning plan. I'd like to get a nice brown bear photo. Falls Creek should be a pretty good bet. I'm sure there are still lots of salmon. There's a ridge I can sit on and watch for feeding bears from thirty feet above and a stone's throw away from the creek. It will add a margin of safety and should keep me out of their line of sight. I'd like a fresh salmon to grill, too.

After breakfast I paddle for Falls Creek. I haven't been there for a while. Murrelets cruise by, low over the water, lemon-shaped bodies and rapid wing beats. I stash my boat above high tide and with my rifle in hand, just in case, walk quietly towards the mouth of Falls Creek. I try to walk where I can see a bear far enough away so it will be reasonably safe. There are scores of seagulls near the creek mouth, and hundreds of pink salmon in the creek. Many of them that have been in fresh water the longest now have white fungus on them as they near the ends of their lives. The males have high humps on their backs and dramatically hooked jaws. Spawning salmon charge back and forth, chasing one another in the shallow water. Some salmon hold in water so shallow their backs stick out an inch or two.

Surprisingly I don't see any bears. Perhaps they smelled me. Although the wind seems favorable it can swirl in unpredictable ways. It's also likely there just weren't any bears here when I arrived. With so many salmon in the shallows it wouldn't take a skilled bear long to catch his fill.

I walk slowly up to the falls, wading the creek where the cliff meets the water. I watch ahead and to the sides for bears, and into the clear water for salmon, healthy looking ones freshly in from saltwater. They are the ones I want to eat. I catch glimpses of salmon swimming in the clear water near the boil of the roaring falls. The twenty foot cascades form an impassible barrier less than a quarter mile from the ocean. The pool's bottom is rocky and green until it disappears into the blackness of the depths. The air is cool and damp from the fall's mist and the wet rocks glisten darkly. The air is heavy with the smell of wet earth and vegetation.

I make a few casts into the deep pool, then walk downstream a few steps to fish the pools just below. I've never fished a prettier spot. The wide white veil of the main falls is joined by a smaller cascade falling from the right. Most of the scene is in cool shade, but the morning sun is just hitting the falls and there are patches of sun on mossy rocks and tree branches draped with hanging moss. Rich green Devil's club and delicate ferns carpet the hillsides. The gravel bar behind me provides plenty of room for my back cast. Below the falls pool is a set of riffles, then another shallower pool below it, a pool two or three feet deep. Dozens of salmon are holding there.

I cast to the head of that pool and strip the purple leech back towards me. The first cast there are no takers, but then a fish grabs it and shoots downstream, determined to get tangled in overhanging brush and sunken

logs. I tighten the drag and stop him in time. When he tires I quickly release him without taking him out of the shallow water.

Someone once said that many fishermen aren't just looking to catch a fish, they are searching for the perfect pool and the perfect cast and the perfect day. This setting is so perfect, so magnificent, so dramatic, I set up my camera to record a few shots. There are countless days of fishing I've forgotten, but I will never forget this day at Falls Creek, here alone in the Alaska wilderness, fishing for my food.

After catching and releasing several fish I hook a nice male with smooth, healthy skin. That's my meal. My camera is still on its mini tripod. I take a self-timer shot of me holding the fish, the fly still in his mouth, the falls behind us.

I stand in the shade of giant spruce and hemlocks, watching the sun on the falling cascades, salmon splashing in the stream beside me. I'm lucky to be here. We all have treasured experiences that no one can take away from us. I think of John Dryden's poem:

*Happy the man, and happy he alone,*
*He who can call today his own:*

*He who, secure within, can say,*
*Tomorrow do thy worst, for I have lived today.*
*Be fair or foul or rain or shine*
*The joys I have possessed, in spite of fate, are mine.*
*Not Heaven itself upon the past has power,*
*But what has been, has been, and I have had my hour.*

I sling on my daypack and pick up my rifle in my right hand, and the rod in my left, hooking two fingers underneath the gills of my fish. I walk back to the kayak where I stop to fillet the fish, keeping the head and guts for bait.

My crab trap is a mile paddle or so. When I get there it holds nothing but a starfish. At Big Island I land and carry everything above high tide into the shade. I do my traditional half circuit of Big Island, picking thimbleberries at the now familiar patches. Numbers are waning but I still do well. I sit on the edge of the kayak taking a break, drinking cool water from my canteen. Man, what a beautiful day!

I dump out all the old crab bait and rebait with the salmon parts, wiring the fresh head to the inside-top of the trap. A stiff breeze has come up as I paddle home. There's usually an up-bay wind around here. There isn't a boat in sight. I haven't seen a boat in days! Not a soul.

Back at camp I lay out the solar chargers. When I get there I'm missing a cord. I grabbed that cord, didn't I? Apparently not, because it's not here. I walk back to camp and come back with a cord, stumbling across the one I'd dropped! Cords are light, it's wise to have spares. It's also wise not to lose the ones I have. I hang up my sleeping bag, waders, and all the clothes that got wet in the evening dew.

At cook camp I start the stove and soon have salmon fillets grilling over hot coals. The canned salmon I've been eating is good, but the fresh grilled fish, nice and crispy on the outside and steaming hot, tastes even better. When I'm done eating I walk over and lower the food cache, taking out six jars. When these are empty I'll have eighteen total empty jars, minus two that are chipped. I'll do some more halibut fishing then.

Back at the tent I organize things a bit, then grab the five-gallon blue bucket that I found and wander around gathering up good, dry kindling and stash it under the cook camp tarp, restacking the wood a little more neatly while I'm at it.

*Whoosh!* Out in Wild Bay a humpback whale spout drifts over the water. Another whale back arches above the water. It spouts and sinks beneath the surface, followed by a smaller one, a calf. They are hunting near camp. With my binos I run out on the point and watch them feeding up and down the bay. Few things are more random and exciting out here than whale sightings.

On a visit to my prior camp, checking for overlooked trash or forgotten items, I find some fishing gear leaning against a tree. Looks like I need to do better keeping my stuff rounded up! Looking out over My Cove I spot three brownish deer feeding in the grass along the timber. I pluck and eat a bit of goose tongue while I watch them.

It's been a big day. A memorable day. I'm lying on my cot. The sun is just about to go behind the mountains, but now it is still seeping through the trees onto the tent fly and screen door. A spider is chasing bugs trapped at the peak of the tent. A squirrel is scampering around. Geese are honking in the distance. Through the screen, patches of golden light flicker on massive tree trunks.

August 22, Day 54

It's a calm, pleasant, sunny morning, a break from the dreary, rainy days. I find a nice opening to hang the latrine tarp and use the trowel dig a hole in the soft soil. Over the hole I tie the tarp off in a nice, taut, square A-frame setup with plenty of headroom. It's a big improvement.

At cook camp I use my head net to filter rainwater into the plastic jug, then suspend it from a big tree next to the tent. I notice a very, very slow drip resulting from a flaw in the valve. It's annoying, but with a plentiful supply of rainwater it's unimportant.

I paddle towards Falls Creek to pick berries but change my mind to explore for berries nearer the head of the bay. I paddle towards a small cove to land. Something's moving along the grassy shore. Bears! A sow and small cub. It looks like they have just come from Falls Creek where they've undoubtedly gorged on fresh salmon. The grass along the shore is vivid green in the low morning light and they rip up mouthfuls enthusiastically. It doesn't seem like these giant (the mother, anyway!) predators with their savage canine teeth would feed on so much grass. I slowly drift, watching, until they wander away into the big timber.

Along the mainland I pick a few sparse thimbleberries and highbush cranberries, then explore a tiny island for the first time. Here I find thimbleberries and also some stinging nettles, which I notice as I pull a length of old weather-worn rope out of the grass for possible use. There are some beautiful elderberries. They are only marginally edible, some even say they can be toxic. I sample a couple. Toxic or not I don't care to eat any more. They taste terrible!

The crab trap holds a single crab. A female! I wonder what has changed that I'm suddenly catching some females?

I enjoy the rest of the day puttering around, solar-charging, reading. I store a few items under the roomy latrine tarp including extra fishing gear and the spare paddle. I saw up a pole of dead wood into stove lengths and stash them under the tarp as well.

As I relax on the cot, reading, I look out through the screen of the tent, the door flaps tied open, watching the play of evening sunlight on the trees. The days are getting noticeably shorter.

# CHAPTER 24

# Paleo Diet

August 23, Day 55

In camp moves like I've been doing on this trip, I usually end up well organized with everything back in its assigned place. This morning I'm getting caught up on that, sorting out gear that got plopped down in a general area rather than where it should be. I'm reorganizing my hard-sided gun case. I've opened it up and removed the padding so that the clam-shell halves form a giant, waterproof tray. Canning supplies (lids, rings and so on) go in one area, ammunition and gun cleaning supplies in another, chargers and cords in a third, etc. I take a look at my rubber boots. The tops of both have cracked so much that they are halfway to falling off. I pick one up and rip it the rest of the way off. Not too difficult. I do the same with the second. The foot part will actually make decent wet-weather shoes for walking around camp. I'm still appalled at their precipitous and profound failure.

My tipi-shaped tent is held up by a single center pole. Simple is good but having no pole at all would be even simpler and it would be cool to have no pole to step around. There's a loop on top of the tent. I remove the pole, tie a cord to the loop and pull up. The tent liner sags. I experiment with ways to evenly lift both liner and fly with that single

cord, but it's not working out. Instead, I apply the time honored "if it ain't broke, don't fix it" rule. I put the pole back, and rearrange things slightly so any pole issue is minimized.

I paddle across the bay to look for and hopefully photograph bears at Falls Creek. The creek is loaded with pinks, of course. The light is good so I take some photos and video of the salmon. My batteries have gone dead. No problem, I have spares. Unfortunately the spares go dead immediately as well. Bummer. My camera, as I've just proved again, will run on nothing but full-power batteries. My mistake. Now I'm guaranteed to see a bear. My GPS also uses AA batteries though. I try them, and they work. Yes!

I look upstream and see bushes waving. A dark-colored brown bear is climbing the steep slope. I don't think he knows I'm here. I head up the ridge. A few minutes later I see a bear, perhaps the same one, hustling up a trail on the opposite slope, with a salmon flopping in his jaws. *Cool!*

Walking along the ridge, rifle in hand, I find a great lookout at a big stump on the top edge of a twenty-foot cliff. There is a great view from the falls all the way down to the grassy opening leading out to saltwater. The bear trail is right across from me, 30 yards away. This is a nearly perfect setup. I wait, camera in hand, confident I'll soon see a bear. Bear or no bear, there's plenty to see, seagulls flying up and downstream, eagles flapping heavily down the little canyon, and salmon holding in the clear water or zipping up and downstream chasing one another.

As I wait I study the ground around me. I have to be careful. What appears to be solid earth three feet away is actually moss draped over a root wad hanging over the cliff. Falling is a greater risk than bears out here!

After an hour or two it's clear the bear isn't coming back. He's either gotten his fill of salmon or he smelled me. I think I'll go berry picking. I can check for bears again on my way back.

There's a narrow but long meadow running up the gently sloped mountainside, only a hundred yards from the falls. I follow a bear trail that threads through the meadow. There are deer tracks on top of bear prints in muddy spots. Mostly the trail goes through open, largely dry tundra. I notice a tiny blueberry on the trail. When I look around I find more of them, growing on diminutive bushes, the berries in ones and twos only an inch or two off the ground. They are the sweetest blueberries of the whole trip! Now as I follow the trail I watch carefully for more of these little berries and eat every one I spot. There are numerous crowberries here as well. They grow on plants about four inches high, each stem looking like the end of a little spruce tree branch. The berries are a dull black. They are as bland as the tiny blueberries are sweet. I eat some nonetheless because they are food and it's good to vary my diet. The crowberry plants are easier to spot than these tiny blueberry bushes. Since they tend to grow in the same habitat I look for crowberries to find the little blueberries.

As I follow the meadow it becomes clear that it runs all the way up to The Bench where I've picked so many berries before. My legs feel heavy today. I've noticed that before sometimes. I'd suspect there was a cause, a vitamin deficiency or something, but it doesn't happen often and I seem to notice it after a kayak paddle. Where The Bench meets this long meadow, I look for a spot where I can see both directions, along The Bench and far down the long meadow. A guy would see a deer here if he was patient. Or a bear.

I walk to the end of The Bench where the best blueberry pickings are, the best tall-bush blueberries that is. They may not be quite as sweet as the tiny ones but there are a lot more and I relish chowing down on them. I pick some of the bigger black huckleberries, too. Steller's jays are eating berries here too, hopping through the bushes and scolding me. Their blue and black bodies are strikingly beautiful. It's fascinating how their hues change with the quality of the light.

On the way back to The Falls I eat some red huckleberries and more of the sweet little blueberries. Today has been a cornucopia of berry varieties! I sneak quietly to the edge of the lookout, where I sit with binos ready and camera in hand watching the zoo of birds and salmon. But the bears fail to make another appearance.

A good breeze springs up as I paddle for home, an unusual down-bay wind. As quick as it arises it fades away to gentle puffs. It was going to be a cloudy day but the sun has come out, a nice bonus for the day. I set up a solar panel to top off my rechargeable AA batteries. I will try to keep them near 100 per cent. They will be my go-to camera batteries if I have any problems.

I hear the now familiar sound of a whale blowing. Three hundred yards away, across the bay a plume of warm breath drifts against the sun, followed by several more blows. There are at least three humpbacks cruising along the bay. The whale population around here seems to be doing well!

Despite all the berries I'm hungry. I finish off the last of a jar of halibut and put a big dent in a jar of venison. The thought comes to me: I'm on a Paleo diet. A 100 per cent, no cheating Paleo diet! It works, too, as a diet. I've lost a lot of fat. I don't know what the long-term consequences of this diet of wild foods would be, pro or con, but I feel fine. Certainly being lean must be healthy.

I'm reading this evening. Patches of sun illuminate the tent. I set down my book and walk outside. The low sun is shining through the tall green grass. Seaweed glows yellow-green against the sun. The mountains

near the sun are a smoky blue above the green timber. Rays of sun pierce a white haze of moisture laden air. I sit on a boulder and look across the smooth water, watching the sunset.

"Light is really important in photography, isn't it?" I once said to a friend, an expert photographer.

"Light is *everything*." he said.

These mountains, those trees, Wild Bay, are here day after day, but it's the quality of the light this evening, this very minute, that makes the experience of being here so magical.

I tend to fall asleep easily at bedtime, early compared to most people. Tonight I'm snuggled into my warm down bag, as usual, just drifting off when I hear something outside. What's that? A stick cracks. *Something big!* I roll over and grab my rifle, closing the bolt and locking in a live round. I listen, hearing nothing. With my rifle in my right hand I unzip the tent door with my left, and step outside, ready to shoot. There's just enough light to see... nothing. Whatever it was it ran off. It was probably a deer. Or bear. I wait few more minutes and go back into the tent and lay my rifle close at hand.

August 24, Day 56

It's a gray day. The faint moan of a foghorn drifts over the water, a ship passing miles away out on the Sound. I eat venison while listening to the weather. Sounds pretty rainy.

I'm going to head for Falls Creek: pick some more berries, look for bears. Rather than switching from waders for the trip over, then to boots for easier walking while berry picking, then back to waders again for the paddle home, I'm not going to wear waders at all. I'll just bring them with, just in case.

With my rubber boots completely shot, and my camp shoes (actually running shoes) sure to immediately get wet, I opt for a "field expedient" again. I put on wool socks, and slip lightweight plastic shopping bags over each one, then another set of my most beat-up wool socks over the top of them. This way I can use my nearly always wet wading boots. The inner socks are for warmth, the shopping bags for waterproofness, and the outer wool socks to prevent the bags from being abraded. If I don't step into water over ankle deep my feet should stay reasonably dry. The bags will eventually wear out, probably in a day or two or three. When they do I'll simply replace them.

I paddle across calm water. The tide is low. Hey there's a crab! The water is about three feet deep. I try to herd him with my paddle with no success. It's tough from a boat without a net. I see another crab and fail again. Lots of crabs! I slide the boat ten feet onto shore and change out of my rain pants and into my waders. Wouldn't you know it, one of the few times I don't wear them and I need them! I unscrew the paddle halves to use half as a crab herding tool.

Wading thigh deep I watch for crabs in the clear water. Seagulls eye me curiously. *There's one!* I push and scoop him towards shallow water and succeed in capturing him but he's too small. In a few minutes I spot another one. Successful again, but this time I can see he's too small even without measuring. I look back at the boat. It makes me nervous walking away from it with the tide coming in. It looks OK so far. *There's another one!* He scrambles around trying to reach deeper water but I steadily gain until I scoop him onto shore. He too, is barely too small. Dagnabbit!

I hustle towards the boat. It starts floating just before I get there. I pull it way up to where I won't have to worry about it, still determined to catch some legal crabs today. Wading back the other direction I soon spot some eel grass with vegetation floating over it. Watching carefully I find a crab, and get it. Too small. Its back is mossy. I don't think I've seen that before. Is it possible that algae grows on crabs that live in shallower water? I catch its twin in a few more minutes, even down to the "moss." They like the eel grass with floating vegetation over it. Good places to hide from predators, presumably. After catching another too-small crab, the water looks less favorable so I head back to the kayak. I didn't get any legal crabs, but it was still fun hunting them. Heading back I find a nice, foldable foot stool! It's gray, it would have been easy to miss. It must have fallen off a crab boat. Funny it didn't sink! Like always I think "what can I use this for?" I can't think of any real need, but I take it with me, just in case.

After carrying my kayak all the way to the trees I change out of my waders and head upstream with rifle, daypack and camera. A pink salmon lies dead on the gravel bar, punctured with two enormous canine teeth holes! I wonder why the bear abandoned it? There are still zillions of salmon. I start to take photos, I can't resist, but the batteries are dead again. I just tested them, they were 100 per cent according to my tester. Whatever the reason I change to the fully charged rechargeables. Bingo. The camera is back in action.

I'm watching for bears but don't see any. I follow the well-established bear trail up the ridge before veering off it to the lookout point. I take a break there, enjoying the falls and the salmon and eagles and watching for a bear that never shows up. Berry time.

It's started to rain. I've got this berry-picking route scouted now but vary it a bit to look for new berry concentrations. I get some of my favorites, the sweet little blueberries that grow barely off the ground. Their relative rarity makes them even more precious and appreciated. The bulk of my berry feast is provided by the taller variety of blueberries, huckleberries and the less common red huckleberries. It's wet picking in the rain. The bushes are soaked and they rain down even more water every time they are bumped and sometimes fling water in my face when branches snap back. Water runs down my rain jacket sleeves as I pick higher berries. When I've eaten my fill I follow the long meadow down to the falls, and walk to the the lookout point again. Where are those elusive bears anyway? There's a plethora of easy-to-catch salmon here! That's probably just it, though. The bears get their fill in short order and are sleeping it off in some forest nest right now.

Back at the kayak I forgo changing into my waders. Instead I leave on my rain pants and sit on the waders to keep my butt out of any water on the boat bottom. The crab buoy is visible a half mile away. The trap holds only a starfish.

I paddle hard for home, intent on getting out of the cold rain. When the bow crunches ashore I lift my feet to step out and cold water runs out of each boot and along my pant legs to soak my butt. When people think of the glory of outdoor adventures they tend to overlook moments like this!

With the kayak safely stashed I walk over to the food cache, lower it, and retrieve a plastic jarbox with six jars of food. After pulling the remaining cache back up I bring the jarbox back to the tent.

I'm chilled changing out of my wet clothes. It's so nice getting into warm, dry fleece! I soon warm up, snuggled in my bag, reading a back issue of an old magazine. I run across the story about an old smokejumper buddy guiding up on the Noatak River. It's a small world! I have a big venison supper while listening to a recording of *This American Life*. I spend the rest of the day mostly napping and reading. It's such a luxury enjoying the warmth and the dry tent and a simple jar of salt-and-peppered venison with a chaser of cold water!

August 25, Day 57

Raining again. If all goes according to plan, I fly out two weeks from today! *Wow!*

My rain gear is soaked on the outside and pretty wet on the inside, too, due to water running up my sleeves, in around the hood, and up my rain pants when I climbed out of the kayak. I am loathe to immediately get wet again. Unlike when I backpack, I've brought lots of spare clothes. I'll sacrifice a set of fleece to the wet. I put on my hooded fleece jacket and fleece pants. When I put on my rain gear over it I can't even feel the wet. Fleece is great for things like this! It will keep me nice and warm as well.

I've got a whole bunch of jars to wash. They build up fast because I eat about three pounds of meat a day! My jar washing is a chore. I think of ways to replicate the kind of jar brush I use at home. It's mostly foam. What do I have for foam? The padding foam of my gun case is very similar. I cut out a strip, wrap it around a stick and wire the center tightly in place. It creates a cylinder just bigger than the inside of the jar, but with the middle of the foam squished in. I give it a try. It works pretty well. Definitely the best method I've used. A small bottle of dish-washing detergent would be handy, though.

When I'm done I line up all the empty jars, including the ones I'd washed previously. There are seventeen. So what do I have left for canned meat? About four jars of venison. Wow! It's only eighteen days since I got the deer and he's almost eaten up already! Amazing. There should also be about three jars of crab, and seven jars of halibut. So what is that? 17 empties +4+3+7+2 chipped ones. 33. I started with 36 jars. Either there is a bit more canned food left or there's some empty jars I haven't rounded up, or a little of each. Either way, I've got enough jars to can a pretty big halibut. Cool. I'll ration out my venison, eat a jar every third day or so for a treat.

I think about Chris McCandless often on this trip. He was the fellow who hiked twenty-some miles into the Alaska bush, north of Denali National Park, back in '92. His emaciated body, weighing about 83 pounds, was found a few months later in an old abandoned bus where he'd been living. He'd carried in a ten pound bag of rice but otherwise had been trying to "live off the land." According to the most-read book on McCandless, in one three-week period he'd eaten 35 pine squirrels, four spruce grouse, five woodpeckers and jays and two frogs, which he supplemented with some wild plants and berries and lots of mushrooms. In contrast to that, in eighteen days I've eaten most of an adult *deer*, plus large amounts of salmon and halibut and crabs and plants and berries, vastly more food. I've still lost about fifteen pounds on this trip.

It would have been extremely difficult to survive a trip like McCandless attempted, starting in the spring, when he did. Legally anyway. Even for an expert. Caribou and moose season don't start until August or September. He did kill a moose well before legal season but didn't know how to preserve it and nearly all of it spoiled. If he'd been able to salvage the meat he might have survived.

Despite varying theories of causes contributing to his death, I think the coroner was right: he died of starvation. He simply wasn't getting enough calories. Wild meat runs lean, especially squirrels and most of the other game he was eating. Regardless, I can relate to many aspects of his adventure. I'm certainly out here for many of the same reasons.

My halibut landing technique needs improvement. In hindsight, a halibut harpoon would have been really nice to have. How can I make one? I've got that old wooden boat oar I found. That would be strong and straight and the oar is pretty beat-up and not worth much. I get my saw and, working out of the rain under the protection of the tarp, saw off the paddle blade, leaving a four foot pole. That should work! I can't think of a way to make a proper, simple harpoon, one with a head that will pull off and stay in the fish. I've got these huge halibut hooks though. How about tying a huge hook to one of my sealed five-gallon buckets, with the bucket acting as a buoy? I could fasten the hook to the end of the pole and when the fish is tired, quickly hook/gaff him in the jaw and throw the bucket overboard. Then he'd be fighting the bucket, and the fishing rod, and he'd still be hooked if one hook fell out. Seems like that would work! I tie a length of parachute cord to the hook with a figure-8 follow-through knot with six feet of cord that I'll tie to a bucket later. How can I attach the hook so that it will pull off of the pole when I've got the halibut "gaffed"? Duct tape! I put a wrap and a half of duct tape around the hook shank and the pole. That should hold it in place but rip loose with the fish on. I flip the point of the hook around so it's touching the pole so it can't puncture the boat. I'm going to fasten a knife on the other end to spear the halibut through the gills, to get him bleeding and kill him as fast as possible. I'll use my bucket/hook/gaff first, because he'll go berserk when I spear him, and there's the risk of cutting the fishing line with the blade. I tape a filet knife to the other end of the pole. It's a little wobbly that way, though-there's too much wiggle. I fetch some wire and wrap the knife handle in two places, nice and tight. Now it's a spear! Lastly I tape the fillet knife sheath in place on top of the blade. Protecting my inflatable kayak from the harpoon's big spear blade and gaff hook is a major priority! People make foolish mistakes in exciting situations.

It's still raining with no end in sight. I take off my rain gear. My fleece is barely damp. That was a good way to protect myself from my wet rain-gear. I relax in my sleeping bag for awhile, reading, with the rain pattering steadily on the tent fly. I've got backpacking magazines, history magazines, and many unread and partially read books. I like "mixing it up" a bit. I'm usually reading two or more books and a magazine or two or three. I'll finish off the jar of venison from yesterday.

On the rainiest days like this, hanging out in camp, I usually listen to the weather several times a day. It's entertaining and it's nice to have a goal, to know when I'll see the sun again. I often jot down the forecast. I printed a bunch of Sudoku puzzles for this trip and I add the current forecast to the margins below a half dozen forecasts from previous days. Here's what I write:

| 26 | T  | MC Scatter showers, H 61, SE 10 to NW |
|----|----|----------------------------------------|
| 27 | W  | MC SS, NW 10                           |
| 28 | Th | MC chance rain                         |
| 29 | F  | Rain                                   |
| 30 | S  | MC, chance rain (to lodge?)            |
| 31 | S  | Rain                                   |
| 1  | M  | "Labor Day" rain                       |

I change into rain gear to stretch my legs and take a look around. At my favorite goose tongue patch I look for especially nice plants and pick and eat them. It's good to get some fresh greens. There isn't a boat in sight. When I walk past the tarp I notice moisture has misted under it and the shotgun is beaded up. Gee, I wonder if it will rust? I'll clean it again when the sun comes out.

As I eat a halibut supper I think about tomorrow's plan. I think it rained all day today.

August 26, Day 58

Wild Bay is calm. I hear the haunting call of a loon and spot two of them fishing nearby. Bald eagles are chattering in the tall timber, others are flying around the mouth of Falls Creek, identifiable from this distance only by their great size. The ubiquitous seagulls are hunting or resting near the low tide mark. Scoters cruise past, their white wing bars flashing against their black bodies. Marbled murrelets paddle around, plump little guys with their beaks tilted up just enough so they look snooty or like they're trying to get a better look at me until *bloop*! They're gone underwater.

After a halibut breakfast I go with "Plan A," crab netting. The usual story would be "Wouldn't you know it started raining just in time so I couldn't see to catch any crabs?" Instead it's the opposite: it's raining lightly as I paddle across but it stops just in time so the water is undimpled by raindrops. It's easy to see into the clear water. I'm right on time, too, just before low tide.

I'm wearing my waders and I've got the landing net. I carry the kayak far enough up so I won't have to keep an eye on it. I tie the crab caliper to my wading belt and go hunting. I'm having good luck spotting crabs, and the net usually makes short work of catching them. The only challenge with the landing net is they can get tangled in the mesh, legs every which way and big claws grabbing on. Although I'm catching crab after crab, time after time I measure them to find that they are only 6 1/4" or so, just shy of legal. Among the eel grass I finally find what I'm looking for and get two legal crabs in a row. *Nice!* When I reach the end of the good area I stop and pick up my legal crabs. I'd left them belly up on the beach, and stash them in the bucket at the kayak. Then I hunt the opposite direction. There aren't as many crabs this way but then I see him: the granddaddy of crabs. By far the biggest one I've caught the whole trip. His claws are massive and when I pick him up I'm surprised at his heft. There's going to be a whole bunch of good meat on this guy!

Time for some halibut fishing! I slosh fresh water over the three crabs in their bucket, then set it in the back of the boat. After checking the rigging of my halibut rod and jig I drip a few drops of bait scent oil on the jig and paddle for the the Hump. Soon I'm jigging over "the sweet spot." After drifting over the best area, I leave the jig in the water to paddle back for another run. The rod starts bouncing. *Fish on!* Nope. Fish off. I think that was a halibut, too. Just as I start back into the good area I get a snag. I got snagged here before, too. There is something down there, rocks or a sunken boat or something. I'm pulling, trying to free it, when the first boat I've seen in about ten days comes cruising by two hundred yards away. They are watching me curiously, a guy in a little inflatable kayak fighting something. I hope they think I'm fighting a monster halibut. I let out a whole bunch of line and pull from way upwind but it's stuck solid. I try another direction and another. *I think it's loose! Yup!* Very cool. No more halibut strikes though.

The sun is trying to struggle through the clouds as I near the crab trap. It holds a starfish, and a nice legal crab! Today's crabbing has treated me well. I sweeten the bait with a little bait oil and move the trap a bit just for the heck of it. On the way back a headwind springs up but my paddling muscles are in good shape now.

The sun makes a glorious appearance. I set the crabs in the shade at camp and hang up my sleeping bag, pad, rain gear, waders and lay out the solar chargers, the usual drill. This has got to be one of my favorite chores, drying stuff out after a stretch of rain and clouds. The sun puts me in the mood to see everything soaking up its warmth, and to have everything dry and stashed safely away when it's done.

It's a nice mess of crabs in the canner/cooker. I start heating with smaller, faster burning sticks. I boil them for twelve minutes. The humongous crab isn't quite done, so I boil them a bit more, then pull them off the fire. I eat a whole, delicious crab right away, and bring the rest back to camp to eat cold.

I pick up another book I've brought, an account of hiking the Appalachian Trail. The author wrote about being a bit frightened, low on food a day away from the next food resupply. It's easy to feel smug, to think "So what? So you might miss a meal! Big deal!" But how many people in the real world are faced with running out of food with nothing at hand to eat? I remember a time, years ago, when a very experienced backpacking buddy and I were going hiking in the Elk Mountains of Colorado.

"What should I bring for food?" I asked him. I could tell that struck him as a silly question.

"You know, regular backpacking food!" he said. All of us are greenhorns at some point. This being a thru-hiking book, there is lots of talk about big feasts in town, feasts featuring the exact type of food that sounds good right now: a large pizza with everything on it, a big tub of Rocky Road ice cream, a huge plate of pancakes with butter and syrup. Foods like this are usually "out-of-sight, out-of-mind" for me out here, but not when I'm reading about them!

I enjoy crab for supper, then go out and collect everything that's drying and charging, making a second check to make sure nothing is forgotten. While I'm at it I pick some goose tongue on the beach and even a few huckleberries on the ridge above camp. It might not be a large combo pizza, but any day a guy can eat halibut, crab, and huckleberries isn't too shabby. 100 per cent organic, too!

# Chapter 25

# Bear Fishing

August 27, Day 59

I woke up about 3 AM. I usually wake up really early but for some reason I didn't fall back asleep again. After an hour or so I decide to just get up and start my day.

It's crab for breakfast. It's cooked and ready to go and I want to get it all eaten up soon. I put on my headlamp and step outside into the dark to fetch the crab halves from the tree branch where they're hanging, and to get a bucket for the shells. When I look down the bay I see banks of distant bright lights. An enormous cruise ship is passing in the Sound, many miles away. What a different world they are in right now!

Where's my crab bucket? I thought it was outside the tent. Maybe I left it by the boat. But it's not there, either. Is it in the tent? Nope. Cook camp? That's my last chance. When I get there I swing the headlamp beam all around. There's a bucket! The wrong one. Bummer. My orange bucket must have floated away. "You idiot," I say out loud. At some point I set it down below low tide. Definitely a mistake but easily done. The ocean and tides don't care about what happens to people or their gear. I still have another bucket with one of those waterproof, screw on lids like the bucket that floated away. And I still have the two old buckets I found that were washed ashore by storms and tides way back when. The biggest downer is the fact that I screwed up and lost a piece of gear.

I fetch the old white bucket. It's got a cracked bottom and holes in it from when I sighted in my rifle but it will still work fine for holding crab shells. I grab the bucket and both halves of the monster crab I got yesterday, duck through the tent door and sit down in the camp chair. It's a fine, filling breakfast with big chunks of luscious white meat.

This is a much darker camp, in bigger timber and facing west, away from the morning sun. I tend to get going a bit later in west facing camps because they are darker in the mornings. Despite that, I'm paddling across the bay by about 6 AM. It's still too early for netting crabs so I carry my kayak up to the timber and bring my camera in hopes of getting bear photos. I take my rifle as well, just in case.

I love early mornings along running water. The riffles are murmuring merrily. Gulls waddle along the banks and cruise low over the water, squawking excitedly. The air smells great, cool and clean and damp. Scores of salmon are swirling and splashing, backs and tails sticking out in the shallower spots. I walk upstream, keeping a sharp lookout for bears. There! A big brown bear is patrolling along the opposite bank, facing the

other way, too far away for good photos. This is a good opportunity. I can use the tall grass for cover. I sink down in the tall grass. I sling off my pack and crawl on my hands and knees through the grass. After fifty yards I crawl towards the stream bank, watching for the bear. Through the grass I spot him. He's standing in the shallow water, watching salmon splashing all around him. He must be getting plenty to eat. It looks like he's practically waiting for one to swim into his mouth. With optical zoom he's close enough for good photos, but there's still enough distance between us for decent safety buffer.

This is awesome! I zoom in and take a shot. When I look at the photo the grass is sharp and the bear is blurry. Autofocus! It's focusing on the grass. I crawl to the side a bit but the same thing happens. How do I manually focus this thing, anyway? I've forgotten. I rarely use that feature. While I mess with the settings he pounces on a fish, pinning it the bottom with his paws, then grabs it in his jaws and takes a few steps and drops it on the shore, still standing in the water. He pulls off a strip of meat from the still-struggling fish and swallows it. With his feet up on shore his prominent shoulder hump looks even taller and more powerful than usual. He swings his massive head around to watch for danger. He freezes when his gaze hits me, still up on my elbows fiddling with the camera settings, only half-hidden by grass. For a long moment neither of us moves. What's he going to do? He stands up on his hind feet, a towering pillar of brown hair and muscle. He's already turning as he drops down. In a few short bounds he's into the trees and gone.

I'd like to say that just as he was standing up I find the manual focus, and snapped off a series of sharp photos that I will be submitting to *National Geographic*. Nope. I was still fumbling. I did get some shots though, and more importantly, I got the experience. That was really exciting!

I fetch my daypack and follow the bear trail that leads past the falls. I stop to examine a waist-high log that lies across the trail. There are claw marks from bears crawling over. This would be a fun spot to put a trail camera! A bear would be likely to chew the camera up if it was low enough though.

I weave my way through twenty yards of sparse berry bushes to reach the overlook. I wait for a bit but no other bears make an appearance.

I head over to the meadow and start out on what has become my "usual route" but then veer over to a parallel meadow that runs roughly up and down the mountain on a gentle slope. I find a nice patch of dwarf blueberries that grow on the tiniest bushes. The picking is great, but the no-see-ums are the worst of the whole trip. I'm getting too hot with my hood up but I have to keep my skin covered or the bugs will chew me to pieces. I take off my Micro Puff jacket and wear my rain jacket over my bare skin. The no-see-ums crawl through the vents and attack me from all angles. *Those little #@$%*&!* For the first time on the whole trip I pull out my little bottle of DEET and spray a general light mist over the backs of my hands and my cap and its bandana hanging down and lastly the jacket vent areas. That helps a lot.

For forty-five minutes I crawl around picking the sweet little berries. In especially good spots I sit down and eat every berry within reach. I feel like a big ole bear. The no-see-ums have nearly vanished. Just for the heck of it I eat a leaf of Labrador tea. It's got a strong taste, not surprisingly a taste something like the smell of the crushed leaves. Not something I'll be adding to a salad.

When I've picked the area clean I walk over towards a good spot I'd found a few weeks ago. I top off a jar with these "highbush" blueberries. When I find a patch of huckleberries, big and shiny black, I top of a second jar as well. By the time I've got the easy pickings, I'm well into a third jar. That'll do! One of my best days of berry picking. I ate a whole bunch of those sweet little blueberries, too.

On the way back to the falls I graze my way down the middle of the meadow, focusing on the "dwarf blueberries." The size of many of these berries are ludicrous compared to the tiny bushes. They look like blue pumpkins growing on apple trees.

I follow the meadow down to the trail leading to the overlook. A few minutes later my trail is dwindling to nothing. How did that happen? No matter. I'll just head cross slope until I hit the right trail. I'm soon in thick brush, weaving my way around Devil's club and climbing over wet logs. When I've gone twice as far as I expected I'm still not there. It's amazing how quickly a guy can get off track if you follow a spur ridge or trail that veers off in the wrong direction! At last I hit the trail I should have been on, and walk to the overlook for a rest.

There isn't a moment where I can't see dozens of critters: gulls, eagles, pink salmon, but no bears. I walk back to the trail, down to the flats and along the creek towards Wild Bay. A brown bear sits up in the tall grass in front of me! He immediately bolts, running flat out, disappearing over the sandy spit. He must have been sleeping in the grass. On the other side of the spit it's easy to see his tracks. His long claws have sliced the soft ground, flinging sand and mud with every stride. He wasn't messing around!

The few passing showers made the brush wet, so when I get back to camp I hang stuff to dry, then head over to cook camp to take stock of the food cache. There's three jars of venison left, with three more in camp. More than I thought. If things go according to plan I'll be out here for about twelve more days. That's a jar every other day. Nice!

I putter around camp organizing stuff. For supper I have halibut and goose tongue. Despite the lack of sun, my gear has dried in the breeze.

August 28, Day 60

It's Dad's birthday. Last night I heard something splashing near the tent. Actually several somethings. Maybe otters?

I'm zipping up the tent flap, headed out halibut fishing. The 6 AM alarm is going off on my watch, hanging from its lanyard in my right shirt pocket. The tide table booklet is in the left pocket. It's chilly this morning so I'm wearing fleece under my rain jacket. Last night I was pondering how to keep my butt dry now that water is slowly seeping through the seat of my waders. I took a piece of plastic about eighteen inches square and tied an elastic cord to two adjacent corners. This morning I stepped into it so it's hanging down over my butt. Seems like that should work. Guess I'll find out!

The tide is falling and the rocks near the Hump appear just as I approach. I drop the heavy jig overboard and let the light breeze carry me along. I avoid the snag, but I also don't get any bites. I'm on the third pass now. Hey, I think I got something! I set the hook and start to reel. Not very big whatever it is. A sculpin, it turns out.

I paddle over to the other side of the rocks and try a new area. On an upward jig the line goes slack. What the heck? Finally I feel the weight of the jig. I bet that was a halibut rushing up and grabbing it then spitting it out.

What time is it? 8:20. I decide to check the crab trap. I can't find the buoy. I've got a bad feeling. Did a knot come loose? Hardly seems possible. A whale get tangled in the line? Theft? I've got to be almost on top of it! Then I see the buoy's red bottom. It's swung around so it's facing exactly away, the white top hidden behind the red bottom.

The trap line feels heavy, but all it holds is a huge starfish. Low tide is coming up. I'll try netting.

I land the kayak at Big Island. To avoid having to carry the boat way up I carry the trap well above the water and tie it off to the boat using parachute cord and a Prusik knot, resulting in a crude anchor. I grab my net and reach for the crab caliper cord. Now where the heck is the caliper? It's not anywhere in the boat. I must not have tied it back in place after using it while walking around netting crabs over at Falls Creek last time. All these weeks I'd been doing pretty darn good not losing stuff, now I've lost two items this week.

"You idiot." It's one of my favorite things to say out loud. I'm pretty good to judge crab size now. I'll let any marginal crabs go and just keep ones I'm sure are legal.

When I begin wading around I see several crabs, but most are clearly too small. I net one, but once it's out of the water I see it's too small. The next one too. And the third.

Since I'm here at Big Island I check out the thimbleberry patches. Most of the patches elsewhere are long since past their prime. The Big Island patches are fading too, but I still find a nice meal of red, sweet berries.

Before I launch the boat I dig out three clams. I crush their shells and add them to the trap's bait cage, with a few drops of bait oil for good measure. I drop the trap in a spot I haven't tried before, nearer the mainland and farther from My Creek.

I'm fighting a stiff breeze on the way home. I try hugging the shore, thinking the wind might be lighter there. If staying near shore is helping, I sure don't notice it. Four deer are feeding in a grassy corner of My Cove: a doe and two fawns with their spots nearly gone, and a yearling. This is a favorite feeding area. It's where I got my buck.

Back at camp I change out of my waders. Hey, my butt stayed nice and dry! That idea, hanging the plastic down in back, looks silly but I think it's going to work well.

I look around for the crab caliber. What I'm hoping is that it was loose in the bottom of the boat and it fell out when I was carrying the boat up to tree line. No luck.

The sun is trying to come out. I hang stuff to dry. I've got the good solar charger spots figured out. Certain boulders, angled just right, still have their smaller rocks I have used to hold the foldable panels in place.

While things dry I brainstorm on how to make a replacement caliper. A tape or stick is impractical due to the curve of the shell. Looking around I see a piece of clear plastic that held my gun cleaning kit. I use a tape measure to mark off six and a half inches then use a Swiss army knife scissors to cut out the squared off notches and a curve that will fit over a shell. It's wimpy, but it will work. While I'm at it I cut out a spare caliper as well. A spare crab caliper is something I would know to bring next time. They are cheap, light, and easily lost.

I think about other things I should get done. I look at my halibut harpoon. I've got the sheath tied on. I replace the cord with a mini bungee. Now I can pull it off in an instant and it will stay nice and tight until I do.

While I'm working around camp I listen to another episode of *This American Life*. It's amazing how it takes me back to the time I first heard it, when I was hiking the Desert Trail, that day through the Sheldon National Wildlife Refuge in northern Nevada. In the morning I'd found a black obsidian spear point, or perhaps it was used as a knife. I would have loved to keep it but I left it due to the law and my conscience. I was hiking down a gentle sagebrush slope. Ranks of dark storm clouds were piled up to the north. Four wild horses appeared, each a different color. They galloped past, long manes and tails streaming in the cold wind. The first snow showers were glittering through splinters of sunlight, all against a backdrop of stepped mesas and brown rimrock. It was a painting brought to life.

A few minutes later that day I was walking past the black mouth of a cave. Caves are a magnet to me so I stopped to check it out. In front of the cave were horse bones. It was easy to imagine the story. A mountain lion had ambushed a horse from the rimrock and dragged it to the cave to eat over the next few days. When he was thirsty, he could drink from a nearby brook. When it was cold, he could lie in the sun. When it was too hot or rainy he could sleep in the cave.

Today I ate one of my jars of venison with thimbleberries, blueberries and huckleberries, I picked some goose tongue, and I started in on a jar of halibut.

After gathering up the chargers and everything that was drying I take a walk along the waterfront. A couple of sea lions are hunting just offshore. They are loud breathers and big animals. What a windfall of food a sea lion would be. I'll bet the meat and fat of a big sea lion has more calories than all the food I've harvested this entire trip.

Thimbleberries are mighty sparse near camp now. As I pick what few berries remain, I find a whole red crab in the grass, a small one. Strange. Here's another one. And another. Suddenly I know what the explanation is: I *did* hear otters last night. They must have smelled me and ran, leaving their food behind. From the looks of things, they must eat well!

Rain starts pattering on the tent soon after I get back. That was good timing! I got everything dried out, and I got home before I got wet. I've been out here for sixty days. Two months! That's a long time. It's a good feeling to have made it this far.

# Chapter 26

# Mind Games

August 29, Day 61

Showers were predicted for today but it's 9 AM and it's been raining more or less straight through since about 5 PM yesterday. I was planning to wait out the rain, but I'm going to go ahead and head out now.

Except for the rain conditions are actually pretty good. Low tide is coming up in less than an hour and it's nearly calm. When I get to the rocks near the Hump I fire up my GPS but the batteries go dead. I think about replacing them but there's no need. I know the sweet spot is about 70 yards out from the rocks. An estimate is close enough. I drift over the Hump several times, and at least three times the jig gets temporarily snagged. I got hung up on that very snag just before I hooked the monster halibut that I lost.

Suddenly the jig pauses and I feel a living vibration. *Fish on!* I set the hook. *I got one!* The line goes slack. He's off. Bummer. Is there something I could be doing differently or is it just one of those things? The hook is sharp. Sometimes when I'm trout fishing I'll fail to get a solid hookup on a string of fish, then land the next half-dozen fish in a row. Who knows?

I gotta pee. I paddle over to the small pile of wet rocks and hang the kayak up so it's half floating. When I step onto the seaweed draped rocks there is cold ocean in all directions. It makes me shudder to think about the boat somehow getting away from me with the tide coming in, inevitably flooding the rocks with fifteen feet of water, the shore too far to swim.

I paddle out on the other side of the rocks and let a light breeze carry me towards the crab trap as I jig. It looks like another day with no landed halibut.

I reel in and paddle the last quarter mile to the buoy. There's forty feet of slack line in the boat before I feel the weight of the trap. Starfish, I bet. Seems like when I try new areas I rarely hit a home-run with crabs but often end up with starfish. Starfish it is, two of them. Both are big with a dozen or more arms. One is reddish and almost looks as if it has a glow to it. Is that possible, for a starfish to glow? Are they ever bioluminescent? I release the starfish and drop the trap back closer to the mouth of My Creek. I paddle for home in the continuing rain.

I land on the close side of the spit and portage my boat up over the top to camp. It would be easier to leave the boat on the other side, but I don't want to leave the kayak unattended for long. Eventually a bear would rip it to pieces. How long that would take is hard to say, but it *would* happen sooner or later. Which reminds me, the bear fence is only on the second set of batteries. Pretty good battery life, I'd say. I should change them out, though. They won't last much longer.

Back at the tent I'm pleased to find how dry my clothes are, even my butt. The only wet spot is the cuffs of my fleece jacket. I'd pushed the sleeves up to my elbow, That helped a lot. Light winds were a big factor as well. A good headwind always drives some rain inside my hood.

I take stock of my canned meat. It looks like five venison, one salmon, three crab and two halibut. I finished off a jar of halibut for breakfast. I open another now for lunch along with almost a quart of blueberries. The blueberries seem to be getting sweeter later in the season.

I think about what gear I need to replace after this trip is over. Rubber knee boots, of course. New waders. This rain jacket is doing pretty well but I need a new lightweight backpacking rain jacket. When I get back home, I'm going to go through every piece of gear before I pack it away. I'll repair it before I forget what needs fixing. If it can't be fixed, I'll replace it.

People often ask me what I think about on trips like this where there's seldom someone to talk to. Not surprisingly I'm doing a lot of scheming and planning for the next few hours or day or days. I think about past events, large and small, people I've known. I often laugh out loud, remembering something funny.

Having time to think is in many ways a luxury. There's no static from coworkers or TV or radio. It's important, however, to try to keep your thoughts positive overall, to not dwell on past wrongs, to not re-fight old battles in your mind, to not worry about things you can do nothing about. With no distractions, it's all too easy to get stuck in your own head, arguing with people who aren't there. On this trip, "negative loops" haven't been an issue. When I was hiking the Pacific Crest Trail four years ago, though, I was in the midst of a relationship meltdown with my best friend and sometimes girlfriend. Most of that summer was great, but many hours of hiking alone were ruined by mental struggles as I thought about how things were spiraling down and wondering what was salvageable. It would have been so much easier if I knew that it was all over or that we would patch things up. If we could talk face to face to iron things out. Instead it was all in limbo, unresolved and ultimately unresolvable.

On this adventure I spend many hours thinking ahead to long trails I'd like to hike some day, rivers I'd like to float.

I turn on the weather radio and wait until it gets to the local weather forecast. They had been calling for "mostly cloudy, chance of showers" but now they are predicting showers. I'm going to the lodge tomorrow regardless. It's supposed to rain Sunday and Monday and I need to do one last update on this trip.

My evening reading, once again, mentions rich, delicious foods.

What would I eat if I were back in the "real world?" For breakfast, pancakes with butter and syrup and coffee. For the rest of the day, in any order, a big salad with grilled chicken, peanut M&Ms, a large pizza with everything, and a half gallon tub of rich chocolate ice cream. That would be a great start!

Before bed I tap out a website update on my iPhone so it's ready to post tomorrow at the lodge.

August 30, Day 62, Saturday

Lodge day! I eat crab for breakfast, fortifying myself for the long paddle ahead. Scattered showers are predicted but the weather looks decent as I launch the kayak onto the smooth waters of Wild Bay. This time I'm not making any stops along the way, and this time there is no fog to disorient me. I beeline for miles, straight down the bay. It felt pretty adventurous weeks ago, first paddling my little kayak far from the nearest land, but now it's as natural as can be. Things can change fast though, if the wind comes up or the fog rolls in or a whale decides to surface nearby!

As usual I take advantage of the short-cut between an island and the mainland, making the fifty-yard portage over the top of the spit, trying not to crush exposed sea life. Just before I launch, I notice my wader belt is missing. I took it off to pee. I must have left it where I landed. I look around but can't find it until I notice that what I'd mistaken for a rock is actually my curled up belt.

By the time I reach the lodge, I'm tired. It's a long trip and the only break was the portage, not really a break at all. I check in with the lodge owners, then head over to the main lodge to update my website. I talk to Marshall, the pilot, about flying, and pretty, cheerful Anna about her adventurous summer in Alaska.

It's nice to have my website update all ready to go. Some more members of the lodge crew file through, snacking or getting an early lunch. It won't be long before I'm back to a world of all-I-can-eat of anything-I-want! I take a quick look at the weather on the internet: seeing the weather for the next week, rather than hearing it, is something my brain processes more easily. In a nutshell, it looks like highs mostly in the high 50s, lows around 50 with a little sun and minimal rain. Sounds pretty good to me!

I say goodbye to the crew, then head over to the office to talk to the owners.

"I really want to thank you for letting me use your internet. It was a big deal, letting people know I was OK, and how I was doing."

"You are certainly welcome. We were glad to do it."

"When are you wrapping your season?"

"In a few days. Some of the crew will be leaving soon. When are you flying out?"

"Hopefully the morning of the 8th. This will be my last visit."

Before I go, I get their winter address. I want to send them a thank-you of some kind. They were mighty kind to me.

As I paddle away, it feels like the end of something. Most likely I'll never see any of these people again. This last lodge visit feels like the beginning of the end of this adventure.

Near the mouth of the cove that leads to Salmon Creek, I give halibut fishing a go, but after jigging my brains out for an hour or so, I have nothing to show for it, not even a bite.

I've still got a supply of canned meat, but my supply of berries always runs out quickly. I paddle over to check out some of the good berry spots I found on the mainland near my old spike camp.

I find is a nice bush of red huckleberries, growing right on the edge of the shore. I chow down, then get a jar from my daypack and pick some more. I pick my way up to a nice meadow. There are some decent patches of blueberries and huckleberries, but red huckleberries have appeared in much greater numbers than before. I stop to admire the blush of oncoming fall colors, faint reds and yellows. As the jar fills I notice beautiful alternating bands of bright red and blue-black berries. When the jar is filled it looks so colorful that I have to take a photo. I look around for a nice setting and find a patch of vivid green moss and tiny ferns. Sprinkled throughout are three-inch-high plants with bright red berries and vivid green leaves. I nestle the jar in amongst them and

snap several photos. They turn out great! What are those mystery berries anyway? I've seen them often, seems like I should know. I bite one for a tiny taste. Not bad. I'll have to look them up.

Out in the cove, I jig in about 50 feet of water. I've got a small fish on. It feels like a sculpin but when I get it to the surface it's a two pound halibut, snagged along one edge. I let him go.

It's nearly 6 PM and time to head home. I beeline straight back to base camp. Murrelets fly by, low over the water, tiny, silvery fish in their beaks, each heading back to its nest to feed a hungry chick. It was the calmest day yet for the long trip to the lodge. Sure made it a whole lot easier.

For supper I finish off the jar of crab. Still hungry, I eat half a jar of venison as well. In the evening I read a book on my Kindle, *How I Found Livingstone*, subtitled *Travels, Adventures and Discoveries in Central Africa including four months residence with Dr. Livingstone* By Sir Henry M. Stanley, G.C.B. Both were remarkable men with remarkable stories. What an experience it must have been to explore such exotic, mysterious and brutally dangerous country!

Suddenly I remember to look up those red berries I found. Flipping through one of my guidebooks I recognize them instantly: bunchberries! Also known as dwarf dogwood. It's says: "*good fresh....sweet, if a little mealy and seedy.*" Amazing to think how frequently I've stepped over them on this trip and yet never eaten one! Tomorrow I will make up for some of those lost opportunities! I wonder how many more things I've been overlooking that are good to eat?

August 31, Day 63

A mouse ran across my head last night!

I'd planned to halibut fish this morning, but there's a stiff wind blowing up the bay. As I think about another plan, I eat a breakfast of venison, blueberries, and huckleberries. Getting another deer wasn't part of my strategy, but I've got enough jars to can one now. I think I'll hunt into the wind, down the peninsula towards Magic Meadow. If I get a good chance at a buck I'll take it. Any meat I have left over-venison, crab, salmon-will be part of my winter food supply. Back in the "real world" almost all the fish and meat I eat are from wild sources. Along the way I'll pick berries, and when I get to Magic Meadow I want to pick a bunch of crab apples. It will be fun to explore new country in the middle of this route.

It starts raining as I pack up to leave. It will be a wet day, deer hunting through the rain and dripping forest, but it will also be quiet walking.

I walk down the beach, looking for a good place to climb the low ridge, finally following a deer trail diagonally up-slope. It weaves through patches of Devil's club and brush through big timber. The trail generally follows the top of the ridge, past a few giant mossy stumps from a hundred years ago. There are even two giant, forgotten logs. It's a tragic waste, those forest monarchs sawed down a century ago, never to be used for their intended purpose. Instead, they are feeding the forest itself, mosses and ferns and bacteria. It's humbling to think this tree might have lived five hundred years before being sawed down. And now it's lain here since long before I was born, throughout my whole lifetime, and this mossy log will certainly be here for at least a generation to come. If this tree sprouted 600 years ago, that would be 1414!

I've been flipping through my guidebooks, looking for wild foods that I have overlooked. One that I noticed was licorice fern, which tends to grow on trees. I've taken photos of them without knowing what they were. The leaflets are short and smooth-looking and grow from the roots individually. When I spot one I peel it, and the moss it is growing from, off the tree. I break the moss apart revealing the knobby roots, breaking off pieces of the newer growth. I brush off bits of dirt and crunch a piece of root between my teeth. It takes a moment for the lightly sweet, licorice taste to hit me. Cool! Now *that's* something new! I enjoy several more pieces before I go. I'll definitely be eating some more.

After a while I come to a well-used bear and deer trail. Looking at the satellite photos before this trip I theorized most bears would take this shortcut across the base of the peninsula. This well-used trail supports that theory. It starts at My Cove. I'm guessing it will come out on Magic Meadow which is itself at the end of a natural route leading away from the cove on the opposite side.

Where logs lay across the trail I notice where brown bear have climbed over them and scraped the moss off with their long claws. There are some good patches of huckleberries. I set down my pack and pick them into a jar, popping some berries directly into my mouth. Good thing I slid up my shirt sleeves because I can feel rain trickling up my sleeves when I reach up for higher berries.

The trail continues on, weaving around the Devil's club and past broad-leafed skunk cabbage. There are deer tracks here and there. Although I watch carefully, I've yet to see or hear a deer. Ahead the forest opens up, and when I get to the meadow I follow along the edge, looking for deer or even slight movements. I sit where I can see across a big expanse of green meadow, partially protected from the rain by overhanging brush. The moisture-laden air is hazy. I try to orient myself. This must be Magic Meadow. Is that tree over there the one I

sat under the day I first came here? I think so. Things can look so different when seen from a different angle! After a while no deer have appeared. I think it's raining too hard. I thought the wind would be steadily in my face but it has been swirling at times so maybe the deer have been smelling me.

From where I'm sitting I look for crab apple trees along the edge of the meadow. They are the trees with the yellowist leaves, I think, round-looking and about fifteen feet tall. I'm going to check them out. When I get to the first one it takes a moment to see the first little apples. I pick a bunch of three and hold them in my teeth, pulling off the long stems. I chew them up and swallow them. It's great to enjoy the tart taste of apples and to be eating another type of food. One of my wild food guides points out that crab apple seeds contain amygdalin, which breaks down into cyanide. Sounds pretty scary until you consider that regular apples seeds contain the same compound. The bottom line, in reasonable amounts it's harmless. As my guide says, just don't eat a whole bowlful of crushed seeds.

It's easy to overlook these little apples. They are mostly a yellowish-green against yellow-green leaves. Clumps of two or three or more seem to magically appear just when I think I've found them all. Since I saw them last many have developed a red blush. They are a bit sweeter now too, it seems. The leaves are definitely more yellow.

As I follow the meadow's edge, I see many crab apple trees overlooked last time. I begin filling a jar with any little apples that I haven't eaten. Here is a nice patch of bunchberries. Unlike the crab apples they are easy to spot, big clumps of bright-red berries. They are fun to pick, too. With one grab I can strip off a whole clump of berries and pop them directly in my mouth. They aren't very sweet, but they are still good, another satisfying way to vary my diet.

When I've filled a jar with crab apples I hunt my way through the Avenue of the Giants. I've had such good luck here before that I expect to see a deer at any moment. It's thrilling just being in this park-like setting among giant monarchs.

When I reach the edge of the grassy cove, I begin following the shoreline back towards camp, watching for deer and good berry-picking. With the wind now mostly at my back I'm unlikely to sneak up on a buck.

I spot highbush cranberries growing on a rocky outcropping. There are large clumps of the tart, bright-red berries. It's the fastest berry-picking of the whole trip, a handful of berries at a time. I climb up the rocks to get at bushes that are too high to reach. It's fun seeing the jar fill so fast. In minutes I've filled it to the top!

As I continue along the beach I notice bladderwrack. It's a greenish-brown "seaweed," actually a type of algae, with distinctive double-bladed tips. My guidebook says it's rich with protein and trace minerals. I pick a piece and try it. Not a particularly appealing name but it's not too bad! Another prolific food I've been walking right past. There are countless things a local wild-foods expert could have taught me, yet it's fun figuring things out on my own. I eat more bladderwrack as I walk.

It's nice to get back to the tent and out of the rain. I stayed remarkably dry despite the hours of rain. Lunch is salt-and-peppered halibut. After that long walk, the good food and the patter of rain on the tent makes me sleepy. I put on my warm balaclava and snuggle into my toasty sleeping bag and fall asleep.

When I wake up I read about Stanley in Africa. What an adventure he had, but what a heavy toll of human life he witnessed: disease, war, banditry, and wild animal attacks. I wonder what things are like there today?

Last night I noticed a faint glow from my headlamp. It is somehow shorting itself a little bit. I fiddle with it but can't find a problem. Maybe it's just general dampness. Using the charger and a USB battery I recharge the AAA batteries the headlamp uses.

The weather radio is predicting quite a bit of rain ahead. The best day for my last camp move looks like two days from now. Partly cloudy and no rain. That's what I'll shoot for.

# CHAPTER 27

---

# September

September 1, 2014 Day 64

It's incredible to think that this adventure started the last day of June. In Alaska, September is autumn. I can sense the coming of fall in gathering flocks of geese, in faded summer flowers, in berry patches long past their prime. I feel autumn in the cooler days and smell it in the air. Fall is in the changing leaves, in dying salmon, the graying hair of blacktails and in the shortening days. The days were nearly eighteen hours long when I got here. They are about fourteen hours long now, every day about five minutes shorter.

It's 8:39 PM right now. A week from now, weather permitting, I will be back in a nice, warm, dry Petersburg motel room. I'll have enjoyed a long hot shower. I will have been to the grocery store, and a restaurant or two and will have eaten my fill of favorite foods. I will have heard the news of the world. It's amazing how different these two worlds are.

I made two halibut fishing trips today. The wind gave me a break on the first trip, but there were some wetting showers. I struck out on both halibut and the crab trap, which I rebaited with mussels and clams. At Big Island I picked thimbleberries. It's my last decent patch and still yielded moderate amounts. My hands were stiff from the cold showers and the wet bushes. Even the light breeze made them colder.

I was surprised to see a skiff come roaring down the bay. It went into the little cove past Big Island, and then veered my way on the return trip, cut the engine and drifted towards me. A beefy fellow with a big gray beard leaned out, his dog looking at me curiously. I'd met him at the Lodge weeks back. He has his own place somewhere next to the lodge.

"How's fishing?"

"Nothing today. Halibut fishing has been slow but I don't really know what I'm doing for halibut. I landed one nice fish out here, a fifty pounder. Do you think this is a good spot?"

"Might be. Just keep at it. You'll catch more."

"What are you up to?"

"Just taking a look around. Mostly looking for deer."

"I got my buck August 7. I've been catching plenty of salmon when I want them. When do you think the silvers will be in?"

"Silvers? I don't think you'll see any silvers in these streams."

"Really? I guess you'd know. The fish run-maps shows them in some of these creeks."

"I'm afraid they're wrong. How much longer are you out here?"

"I'm scheduled to fly out on the 8th."

"All right. Have fun out here. Stay safe!"

"You too. Good luck on your fall hunts."

With that he was off. It was really strange to talk to someone. Other than the biweekly lodge trip days, it was the only time I talked to someone all summer.

About noon the wind came up. I gave up and paddled for home.

The sun was peeking out occasionally so I hung up my rain gear and waders for awhile. I got caught up on "the dishes" by washing six dirty jars, using my homemade sponge brush. Those empty jars sure do accumulate fast. I want to do at least one more major canning operation before I leave.

With glimpses of sun and the breeze dying down, I headed out on another halibut trip at 5 PM. A mink ran right behind me when I launched, completely ignoring me as if I were a tree. That mink explained the dead shrews I found on the path. Shrews must really taste bad. They are often killed and abandoned by predators.

Out over the Hump my heart skipped a beat when I felt a fish, but it turned out to be a three pound sculpin. If sculpins were halibut I'd be real killer!

At about seven I called it a day and returned to the tent for a supper of halibut, crab-apples and goose tongue. Earlier in the day I had venison and salmon and thimbleberries.

I'm reading the Stanley-Livingston book this evening and thinking about tomorrow's plan. Despite the glimpses of sun today, there was enough rain and humidity to make it pretty wet. Yesterday was rainy, too, enough to fill the cook camp water jug full to overflowing. If the weather cooperates tomorrow I'll do a camp move as well as a major drying operation.

September 2, Day 65

When I step out of the tent to pee this morning, it looks like a pretty nice day. What should I have for breakfast? Venison! I'm definitely not at all tired of blacktail meat. After eating my fill I walk to the edge of the water and break off pieces of bladderwrack, eating it raw, fast and easy.

I launch my kayak into the barely rippled waters of the bay. It's 6 AM. Clouds on the western mountaintops glow orange in the morning sun. Water dogs drift over the water. I paddle out to the middle of the bay, planning to drift along while jigging, hoping to find a good halibut spot by chance. As the kayak slowly drifts toward the head of the bay I jig steadily, watching the sun flow slowly down the green alpine tundra until it reaches the timberline.

Although the sky is blue overhead, fog rolls in until the mountains and shore are half obscured by white mists. The sun is doing its best to shine through. A partial "fog bow" appears to the west. I pull out my camera to take a photo. The photo shows rugged peaks in the background, barely visible through the fog. The sky, a robin's egg blue, peeks through wispy clouds. There is the bright-white shard of fog rainbow, an arc one hundred feet high and two hundred yards away. In the foreground everything is in a beautiful morning sun: the cuffs of my waders, my wading boots and the green and gray bow of my kayak. My fishing rod is bowed by the heavy halibut jig.

I can hear geese honking in the distance, passing ravens are croaking, eagles are calling, and seagulls squawking. There is no human sound except the occasional splash of my paddle as I straighten the boat. The smell of the ocean permeates everything.

I turn on the GPS hanging around my neck-I'll need it to find the Hump this foggy morning! I follow the GPS until I get close, then, after getting a heading reading, switch to using magnetic compass. It's less confusing to me that way. I watch the GPS to see how much farther I have to go: 58 feet, 32 feet, 15 feet, right here!

The jigging is going well, but the halibut fishing... not so much. When I check the jig I find the tail has been torn clean off! I can see teeth marks, the sharp teeth of a halibut, no doubt. I don't have any more of the giant plastic halibut jigs. How about if I tie a rockfish jig to the halibut jig? I lay the white rockfish jig on top of the halibut jig, then, using fishing line, I tie a tight knot around both bodies followed by a dozen wraps around the length of them, then tie it off again at the other end. It looks like it will work pretty well. I dunk it in the water and swim it back and forth. The rockfish jig tail now acts as a tail on the big jig and it isn't a whole lot smaller than the original. Seems like it should work fine!

I keep jigging, letting the light breeze carry me nearly to the crab trap. I must have jigged most of the way for nearly two miles. Early on in the trip it was no surprise I wasn't catching halibut. I wasn't putting in much effort. Now though? My halibut fishing luck is bound to improve. It really is.

Speaking of luck, today I'm luckless for crab catching, the trap is empty. I land on Big Island to pee and to pick thimbleberries. Despite the decline in ripe berries, I get enough for a nice brunch. It's nearly noon and the fog is burning off. Camp move!

After stashing the boat I change out of my waders and slip into the

foot parts of my trashed rubber boots. I next hang up and lay out everything to dry part way to the new campsite I've scouted out. I turn both my rain jacket and my sleeping bag inside out to expose their black interior. The black will soak up more heat and obviously the inside is more of a priority to dry than the outside. My sleeping bag uses Pertex in the shell. It's water resistant so turning the bag inside out will also help it dry. Next I set up the solar panels and check to see the charging lights are lit. With all my gear toasting in the sun, I move the tent. It goes faster each time. It's satisfying to have it set up and ready to go with a nice, taut pitch. I leave the silnylon doors open with the screen door zipped shut so any lingering moisture can dissipate.

I sit in the sun to clean the guns for what I hope is the last time on this trip. I reach for the cleaning supplies. Where is that bore brush I was using to scrub rust spots? I can't find it anywhere, so I make do without it. It's a good feeling to have the guns gleaming with gun oil again. When I get back, I'm going to take both guns apart as far as I dare once more and give them a good scrubbing with the best rust inhibitor I can find.

The beautiful sun is still out so I make the rounds of all my gear, repositioning each item as necessary to expose the dampest area to the drying sunlight. This is a happy, pleasant chore, getting everything crispy dry in the friendly sun. It looks like a hobo camp though, gear draped here and there, colorful and chaotic.

It's about 5 PM. I just noticed ominous rain clouds rolling in fast. I scramble around madly, gathering up gear at top speed, frantically trying to beat the rain. I dash about stuffing clothing into my big, red dry-bag. Lastly I gather up the solar panels, and fifteen minutes after I noticed the fast approach of the clouds everything is secured in the tent, albeit in a bit of a jumble. After a quick check to make sure I haven't forgotten anything, I move the electric fence. I beat the rain!

I take a break to look for licorice fern. It's nearly ubiquitous and easy to find, I peel a strip of moss off a tree branch along with several fronds of licorice fern, pulling the moss apart to separate out the roots. I chew, enjoying the sweet, distinctive taste.

Back at the tent I put on my sun-dried camp shoes and sort things out, taking a break to open the last jar of venison. It's nearly 9 PM before the tent is fully organized. I'm tired. Camp moves are always big days. It's great to have the last camp move done.

# CHAPTER 28

## Victory and Defeat

September 3, Day 66

It's Leah's birthday. She's my little sister. It doesn't seem so long ago that she was a little kid, all excited about the candles on her cake, tearing the wrapping off her birthday gifts with great excitement, thrilled to be the center of attention. Just being alive is an adventure when you're three years old!

There is fog down towards the Sound. I walk down to cook camp with the water jug, straining the gathered rainwater through my headnet. Back at camp I suspend the water jug from a stout tree branch. Turning the spigot = running water!

I finish off the last of the venison for breakfast, with some fresh picked goose tongue and cranberries for my breakfast vitamin C. Hey, I ate that whole deer! I'm getting low on canned meat. Maybe that's an understatement. I've got some crab meat left, that's it for meat. I've also got some crab apples, huckleberries, highbush cranberries and blueberries. I've given halibut fishing a good go of it, but I need more food in the bank. I'm going after salmon today at Salmon Creek.

Halfway there and I'm paddling across calm water into a gentle breeze. There is a feeding frenzy nearby. Two or three species of gulls and a handful of murrelets are after some kind of small, silvery fish that are dimpling the sea. Why they don't dive to escape the birds is a mystery. The murrelets seem focused on catching their own fish, while most of the gulls seem primarily interested in stealing fish from one another.

I turn into the cove leading to Salmon Creek, passing eagles and seals and salmon cruising right below the surface. Nearing the creek, I see something: *A brown bear!* I paddle behind a little island and carry the kayak up to the treeline. I want to get a photo of the bear if I can. I put on my daypack and start walking around the island, rifle in one hand, a jarbox full of empty jars under the other arm with a bucket in my hand.

As I round the island my heart jumps. Nearby two brown objects are streaking away. *A sow and cub!* They must have been on the other side of the island when I landed! I'm not sure which of us is more surprised. Charging is not the default reaction for a sow with cubs, running is. She had all the room in the world and fled. Still, surprising a bear at close range is something best avoided.

I stand looking for the lone bear I first spotted. A huge brown object is swimming downstream, just underwater, making the brackish water bulge upwards. It disappears around the corner. What the heck was *that!?* A huge halibut? That's my first thought. I've seen flatfish in the shallows a bunch of times, but never one that big. Maybe it was a seal or sea lion? I've never seen one of those that far upstream, either. That seems the likeliest explanation, though.

I wade across an oxbow of the creek and climb the other bank. *There he is!* I slowly sink to my knees and un-sling my pack. He doesn't see me. Bear photo, here I come. I unzip the front pocket of my pack and pull out the dry box, flipping both latches... where's my camera? I definitely had it, didn't I? I take a quick look through everything. Nope, I don't have it. I reach for my iPhone, but I don't want to get close enough to him to get good photos with no optical zoom. It's not going to stop me from enjoying watching him though. He wades into the shallows, salmon zipping all around him, their backs and tails sticking out of the water. It's like shooting fish in a barrel. He pounces and pins one to the bottom with his paws, then grabs it in his huge teeth, carrying the flopping fish up on the opposite bank. The big brownie sinks down on his butt, facing away from me. He lowers the fish so he can hold it down with one paw and strip meat away with his teeth. He's the picture of contentment, chewing leisurely and looking about lazily.

When he's done eating he stands up, staring upstream. I hear a deep warning rumble. There must be another bear coming! I'm glad he's not growling at me! There's another bear! It strides out of the trees and down the bank. Another male I'll bet. It's alone, anyway. When he spots my bear he veers away slightly so their paths won't converge, then hustles into the trees. My bear is the dominant one. He stiffens again, nose in the air, and swings his head around towards me. He sees me. I put my hand on my rifle. Without the wind I'd be a suspicious lump on the bank, but now with my scent blowing his way he knows exactly what I am. He turns and lopes into the trees.

Now I concentrate on fish spotting. The creek is loaded with countless pink salmon but also numerous bigger fish, fresh-looking, with none of those white patches giving them a battered look. Are the silvers here at last?

I walk upstream, looking for a perfect spot, one with plenty of fish and not too deep. Here's a good spot, just below a confluence, loaded with fish, plenty of room for a back-cast and a great gravel bar for landing my catch. It's a good spot to see approaching bears, too. Could happen!

This pool is absolutely loaded with pinks, so many that I'm inadvertently snagging some, even with a slow retrieve. Most get loose almost immediately, those that don't I land and release as quickly as possible. Hardly any pinks are actually biting today. What I want to catch, if they're in here, are some silvers. There are at least some chums. I've seen their tiger stripes. Some are in good shape, too. This must be another, later run of chums. I'd be happy to catch a few.

I notice a big chum among the pinks, acting aggressively. Aggressive salmon are usually the easiest ones to catch. I cast what has become the standard "go-to" fly on this trip, a purple egg-sucking leech. It plops into the clear water six feet beyond him and I begin stripping it back towards me, trying to time the retrieve so it passes inches from his nose. Incredibly, in a pool of a hundred fish or more, the very fish I'm targeting swings his head and the fly disappears. I set the hook and my rod bows, the line taut. He explodes upstream scattering pinks in all directions. *Fish on!*

I manage to keep him in the pool and he slowly tires. I look around for something to stun him and see a rock that will work. When at last he's exhausted I pull him up onto the gravel bar, grab him at the base of the tail, and bonk him on the head with the rock. I pull out my Swiss army knife, flip open the blade, and slash his gills. Dark red blood spurts out onto the gravel.

I walk down to the lower pool again. Many more big salmon are here. I'm still hoping some are silvers. After a few casts I decide the magic has waned with the purple leech. I open a couple of fly boxes and kneel down, pondering my choices. Lots of big flies in various combos of black, orange, green, pink, silver, white, red, and purple. I switch to a black marabou muddler. This is one of my favorite flies for rainbows, but I decide to try it on salmon today, just for something different.

I stand up and make a few false casts, then lay the fly out beyond several big salmon near the head of the pool. The line tightens and I set the hook. Got em! There are a few big boulders in this pool, so I try to keep my fish away from them so he doesn't wrap the line. It's another chum, a nice, big male. I don't play him any longer than necessary. I want to get him on shore. I reach down and pick up the stout, eighteen inch stick I've broken off for a club, then look for a landing spot far enough from other fish to prevent spooking them. When it's time I pull him flopping onto shore where I pin him down. Most of the first blow is absorbed when the end of the club hits the gravel first but the next instantly stops the flopping. I reach into my raincoat pocket for the knife and slash his gills. Two down! I want about five.

You never know with fishing. Most of the pinks today aren't biting. The chums are biting, but I'm really having to work at it. I try a green woolly bugger with a brass head, a fly I've caught lots of chums with in the past. A group of a half dozen big salmon hold near the head of the pool. I've pretty much conceded that all the big ones are chums, no silvers. I cast out past them and strip the bugger back towards me. Not many pinks in this pool, a big advantage, less unintentional snagging. *Got one!* It makes a short rush, shaking its head and the line goes slack. *#$%! I want to get my fish as soon as possible, to keep them fresh. To give me plenty of time for canning. It's already noon.

The green bugger soon comes through again, though. I see the fly hooked deeply in the corner of the chum's mouth. When the time is right I lead him to the shallows and haul him onto the gravel. He still has a couple of sea lice on him. Fresh in from saltwater! Three down!

I walk upstream to another pool. I land a pink in good shape, a male. He's not nearly as big as a chum but he'll do nicely. Four! I switch back to the black muddler. It does the trick. I slide another chum onto the gravel, the most silvery one I've caught on this trip. Five!

I try to think of a good way to take a photo of the fish and me. My gaze pauses on the root-wad of an old, fallen tree. I carry my salmon over there and hang them on roots and set up my iPhone on its mini-tripod to take a video.

As I narrate the day's events, dozens of pink salmon splash just behind me, some swimming within a few feet, their dorsal fins sticking out of the water. It will be a good setting for a video, I think, with the pleasant sight and sound of running water, and splashing salmon, here in the rich greens of the rain forest.

It's down to business now, though! I lay out the fillet board with a clear piece of plastic under it to keep the fish clean if they slide off to the side of the board. I line up all twelve jars, ready to go, rings and new lids handy. The jars fill quickly, I'm not messing around! Before I throw each carcass in the stream I slice off any meat that I've missed. When I'm done I've gotten ten jars, nearly twenty pounds of boneless meat! I want two more jars, though. It would be nice to have a grill full of fish, too.

I walk down to the lower pool and soon have another nice chum. At the upper pool, the one most loaded with fish, I catch another nice pink. Success! I quickly fillet both fish, filling the last two jars with

enough fish left over for the grill. I put all twelve jars into the jarbox and wire both ends shut. It's heavy, but not as heavy as the whole fish, that's for sure.

I have to switch carrying arms a couple of times, but I'm soon back at the kayak. There, on one tube, is my camera! I'd forgotten I pulled it out of the dry box when I first landed. Good thing it didn't start raining.

It's 7:15 when I get home. Where has the day gone? I haul my canning gear: chair, canner cover, and so on, down to cook camp. I add water and nearly fill the canner with two layers of jars. When I go to tighten the lid, two of the plastic knobs are stuck. I've got pretty good leverage with the "wings" of the knobs, and I'd like to think I'm reasonably strong, but the one will not budge one iota, and the other only a fraction of a turn. *This is not good.* I pull out my Leatherman and, squeezing down on the knob as gently as I can, try turning it. Nope. I walk back to camp and get my larger Gerber tool and a piece of rubber, I wrap the knob with the rubber, then clamp it with the Gerber and turn: it comes free, but not without chipping a little. The other one, though will still not budge. I apply more and more pressure until,

crunch, both wings break off. *Oh oh. So now what?* If I squeeze harder it will just break all the plastic off and it will be useless. I study the knob, thinking. I notice a rim of metal at the very base of the knob.

I walk all the way back to camp, again, and get a little Vice Grip I brought for something just like this. I clamp it around the metal and it reluctantly turns. Yes! I'm back in business. It's nearly dark. It's going to be a long, long day by the time I'm done. I am hungry now. I don't want to grill salmon when the long canning process is done. I walk all the way back to camp. Fourth time. In the dark this time. I get a jar of crab and crab apples for supper. And two jars for canning the fillets I'd saved to grill.

At long last I have the canner ready to go, filled with fourteen jars of fillets and the knobs cranked down nicely. I start the fire. Anxious to expedite the process I feed a steady stream of my best wood into the stove's small door. When it's time to put the pressure regulator on top, I keep feeding wood in and the pressure slowly climbs. Man, this is taking forever! It's a full canner. That's a lot of heating to do. But then the pressure starts *falling*! Now what's up with that? I pull the canner off the fire and look. The stove chimney is mostly choked with coals. I was pushing in the wood so aggressively that the fire wasn't getting enough air. I clear the chimney and feed wood at a much more moderate pace. Soon I'm back on track and the pressure, at last, hits ten pounds and I hear the sweet music of a chattering regulator.

I'm starving. I haven't eaten for about 14 hours or so, since the venison of my long-ago breakfast. Now I have all the time in the world, though. I eat a bunch of crab meat then snack on crab apples, one at a time, spitting out the stems. They are tart, but good.

It's just about midnight when the 110 minutes of pressure canning is done, then a considerable wait for the pressure to drop to zero on that big canner. I am more than ready to go to bed. I keep flipping on my headlamp switch to check the pressure. When it finally hits zero I open the lid to set the jars out to cool.

When I grab the neck of the first jar and lift it crunches. *Oh oh.* Only half a jar comes out. Broken! The next jar makes the same funny crunch. My heart sinks. It sinks farther when the third is also broken. *Oh no!* Are they *all* broken? The fourth jars is OK. I have hope. The next is broken and the next. I am really bummed. Luckily, the rest of the jars are OK. Eight good jars, six broken. A terrible toll of valuable food. What went wrong?

While waiting for the jars to cool I make yet another walk in the dark back to the tent to consult the canner instructions. I read by headlamp light, it says, more or less:

*Q. What causes the jars to break?*

1. *Jars are too tight in canner*
2. *Not using standard jars*
3. *Jars improperly tightened*
4. *Not placing jars on rack [touching bottom of canner]*
5. *Over-filling jars*
6. *Sudden temperature change*
7. *Jars have tiny cracks*
8. *Fluctuation of pressure*

It's either over-tightening, or cracks. Since six broke, it's almost certainly over tightening. Before this trip I'd only done one batch of pressure canning. When I think about it, you're only supposed to tighten them finger tight. I started out like that, but today? I tightened them. Too tight. My mistake. This might be my biggest blunder of the trip. What's maddening is all that good meat is wasted. I don't dare eat it. There might be tiny shards of glass in it.

Isn't there a saying like "You learn to avoid mistakes with experience, you get experience by making mistakes?" At least they didn't all break. I did get eight good jars.

It's 1 AM when I crawl into my sleeping bag. Two long days in a row. Days full-lived.

# CHAPTER 29

## Halibut Heaven

September 4, Day 67

When I check the time it's only 4 AM. Funny how I still wake up early, even though I went to bed so late! Man, I'm tired though. I close my eyes and doze.

I finally sit up at six. I have that not-enough-sleep feeling. I can rarely sleep in late though. It's just the way I'm wired.

I walk outside to pee and to check things out. I brought the jars back to camp last night and set them down just inside the electric fence. One of the broken jars only has a small circle of glass missing off the bottom edge. I decide that it will reasonably safe to eat the top half of the jar. I unscrew the ring, pull off the lid, and deploy my trusty fork and salt and pepper. It's good stuff. I chew carefully. No crunchy glass!

When half the meat is gone I sadly carry all the broken jars down to the bay and dump the meat in the water. What a waste. I suppose it will be a windfall of food to some ocean critters, though.

I clean up cook camp. I put all the broken jars in the bucket with the cracked bottom. Those six broken jars comprise most of the trash I've produced in the last two months.

Counting today, I have only four full days left on this trip! I want to make each remaining day count. Number one on my list is to get another halibut. I've only managed to land one halibut fishing in the upper bay. I was going to rebait the crab trap and fish the Hump today, but instead I'm going to fish the mouth of the cove down by Salmon Creek. I'll bring gear for a spike camp and fish it hard today, and tomorrow, too, if I need to.

I round up supplies for spike camp, halibut fishing gear and enough food for a couple of days. For meat I have half a jar of crab meat and two jars of salmon. Soon I'm beelining into a gentle wind for Salmon Creek. It must be about three miles to get to the island where I'll camp.

I camped here before, so I've got the best landing place dialed, as well as the best place to set up my little tarptent. I like to set up camp while the weather is good. I carry my big dry bag up the slope and set up my shelter on the now familiar spot, ending up with a nice, taut pitch. I roll out my sleeping pad and pull my sleeping bag from its stuff sack and shake it out before laying it out on the pad. A fine camp, ready to go!

I load the fishing gear, rod and homemade halibut harpoon into the kayak and paddle out to the mouth of the cove, and then a couple hundred yards upwind. I'm going to try to fish about twenty fathoms deep, 120 feet. Before I launched I measured out twenty arm-spans of fishing line, then pinched on a tiny split-shot to mark that depth. Drifting across the mouth of the bay should give me twenty fathoms or so according to my nautical chart.

Halibut are sometimes called "butts." I'm using a bait scent called "Butt Juice." Before dropping the jig in, I drip on some more Butt Juice. When the jig hits the water the scent leaves an oily sheen. When I'm in position I drop the heavy jig to the bottom. The depth is pretty close to my 20 fathom target depth. I jig as the gentle breeze slowly carries me along. Perfect. I take a good mental note of landmarks. I'm about 150 yards from shore, and I notice I'm drifting about 125 yards out from some bare rocks that are marked with an asterisk-like "rock awash" symbol on my nautical chart.

I'm just about ready to paddle back upwind for another pass when I feel something, a tug. I lift the rod tip. My rod tip is yanked violently underwater. I got one! A *big* one! He pulls so hard and violently that I'm afraid something is going to break. I flip the big spinning reel's bail to give me a moment, to keep from snapping my rod in half. When I flip the bail back and reel, he's gone. That moment of slack is all it took. It leaves my hands shaking. That was *awesome!* First pass, too. I carefully adjust the drag. Next time I'm hanging on for dear life. No slack. No bail flipping. If something breaks, it will have to break. I mark the spot on my GPS.

I paddle back upwind to do the same drift. I've barely started jigging when I feel a fish, but it soon gets off. I mark that spot on my GPS as well. A couple of minutes later I feel another fish, but again, I fail to hook it. Then it happens: I feel a tug and set the hook. The fish dives, unstoppable, yanking the rod tip into the water. Whoa! I lift the rod tip, the taut line is singing, the rod in a hard arch, the drag screaming. Despite not a moment of slack, this fish too, escapes. *Bummer!* You know what though? Not that big of a bummer. I've hooked at least two big halibut in less than an hour. I set another GPS waypoint. I've finally *really* found a good spot. I look at the screen of my GPS. There's a string of points where I've had strikes. I'll land one. I know I will. Man, this has been an exciting day!

I paddle to shore for a pee break and to stretch my legs. While I'm walking around I notice some good, red huckleberries in some bushes right next to the high-tide mark. I pick and eat several nice handfuls, then pick some goose tongue and bladderwrack.

I check out the jig hook. It seems pretty sharp, but just to be sure I find a fine-grained flat stone about three inches across, and use it to sharpen the point hook a bit more. I'd be curious to ask a halibut expert why I'm not hooking most of these fish. Perhaps it's mostly chance? I don't know.

I paddle back out to start another drift. It's raining now, and the wind is starting to come up. Is that a fish I feel? The jig is so heavy it bends my rod and fools me sometimes. I reel in. It IS a fish. A two pound codfish. I'd eat it if I was hungry, but I'm after bigger game today.

The wind is becoming an issue. My drift is too fast and cold rain is driving into my face. I'm going to call it a day.

It's 4 PM when I get back to my tent. It's nice to have camp set up and everything nice and dry. I dig warm fleece out of the dry bag and put on dry socks and my balaclava and crawl into my sleeping bag. I lean on one elbow and eat crab meat, with cranberries for dessert. Then I burrow into my bag and lie back. This is so cozy with rain pattering on the tent. I am completely dry and toasty warm. With the short night's sleep and all of today's excitement and work, I am a tired puppy. I close my eyes and quickly fall asleep.

When I wake up it's 10 PM. A five-and-half-hour nap! The wind is groaning in the treetops and waves are crashing against the rocks. I pulled the boat up far enough, didn't I? I'm sure I did, but just to reassure myself I put on my headlamp and rain gear and follow the beam of light until I see the boat, safely stashed at the edge of the dripping trees. I climb the wet trail back up to the tent.

For a while I lie awake, looking up into the dark, listening to the waves and wind. I think about a cabin I might build someday, about maybe getting a camper for traveling the West, about making maple syrup again next spring. But for tonight I'm out here on an unnamed island on the coast of Alaska, miles from the nearest person. Tomorrow I'm going to catch me a big ol' halibut. If the wind dies enough. If it's too windy, I'll go salmon fishing.

September 5, Day 68

I don't hear the wind. What time is it? 5:30. I'm going halibut fishing, at least until the wind comes up. They are predicting winds at ten to fifteen.

I eat some salmon for breakfast, then quickly gather my rod, harpoon, bucket, and daypack with spare fishing gear. I launch the kayak, paddling out to the mouth of the cove and into the gentle breeze until I get to the upwind end of yesterday's drift line. Clouds are hanging at treetop level. A thin fog hangs over the water, limiting visibility to a few hundred yards, but that's far enough that I can stay oriented with the shore and islands.

If the light breeze holds, I'll be fishing the same stretch where I got all those strikes yesterday. This is by far the most confident I've been about halibut fishing on the whole trip. The halibut still have to be in a biting mood, though. When the GPS shows I'm in position, I drop the jig until it hits bottom. I get the first bite in minutes. Then another bite a few minutes later. Each fish is on only briefly, but the quick action bodes well for the day.

When I feel another fish I sweep the rod up hard to set the hook. He dives violently for the bottom. The drag screeches. This is it! *It's a nice one!* I hold on for dear life. I think this one is hooked good. Man, do I want to land this fish! It's another vertical fight. The fish wants to go nowhere but to the bottom. I slowly pull up until I drop the rod tip, reeling quickly to maintain tension. Very slowly I gain line, dragging him through over one hundred feet of cold water. After a long struggle I see him. He's a nice one, nearly as big as the first one I landed!

When he sees the boat he dives. There's no stopping him. He fights the drag taking most of the line I've worked so hard to gain. But this time it's not nearly as long until I see him again, big and dark like a giant brown leaf except for the white of his belly.

The fourth time I get him near the surface, I look around to prepare my harpoon plan. I clip the little carabiner to the bucket handle. The bucket, of course, has its waterproof cover screwed down tight. Tied to the carabiner is a length of parachute cord, and at the other end of the cord is tied a huge halibut hook. The shank of the hook is duct-taped to the shaft at the end of the harpoon. I flip the point around so it's faced away from the harpoon shaft, then grab the other end of the harpoon shaft with my right hand and reach the hook out towards the halibut, whose head is only six inches below the surface. I am tense and extremely excited.

I hold the rod tip high with my left hand. With my right hand I slowly reach the hook point to the other side of the halibut's mouth and give a sharp yank. I miss. The hook spun just as it touched him. Surprisingly, the halibut barely reacts. I try again, holding tension on the cord. It will help keep the hook from turning. I aim, and yank. The halibut disappears in an explosion of water. My face and hands are soaked. But the rod still has tension and the bucket is getting dragged beneath the water. *Success!* He's now fighting both the bucket and the drag! The bucket displaces about five gallons of water, so theoretically it should take close to a forty pound pull to drag it underwater. He's already tired. The rod and bucket are keeping him near the surface. With any luck at all, I'll land him.

I get the harpoon ready for its second function. I remove the sheath and carefully aim the blade of the fillet knife I've taped and wired to the opposite end of the shaft. When everything is aligned I spear him down through the mouth and one side of his gills. He thrashes and the knife blade instantly snaps. But now blood swirls in the water.

I work him back towards the boat and ready my Swiss Army knife blade. I slash one side of his gills. Scarlet blood eddies around his gills. The jig falls out when he shakes his head! He's still attached to the bucket but I reach the jig out with my hand and re-hook it in his mouth. I want redundancy! I slash the other side of his gills. The water is red. I wait a few more minutes as his life ebbs away.

I'm still anxious to get him tied off solidly to the boat, though. I ready a heavy, braided stringer. When he's done struggling I drive the stringer's sharp metal point through his mouth. It isn't easy, but when I succeed I run the point through the metal ring on the other end, then tie him solidly to the boat handle. I've got him! He's mine!

Flushed with victory I decide to try to catch a smaller halibut to fill up the rest of the empty jars. I paddle back up to the starting point. I notice something out of my peripheral vision. What the heck was that? A sea lion, right behind the boat! He glides past just under the surface, huge and brown, heading for the halibut. He's after my fish! I spin around, grab the heavy stringer line and heave my heavy fish into the boat. The sea lion surfaces a few feet away, his head out of the water, his big, white canine teeth look menacing. My heart is pounding. I've suddenly got a new perspective on sea lions! He eyes me for a few moments, then sinks away and is gone.

My reel handle is getting loose. When I turn the opposite nut to tighten it, it breaks off! I'll take that as a sign! I've got my halibut. Very fortunate timing, I'd say. It takes a quality reel to stand up to landing heavy fish like a halibut.

I paddle back to the island and break camp. I'm surprised to see some water on the tent floor. This is a great shelter, but you have to watch so the mesh that runs between the fly and the floor doesn't stick out far enough that rain running off the fly can follow the mesh into the tent and onto the floor. That's what happened. Only the tent floor got a little wet though. My sleeping bag is on the pad and stayed high and dry.

Down at the beach I take some photos of my prize catch lying on the shore. He's beautiful, mottled gray and brown and black surrounded by bright green goose tongue, greenish-brown bladderwrack and wet rocks and seashells. In one photo I lay my harpoon and Leatherman next to him. Another shows me holding him up with moss-draped trees in the background. In the next I'm holding him in the more traditional way, his white belly to the camera. He stretches from my chin to well below my knees.

When I stretch the tape along him he is 44 inches long. According to the chart that makes him a 40 pounder!

I flip the boat over to use as a table to fillet him. I'm not worried about puncturing the boat because I'm slicing parallel to the kayak's bottom. Now that I have some halibut filleting experience, it goes even better than last time. I save some steaks to grill today.

I'm hungry. I eat some canned salmon, then I wander along the beach eating goose tongue and bladderwrack. From a jar I brought with me, I eat cranberries and huckleberries.

I load the boat and paddle for home. Good thing I got my halibut fishing done early because the wind has come up. It's a strong, quartering tailwind. Rather than helping, the wind makes the journey much more difficult. I have to paddle hard and steadily, on the right hand side only, to keep the boat from swinging sideways to the wind and waves. It's very hard work and a little unsettling as the cold waves build and I look to the nearest shore, nearly a mile away. On and on I paddle, with no chance to rest.

Despite the hard work and uneasy feeling though, the boat does fine

and I make it safely to base camp. I carry the canning supplies down to cook camp, where I'm surprised at two things: there's a small boat anchored in My Cove, and there are twelve clean jars lined up and ready to go. I forgot that! It's a pleasant surprise. I cover the grill with halibut steaks and then fill ten jars with beautiful, white, halibut fillets. Remembering the recent broken jar fiasco I make sure to be very gentle in tightening the lids. "Fingertip tight" as they say. As a matter of fact, I go back and check each lid once more, just to make sure.

I put the lower rack in the canner, pour in a couple inches of water, put in seven full jars, the second rack, then the last three jars. I've brought some gun oil, and use it to lubricate the threads of the clamp bolts, spinning the knobs on and off a few times to make sure all the threads get a good coating. I make certain to clamp the lid down evenly, then fire up the stove. I feed in a moderate supply of loosely stacked, smaller wood to begin with, feeding it gently. The fire burns hot and, after the required venting, I set the regulator in place. The canner reaches ten pounds pressure much, much faster than last time.

While the regulator chatters, I monitor the fire and write in my little green journal. My hands are cold and stiff. I warm them in wisps of steam escaping above the regulator. It's highly effective. After I'm done writing I round up every dirty jar that I can find. There aren't many. I continue to feed the fire every few minutes.

The operation goes very smoothly. After the allotted time I pull the canner off the fire to cool and set the grill of halibut steaks on top of the coals. I love this method, a large supply of hot coals ready to go!

It's 7 PM on this dark day, darker under the big trees. The coals glow red through the translucent halibut meat. As the meat cooks through it grows opaque. The grill overlaps the stove by a good amount, so I slide the grill to a new area, until that meat, too, is cooked through. When it's done the meat is browned and flakes beautifully. I pull out the salt and pepper. What can be better than fresh, hot halibut steaks? I am living the dream!

I'm just a little anxious about jars not breaking, so I'm excited when the pressure in the canner has dissipated so I can check them out. I pull out the jars one by one and set them in the moss. I am very, very disappointed to find three jars have broken. Why did they break? I didn't tighten them too hard. For sure.

Once again I skim through the list of possible causes of broken jars. *Jars have tiny cracks.* That's it. I've been hauling these jars around for over two months. Occasionally they've clinked against each other or rocks or some other hard object. Some of them I had been swishing small gravel around in for cleaning. And they've all been subjected to excessive pressures before by my lid overtightening. I need to hold each jar up to the light to check for hairline cracks.

Three broken jars is a bummer, no doubt. But eight have survived. It looks like I can eat half of one jar with reasonable safety. It's only broken at the bottom. That'll be breakfast. The other two I'll just have to chuck.

I hang most of the canned food supply in the cache tree and carry my chair and canning supplies back to camp. It's amazing how the hours fly by. It's 9 PM and dark already. Fall is coming on fast.

The weather gave me a break today. There was some rain, but it didn't amount to much. The sky is partially clearing this evening. It seems brighter outside the tent. I unzip the door and walk out through the trees and down to the water. There's a three-quarter moon rising, bright and mysterious, its silver light shimmering off Wild Bay. It's only the second time I've seen a nice bright moon on this trip. It's usually cloudy. Or I'm sleeping. Or both.

As I drift off to sleep I think about tomorrow. Maybe I'll go to My Creek. I wonder if there is a second run of chum salmon there? In less than three days I fly out. Three days...

# CHAPTER 30

# Stormy Seas

September 6, Day 69

I wake up in the dark and check my watch. 4 AM. I put on my headlamp, go outside and bring in the jar of halibut that has a broken bottom. Where should I go today? I've still got empty jars. I'd like to get some more salmon for my winter supply of meat at home. I think Salmon Creek is my best bet. Maybe I can even get some bear photos. Salmon Creek is a long paddle round-trip though, seven miles or so if I beeline it, quite a bit more if I don't. Wind is a big factor. I turn on the weather radio. They are calling for a chance of rain in the morning, and then rain, with SE winds at ten mph. I've found that regardless of the predicted wind direction it tends to blow up or down the bay. Ten mph is no big deal. If I get an early start I might be able to get home before the real rain hits. I follow my headlamp beam to the latrine tarp. It sure was worthwhile establishing a covered latrine at each camp, especially on the rainy days.

It's 5:30 and barely light when I launch into a calm bay. It's a gray, somber light. It feels like impending rain. The wind is starting to come up. I've been paddling only ten minutes or so and I'm already fighting it. No morning calm today, I guess. Now, at 6 AM, it's started to rain. The steady, cold rain blows into my face and trickles up my rain jacket sleeves. I pull the brim of my hat down low to keep the rain off my glasses.

The wind slackens somewhat as I turn into the cove leading to Salmon Creek. It's a relief when my kayak crunches ashore at the island near the creek's mouth. There's a bear! An adult male, likely, hustling along the opposite bank of the creek. I think he smelled me. He hurries into the trees. That's good.

I carry a bucket, my daypack, rifle and fishing rod to the lower pool, the one that's flooded by high tide. I set up my fly rod with a black marabou muddler. I'm standing on the inside of a gentle bend in the creek. When I first visited this spot two months ago, tall grass stood here. Now it's been mostly flattened by brown bears. Pretty soon I get a strike. What have I got? When it gets closer I see it's nice male pink salmon, in good condition, too. If I had some chums already I'd keep him, but who knows how the fishing will be today? I don't want to kill him and then not get enough for canning. If it stays this rainy I'm not going to want to grill a fish, either. I let him go.

I make cast after cast. I know there's plenty of salmon, I can see them sometimes when the wind isn't rippling the water, but I'm not getting any strikes. I switch to a bright green streamer. Strike! It's exciting every time! It's a female chum salmon, I can tell from the dark, horizontal stripe on her side. Suddenly the line goes slack. Oh well, I prefer to keep the males, anyway.

The wind is hitting hard enough here so it's getting to be a hassle to fly fish. Flies aren't working that great anyway. I switch to spinning gear, a green Pixie, easy to cast in the wind. With no takers I walk up to the next pool, where I caught most of the salmon last time. The water has gone way down. Did some of the eggs get left high and dry? Do salmon instinctively know to avoid spots that only run during high water? They are avoiding what's left of this pool now. There isn't a single fish there. I hike up farther, to the first pool in the trees. I love this spot, it's where I caught all the Dollies before. It's much calmer here, tucked back in the trees, but it's still very rainy. There are plenty of salmon here in the deeper water. After many casts, the Pixie fails to produce and I switch to an orange spinner with no better results. You can't make them bite. If I were starving, it would be simple to snag them. But I'm not starving.

*Splash!* Was that a bear? I walk downstream, keeping a sharp watch. *There he is!* A brown bear, fishing in the shallows. My camera is in its dry box, and the dry box is in my pack, and the pack is sitting on the bank, 100 yards past the bear. If you're serious about photos, you have to have your camera ready. I've got my iPhone though, hanging around my neck in its waterproof case. I step over beneath the thick branches of a tree where I can escape the rain.

The bear is standing in riffles watching for passing salmon. As I watch, he catches fish after fish, ripping the orange flesh from their bones. He's calm, unhurried. We are in a similar situation, the bear and me. When the salmon were first running I was nearly frantic to catch some, and I'm sure he was too, both of us needing to stockpile food. Now that there's plenty of salmon in the stream, and now that we both have food in the bank (me in the form of canned salmon, he in the form of fat) the pressure is off. He rarely makes more than a couple of jumps to catch his fish. When he misses one, no problem, another will come shooting through the riffles in a bit.

I take a few photos, and then some video. Seagulls are dashing in to snatch up pieces of fish he's dropped or left behind. The rain is pouring down. Salmon are splashing. His thick coat is matted by moisture. He stops and shakes the rainwater off, like a giant dog, his long hair flinging a gray halo of water in all directions. I bet he's plenty comfortable. That thick, warm hair, with rich salmon in the fuel tank to keep him warm.

He stiffens and warily looks around. He doesn't see me standing motionless beneath the dark trees. But he knows what he's smelled. He stands part way up and then turns to scramble up the steep bank, charging away through the soaked brush. That was exciting!

I try some streamers of various colors but the salmon are having none of it. Why they aren't biting is a mystery. Since salmon don't feed in freshwater anyway it seems like they'd be as aggressive to bite as ever, but they're not.

Fly fishing isn't much fun today, it's too windy. It's raining like crazy, the fish aren't biting. I walk downstream to the lower pool, now flooded by the rising tide. *To heck with it.* I pack everything to the kayak. There, at the island, I see whitecaps out on the cove. If there are whitecaps here, it's going to be really ugly out on the bay. There's no way I'm going out on that big, cold water under conditions like this. Now what?

Well, it won't kill me if I get stuck over here. It *could* kill me if I go out on water that's too rough. If a situation like this makes me uncomfortable, it's probably for good reason. It's taking a significant risk being far away from land in marginal conditions. I'll wait. Maybe it will calm down later in the day. If I get stuck here it won't kill me. I've got my rain gear and a warm jacket and a space blanket (the good, heavy-duty kind) to get out of the rain and/or wrap up in. I can start a fire if I need to. It's barely after 10 AM right now.

As I stand under the dark trees at the edge of the island I'm surprised to see kayaks, six of them. Two-seaters. They are paddling rapidly downwind, each pair in beautiful synchronicity. It is startling to see other people when I've been out here all alone. They must be on some kind of guided trip. They must have launched from a bigger boat anchored in the cove. There's no way a guided group would be out on the bay on a day like this.

They are going to pass within hailing distance but I don't want to break the spell of being out here alone. It would take some of the magic away to talk to them, to explain what I'm doing. Instead I stand quietly in the shadows, watching them look curiously at my nearby kayak. Soon they are out of sight.

For a few minutes I look around for a good hunker spot. Maybe I'll just wrap up in my space blanket under a tree and take a nap. That would make for a long day though. While I'm waiting I might as well pick some berries. I can't really see Wild Bay from here, so maybe I'll pick berries out towards someplace where I can see the bay and monitor conditions-kill two birds with one stone. I paddle across the end of this cove and stash my kayak at the edge of the trees. Just as I'm getting ready to leave I see the kayaks again. They must have been looking for bears at Salmon Creek. Their progress now, into the wind, is painfully slow. I watch as they struggle upwind for ten minutes or so before they land on the opposite shore, likely to take a breather and to talk things over. Compared to me they do have a couple of advantages: hard-shelled, streamlined kayaks being a big one, and two paddlers to share the work. They'll make it back to the boat if they tough it out. I'll bet they'll enjoy getting into dry clothing and eating lunch in the heated galley.

I follow a bear path just inside the treeline for a way, then cut inland to begin berry hunting. I find blue huckleberries and red huckleberries and lots of bunchberries. It's flat here where I'm walking, and in this dark forest it's super easy to lose track of directions. I pull out my GPS to get oriented and to get a compass bearing. It doesn't matter a whole lot exactly where I hit the bay, but at least I want to head in the right general direction.

It takes a surprisingly long time to reach a point where I can see Wild Bay. The berry picking and exploring and meandering around Devil's club patches made for a long walk. The bay looks daunting, whitecaps rolling across the water, wind whipping the tops off the waves. Yikes. This is much, much windier than what they predicted. If it doesn't improve a lot I'll be sleeping over here, without a sleeping bag or tent. It's raining now, too. A hard, cold rain. I'm dressed for it though. I've discovered, at long last, how to properly adjust my rain jacket hood with the barrel locks on each side. The rain isn't a big problem. Big waves are a big problem.

Under the biggest, thickest trees it's mostly protected from the rain. I find a good spot and lie back for nap. It's out of the wind and reasonably comfortable. I doze for a bit.

When I sit up it seems quieter. I think the wind has died down a little. I pick berries to where I can see the bay again. The water is a bit calmer. I think I'll pick my way back to the kayak and play it by ear. Along the water I find and eat some "skunk currants," the berries with the strange aftertaste. As I follow deer trails through the brush I come out on a nice, open bench. I can see plentiful bunchberries from a distance and the tiny "dwarf blueberry" bushes. I end up crawling around on my hands and knees, picking the sweet, tiny blueberries by ones and twos and the bright red bunchberries by the cluster.

Through the trees ahead I see the grassy flats along the cove. A flock of huge Canada geese are waddling around near the edge of the timber. It triggers the hunter instinct in me. It's a perfect setup for sneaking up on them. It's something I'd imagined in planning this trip, before I found out that waterfowl season doesn't open until the 15th. Using the trees for cover, I'd sneak down to the edge of the meadow, undetected by the geese keeping watch. When I stepped out of the trees they'd launch, honking excitedly, loud, powerful wing-beats carrying them away, their long black necks outstretched. Today I lift up one hand and swing it ahead of a white cheek patch. *Bang!* That would have been it. A fine, fat goose.

At the kayak, the cove has calmed considerably. The tide has fallen dramatically as well. I pause to eat goose tongue and bladderwrack. I carry my gear down to a side channel, dragging my kayak through the shallow water until there's enough water to jump in and paddle down the meandering little channel to the main creek.

There must be twenty seals hunting salmon in the cove. I stay near shore as I reach the bay, wanting the option to land if I need to. But the waves have fallen and look manageable. Once again I'm dealing with a strong, quartering tailwind though, and once again I have to paddle hard on the right hand side, with no option but to relentlessly paddle to keep the kayak from swinging sideways to the waves. I don't like that, having to keep paddling to stay safe. I keep up a seemingly endless series of strong, right-side strokes.

I begin to think of foods I most want to eat when I fly out. Bread with melting butter and peanut butter. Hot pancakes with butter and maple syrup! Carbs. A cornucopia of grocery store foods, wandering up and down the aisles, anything I want to buy. It's going to be awesome. I'm experiencing the greatest food cravings of the trip, by far.

For a long time I aim towards an island on the opposite shore, the base camp side, but as the wind carries me up-bay, I have to adjust my target point. Cold waves continue to roll in from towards the Sound. I keep an eye out for taller waves. When I see one I square up the boat to it. One wave slops into the boat but immediately drains out the self-bailing floor. It's a lonely feeling out on the rough, cold water so far from land in this tiny kayak. I hear the wind and the gurgling waves and the sound of my heavy breathing.

I keep paddling hard, making slow but steady progress. At long last I'm within a stone's throw of the opposite shore. I head downwind for the last quarter mile. What a relief. I skim across the water with a full tailwind.

It is so nice to get into dry clothes. To be out of the rain and off the rough water. I'm hungry. Except for the berries I haven't eaten in eleven hours. I've been working hard and I'm hungry. I check out another broken halibut jar. It, too, is only broken at the bottom. I eat most of it, only quitting when I near the break. Not something I'd recommend, but it sure is good.

This day might have gone so much differently. If I decided to leave camp a half hour later this morning I wouldn't have even launched. It would have been a camp day, easier, safer and more comfortable. The day I had will be a lot more memorable than a day in camp, though!

# CHAPTER 31

## Last Expedition

September 7, Day 70

I slept great. Wow, it's my last full day. If my flight is on time, that is. It's hard to believe it's almost over.

My air taxi pick up is scheduled for 8 AM tomorrow so I'll want to start packing things up today. I need to pick up my crab trap, too. Heading to My Creek makes sense. I can get the trap and maybe get a crab or two to eat and a salmon to grill. I'll be too busy to catch enough for a canning operation, although it would be nice to get a little more meat for the winter. I'll start packing this afternoon. The thought of packing gives me a faint homesick feeling. That feeling isn't a longing for home, although I'll be happy for the comforts of home, no doubt. It's a twinge of knowing the adventure is ending, that this place, a place that has been my home for nearly two and a half months, will soon be a memory.

It's a typical morning, foggy, cool and calm. It's a familiar routine, carrying my kayak and gear to the water, loading the boat, and paddling out into Wild Bay to start my day.

It's foggier than usual today, though. I meander when I temporarily lose sight of all landmarks. In just a few minutes of paddling through the drifting, featureless fog, I find I've veered off course. The sight of a well-known island sets me straight.

I finally spot the trap buoy through the fog. Once all the slack line is in the boat the trap feels heavy. Is it starfish, or will luck be on my side this last morning. Crabs! Four of them! I measure each with my homemade caliper. Only one is too small. I drop it into the ocean and watch it kick as it sinks out of sight. One thing I like about crab trapping is it seems to be very easy on crabs that are sublegal. Most get out on their own. I don't think any of the sublegal ones I've released have been injured.

To keep the legal crabs in good shape I put them back in the trap, then bring the trap to the shallows and drop it back in the water. It's almost exactly low tide so it's a long carry bringing the kayak up to the trees.

I grab my fishing rod and pack and hike towards My Creek. I spot three deer a half mile across the head of the bay. Their hair, summer-brown, dully reflects a small patch of sun drifts across the grassy flats. It doesn't seem like animal hair would reflect light, but I've spotted many animals this way through the years.

Coming around a forested point I freeze. Three animals are walking towards me. It's blacktails, a doe and two big fawns, and they haven't noticed me. They are already winter-gray, another indication of the changing seasons. The other deer were so brown, and these are so gray. I stand motionless and watch until one of the fawns spots me. When it freezes, staring, the other two take notice. It's a stare-down. The doe lowers and raises her head to get a different perspective. They lift their noses to scent me but the wind is working against them. I think they sense somehow that I'm not going to hurt them. Instead of bolting frantically they turn and hustle into the thick forest.

The lower pool is empty. I walk past the tiny falls and find the next pool devoid of fish as well. I hike upstream, looking into the clear water. How can so many fish have disappeared so quickly? It looks like it's come full circle on this trip. There were no salmon here when I arrived. Then came the chums, then the pinks, and now they are all gone!

There's movement in the nearby tall grass. A brown bear rises up on his hind feet, towering in the air, huge and powerful. We look each other in the eye for a long moment, then he drops down, turning, and races into the forest. I've barely started walking when I spot another bear, striding through the belly-high grass and willows-a different bear, I'm sure, but equally big. He smells me and in a moment he too vanishes.

"The top of the food chain." That's what people say about brown bears. The way things normally go is that the bear runs. But bears can do foolish things when they are scared. And so can people. Either can turn a simple meeting into something deadly if they make a bad decision.

We're looking for the last fish, the bears and I. Salmon are critical to life in Alaska, and they are the most precious when they are hard to find, like now. I continue upstream. There's a salmon! He's in rough shape though. Not something I want to eat. I follow the clear stream into the shadows of the forest up to the confluence, beyond where I've seen salmon here. Tiny Dollies dimple the water, but no salmon. I follow the stream back down. I'm surprised to see several salmon cruising through the shallows. There's more! Not many fish. I see maybe thirty total. Thirty instead of the thousands not long ago.

I fish some riffles. Most of the salmon are holding around there. I inadvertently snag several pinks and and release them. It feels like there should be some big Dollies in there, a place predatory fish would be waiting to snatch up eggs before the season ends. The leech I'm fishing has an "egg" tied at the head. Maybe that will trigger a strike from a big Dolly.

The fly swings through the riffles on a tight line. The swing stops and I set the hook. A fish rockets upstream wildly. I think it's a big Dolly! This could be epic, catching a huge Dolly the very last day of the trip. I was similarly lucky one time years ago, rainbow fishing. We were fishing a little-floated river in southwest Alaska, five of us, fly fishing in two rafts. We were getting picked up the next morning. The other raft was ahead of us, heading to the pickup point. Two of us stayed behind to fish one last pool. I hooked a giant of a rainbow. My buddy reeled in and watched the action, the huge fish making wild leaps and strong runs. I was desperate to land him. He was twice as big as any trout I'd ever caught. At last he tired and I held him briefly in my hands. Nine pounds based on a quick measurement. I released him back into the cold water. The biggest trout of my life. The last day, last pool, last cast of the trip.

This fish, though, proves less dramatic. It's a female pink salmon, a late spawner, looking remarkably fresh and trout-like. I'd prefer a male but she is in such good condition I decide to keep her. I stun her with a rock then slash her gills to bleed her, sliding her headfirst into the bucket to carry back to the kayak. This will be the last salmon of the trip.

Not far away, on the edge of the forest, there is a short hardwood tree with reddish leaves. Is that a crab apple? When I get closer I spot the tiny fruit, apple-red on one side. I pick and eat a bunch of them. I certainly never dreamt I'd be eating apples of any kind on this trip.

I pack the kayak down to the water, much closer now. Before launching I eat some seaweed and goose tongue. Goose tongue sure looks a lot like crabgrass. I take a photo of a nice patch when the sun peeks out briefly again. It's easy pulling in the crab trap where it's stashed. It was barely under water when I left it and now it's still only a few feet deep. Hey, crab-apples, crabgrass, crab trap. I'm easily amused by things like this!

For the last time I paddle towards base camp. On the way I pause to admire the natural beauty surrounding me. Here and there mountaintops poke through low clouds drifting raggedly above the water. Patches of sunlight sweep across the calm waters of the upper bay.

After landing I pack the crabs, fish, camp chair, and canner cover down to cook camp. I quickly clean the crabs, another now-familiar task, one with the pleasant association of hot, freshly cooked crab meat. I quickly clean the salmon as well, removing the head and tail and splitting it. I lay it on the grill, locking the meat between the two grill halves. It's a nearly perfect fit.

I start the fire and soon the crabs are boiling. When they are done I put the salmon on the hot coals. I lay a piece of foil on top to hold the heat a little bit better. With the salmon grilled to perfection I have to take a photo of my feast atop a mossy log, the six halves of crab on a canner rack and the crispy-brown salmon next to them. With salt and pepper and a full canteen of cool water at hand I polish off the whole salmon in a few minutes. I can honestly say I have not grown tired of salmon on this trip. That was one of my big concerns. I'm going to save the crab to eat the rest of the day, with some for breakfast tomorrow.

After my epic feast I break down cook camp and begin toting everything back to base camp, including my food cache hanging in the tree. Next, I hike over to my latrine tarp and dismantle it, setting it up again next to the tent to store my gear.

The sun is out occasionally so I lay a few items out to dry, then begin packing in earnest. Obviously there's some stuff that can't be packed yet, the tent, sleeping bag, pad and cot for example, but I want to get ahead of the curve for tomorrow's 8 AM flight. In many years of firefighting in Alaska, we would usually fly out from the fire by helicopter. It wasn't uncommon to have the helicopter appear unexpectedly. Helicopter time is expensive, so it usually resulted in a mad scramble to pack, sometimes with the rotor blades still spinning and the engine roaring. I called those times "panic demobs." I didn't like panic demobs, and I want to make sure I'm in no big hurry in the morning.

I wash off the fish grill and break down and fold the crab trap flat. A foldable crab trap is a great feature on a trip like this! I remove the hoop of the landing net. I then stack those three items: hoop, trap, and grill, and zip tie them together. It's a nice, flat, and solid package. It makes me happy.

I gather up all the unbroken jars, full and empty, and pack them away into two jar boxes. During the course of the trip I broke, I believe, eight jars during canning, and chipped the lip of a couple more, and broke two more in handling. That leaves me with two jarboxes full of jars. The broken and chipped jars I put in an old pail to throw out when I get to Petersburg. I use the two extra jarbox halves to "double box" one of the jarboxes. I wire both jarboxes shut when I'm done.

It's almost hard to believe when the valves are open and the air is rushing out of the dependable old kayak. I never had to add a bit of air in seventy days! After squishing the remaining air out I close the valves again and roll the boat up tightly, using a small ratchet strap to hold it snugly together.

I break down each of my fishing rods and start packing fishing gear into a bucket. I fill the canner with breakable items that I won't be needing in the morning or in Petersburg, things like the kayak pump. Ironically, one fragile item is the canner cover with its pressure gauge sticking up. I use the same method I used on the flight down. I top the various "breakables" with some spare clothing for padding, then flip the canner lid upside down, so the fragile gauge is inside, using the knobs to bolt it in place. Nice!

Storm clouds are rolling in. I hear the first thunder of the whole trip. I scramble around, gathering up gear that was drying. A rainbow appears over My Cove just as the rain hits. I duck into the tent.

The rain doesn't last. The storm passes. I think it will be, as predicted, a nice morning tomorrow. Night is falling. With most of my gear packed up, I bring my camp chair, crab meat and daypack down to the good old cook camp. I build a nice campfire on the gravelly shore. There's no need to conserve firewood now. It's a beautiful, bright, cheerful fire. I sit and watch the flames flicker in the dark, the coals glowing, sparks spiraling up into the clearing sky. Shadows dance on the surrounding old growth timber. It's my last night alone in The Fortress of the Bears.

When I'm sleepy I let the fire die, then carry the remaining firewood to the water's edge where it can float away.

There is a glow behind the trees as I near camp. I cross the narrow spit and watch the full, silvery moon rising over the treetops, bathing Wild Bay in a cool light.

# CHAPTER 32

## Farewell to Wild Bay

September 8, Day 71

As usual, it's just about 4 AM when I wake up. But today I'm not making plans for fishing or berry-picking or crabbing or a deer hunting expedition. If all goes according to plan, today I'm flying out. I unzip the tent door and step outside and walk down to the water.

The black sky is sprinkled with a million stars. Looks like it will be a beautiful day. The plane should be here this morning. The weather radio says it's 43 degrees, the coldest morning of the trip. Nearly the whole time the temps have been cool. Not cold, usually not very warm, not hot, remarkably moderate.

Breakfast is an easy choice: I chow down on the last three crab halves. It's time consuming, cracking all those shells. Good thing I woke up early. When I'm done I take the bucket of shells and throw them in the ocean.

By headlamp light I stuff my sleeping bag in its sack, then into the big dry bag along with my sleeping pad and spare clothing. I break down the cot and slide it into its carrying bag. The lengthiest items go in the longest pack bag: cot bag, kayak paddle, spare paddle, landing net handle, the folded-up chair.

The tide is falling. If my plane is on time (and as the first pickup of the day in this nice weather, I think it will be) it will be just past low tide. As I get things ready to go I carry them down to the pick-up point and stash them near the receding water. About 5:30 the sky begins to brighten. I break down the tent, counting all the tent stakes to make sure I've got them all. I roll up the electric bear fence. I wonder if a bear ever touched it while I was gone? Or sleeping?!

Beautiful sunlight hits the mountains across the bay. What a day! I'm so lucky to fly out on a day like this, and to have arrived when it wasn't pouring rain, too, way back in June.

Everything is packed up and stacked up, ready to go on the beach. I've checked before but I take a final look around my camp for bits of trash or forgotten gear. I walk down to the previous campsite, and then to the last cook camp. Lastly I walk the shore where I had been drying gear and solar-charging batteries. What's this? It's my good old fleece hooded sweatshirt, the camo one, veteran of countless adventures. It darn near got left behind.

Walking back to camp I hear it: the faint buzzing of a distant motor, slowly getting louder. It's exciting, standing on the gravel of the sloping shore, watching for the plane down Wild Bay, now so familiar. There's a glint of sunlight off a shiny wing. The tiny dot grows with the sound. He's right on time.

The plane passes in front of the blue-green mountains, descending, then banks sharply, its blue and white fuselage gleaming in the low morning sun. It skims just above the surface of the water then touches down, plumes of white water gracefully arching up from each float.

I'm going home.

# Afterword

As I was checking into my motel in Petersburg there was a tray of fresh muffins about to be whisked away. Breakfast was over.

"Do you mind if I grab one of those?" I asked.

"Sure, go right ahead."

I peeled the paper from my prize and took a big bite. I was back to the luxuries of civilization.

I flopped my bags down in my room, and started filling the bathtub with hot water while I took off my dirty clothes. I stopped at the bathroom mirror to see how I'd fared. I looked lean, grizzled and happy. I sank into the glorious hot water of the tub and leaned back. The TV news was on. Something about unrest in Ferguson, Missouri. The troubles of the wider world were something I'd escaped out on Wild Bay.

Freshly scrubbed and in a clean set of clothes I went down to the front desk to ask about a laundromat, grocery store and restaurants. On the corner of the counter sat two muffins.

"I saved you a couple of muffins."

They'd heard about my trip. Very nice of them!

Twenty minutes later I was sitting in a cafe. Butter melted into a warm stack of pancakes slathered in syrup, and I sipped my first cup of coffee since June. Before the day was over I'd demolished most of a carton of ice cream and the majority of a large pizza.

Nearly a year has passed since I last saw Wild Bay. It's mid-August in Fairbanks and the leaves are just beginning to change. I think about my adventure every day. Here are some thoughts now that I'm looking back...

- I lost about twenty pounds, virtually all of that in the first month, I'm sure. At the end I think my weight was holding steady. I was healthy-lean.
- The hardest part of the trip was eating what I could get rather than what I might want. The next biggest challenge was the rain and wet. The solitude was a minor issue for me.
- My best gear decision was bringing the pressure canner. It was, by far, the most practical way to preserve windfalls of fish and game.
- My worst gear decision was not bringing a satellite phone, although that decision was based on bad information that said there would be pockets of cell coverage. A sat. phone would have saved me the biweekly trips to the lodge. It would also have been a significant safety hedge. However, being completely cut off from communications is a valuable experience in itself.
- The best piece of gear I had was my kayak. I inflated it the first morning, and it was maintenance-free the rest of the trip. The worst piece of gear was my rubber knee boots which completely disintegrated. (See my website at www.bucktrack.com for more gear information.)
- The best part of the trip was undoubtedly "Living the Dream." I'd wanted to take a trip like this since I was a kid. It was at the very top of my bucket list. It was an incredible, invaluable experience.
- Takeaway lessons? I think it's realizing how lucky we are nowadays. We have easy access to a wide variety of inexpensive,

high quality foods. We can turn a knob for instant access to clean water, cold or hot. We are to be able to sleep warm and dry every night. We have the best medical care in human history and face so little danger compared to the past where saber toothed tigers or cave bears or lions would be stalking us at night, or when enemy tribes might attack at any moment.

Perhaps, more than anything, it's good to know that there are still epic adventures to be had and a wide, natural world waiting to be explored.

"All America lies at the end of the wilderness road, and our past is not a dead past, but still lives in us. Our forefathers had civilization inside themselves, the wild outside. We live in the civilization they created, but within us the wilderness still lingers. What they dreamed, we live, and what they lived, we dream."

— T.K. Whipple *Study Out the Land*

If you enjoyed this book please consider writing a brief review on Amazon.com.

Please visit www.bucktrack.com to see my other books and films including:

*Alaska Hunting Adventure: 700 Miles Alone by Backpack and Raft*, my video documentary of an epic hunt for caribou, moose and sheep;

*Alone Across Alaska: 1,000 Miles of Wilderness*, a film of my traverse of Alaska, from Canada to the sea.

*Hunting Big Whitetails*, one of my books now in it's third printing;

You can also explore www.bucktrack.com for journals and photos of my other adventures, including hikes of the Pacific Crest Trail, the Continental Divide Trail, paddling the Mississippi from its source to the sea, and much more.

Made in the USA
Lexington, KY
12 December 2016